*This book is dedicated to all the broken hearts
who have had the privilege of knowing what it means to truly love.
It is also dedicated to those who have truly loved another individual,
yet in their human frailty have failed that person.*

Design and typesetting by Brent Flink. Indivisual Design Inc. Vancouver, British Columbia, Canada. www.indivisual.ca

† Page 123 Lyrics © 1998 Reuben Morgan/Hillsong Publishing (adm in the US & Canada by Integrity's Hosanna! Music)/ASCAP c/o Integrity Media, Inc., 1000 Cody Road, Mobile, AL 36695

† Page 303 Lyrics ©1997 Universal - Songs of Polygram Int'l Inc./Loon Echo Inc (BMI); Out of Pocket Productions Ltd., all rights on behalf of Out of Pocket Productions Ltd. controlled by Zomba Enterprises Inc. (ASCAP) for the U.S. and Canada

For information visit www.passionatelife.ca.

Note for Librarians: a cataloguing record for this book that includes Dewey Classification and US Library of Congress numbers is available from the National Library of Canada. The complete cataloguing record can be obtained from the National Library's online database at: www.nlc-bnc.ca/amicus/index-e.html

ISBN: 1-4120-3320-9

TRAFFORD

This book was published _on-demand_ in cooperation with Trafford Publishing. On-demand publishing is a unique process and service of making a book available for retail sale to the public taking advantage of on-demand manufacturing and Internet marketing. **On-demand publishing** includes promotions, retail sales, manufacturing, order fulfilment, accounting and collecting royalties on behalf of the author.

Suite 6E, 2333 Government St., Victoria, B.C. V8T 4P4, CANADA
Phone   250-383-6864   Toll-free   1-888-232-4444 (Canada & US)
Fax   250-383-6804   E-mail   sales@trafford.com
Web site www.trafford.com   TRAFFORD PUBLISHING IS A DIVISION OF TRAFFORD HOLDINGS, LTD.
Trafford Catalogue # 04-1147   www.trafford.com/robots/04-1147.html

10   9   8   7   6   5   4   3   2   1

To Brian,

In your youth, you gave me your strength,
And you gave me a promise that was to last a lifetime.
In your heart you pledged to yourself that you would always
Love me, respect me, protect me and take care of me
And you worked very hard to make all of this come true.
In midlife once you failed me, but then you redeemed yourself.
You faced your failure with courage, you did not run away.
In my struggle to understand, you granted me honesty,
And you never ran from the pain.
To you, I was worth the work of rebuilding, and you gave to me
tirelessly, more than any man could ever be expected to give.
Now as together we live the second half of our lives,
You have won all of my admiration and all of my respect.
Now you have made my dreams come true.
The thing that you worked so hard to achieve, you have achieved.
I trust you completely.
The greatest man of all is the man who is willing for this story to
be told, that others may be helped.
You are my best friend, my lover, the father of my children.
You are strong, intelligent, romantic, and full of humor.
You are my man of steel and of velvet.
If I had my life to live over, I would marry you all over again,
Even if I could see the future. It's all been worth it.
You have made me very happy. Thank you for an amazing life.

Anne

CONTENTS

Acknowledgements 7

Foreword 9

Prologue.. 11

ONE   Cinderella ... not 13

TWO   Before the Affair 23

THREE   Surviving the First Day 37

FOUR   Forgiving the Other Woman 47

FIVE   It's Over 65

SIX   When Life Doesn't Make Any Sense........................... 75

SEVEN   The Vision 87

EIGHT   Friendship in Adversity.. 91

NINE   Crazy Making.. 105

TEN   Small Miracles 117

ELEVEN   Danielle Calls the Other Woman 127

TWELVE   Our Children.. 139

THIRTEEN   Meeting the Other Woman 149

FOURTEEN   Unseen Forces Pulling Brian Home 165

FIFTEEN   Success – and an Ultimatum 177

SIXTEEN   Trouble with the Law 201

SEVENTEEN   Fire 217

EIGHTEEN   Suicide Attempt.. 223

NINETEEN   Let the Fights Begin 243

TWENTY   Chicago?... 255

TWENTY-ONE   9-1-1 267

TWENTY-TWO   From Fighting To Healing... 283

TWENTY-THREE   Should I Stay or Go 295

TWENTY-FOUR   The Rewards 303

TWENTY-FIVE   Lessons Learned 313

Epilogue... 327

ACKNOWLEDGEMENTS

In the past, I have always wondered why authors go to such extremes to thank their family members in their books. Now I understand. Writing this book has been a huge undertaking.

When asked to speak at a marriage seminar recently, our host commented that he had been looking so forward to meeting Brian, because, he said, he knew he would be meeting one of the most courageous men he'd ever met. That's the truth. It takes an exceptional individual to share failure publicly. Brian has been my number one cheerleader throughout this project. This book could not have been written without his encouragement and support.

I would also like to thank my three exceptional children, Danielle, Dustin and Tamara for their patience and sacrifices, during the many months it took me to write. (And for putting up with roast chicken and bagged salad more times than they care to remember.) I commend them also for their willingness to share such a personal family story with the world, so that others can be helped. I am very proud of all three of them.

Especially, I want to thank Danielle for not only sharing so much of herself with the world, but for writing pieces for the book, which offer readers a unique perspective into another side of affairs. It is our hope that her contributions will inspire hope for the many overlooked teenagers in the world, whose parents are struggling with similar challenges.

So many people have participated in my vision to make this book a reality. Writing a book like this one is not like writing other books.

When stepping out of the ordinary, and talking about subjects normally considered taboo, one's personal network of support becomes essential. I therefore want to thank our friends for cheering us on and being there for us during this writing endeavor: Jacques and Judy Belzile, Sean and Heather Upshaw, Victor and Alanna Klassen, Doug and Karin Elrick, Kevin and Annabel

Bessenger, Lindsay Brooks and Adrian Lee.

Margot Silk Forrest has been my writing coach. Her professional insight and experience, coupled with kindness, wisdom and encouragement have assisted me in bringing to paper the truth about the events that transpired in my life.

Marital affairs expert Peggy Vaughan has been my mentor. She took time to read the entire manuscript at an early stage and offered praise and constructive feedback. She is a tremendously giving individual, who has shared invaluable wisdom, knowledge and understanding with me, through ongoing correspondence.

I would also like to thank my friends and colleagues, who read the manuscript and provided valuable feedback and encouragement: Margie Thaler, Deidra Robertson, Monica Columbus, Michelle Elrick, Jan Mosley, Karen Anderson, Chris Hildebrandt, Shirley Clark and Gail Ostiguy. This book would not have been as good without their valuable input.

My editor Andrea Scott-Bigsby did an outstanding job of making the text flow smoothly, clearly and chronologically. Her detailed editorial advice has greatly enhanced this manuscript. She helped me to include important nuggets in the story, avoid getting bogged down in unnecessary details and to avoid being offensive in a few places. We affair survivors have strong emotions sometimes.

F O R E W O R D

Every individual is unique, every marriage is unique, and no two affairs are exactly the same. Nonetheless, the devastation and emotions experienced by those on all ends of an affair are sadly similar.

In this book, I have recounted the events that took place in my life after learning that my husband had an affair. I have told my story as accurately as possible.

To preserve anonymity of the other people involved in our lives at that time, the names of all characters in the book have been changed, except for those of our own family. Also many of the particulars have been altered to preserve confidentiality without distorting important facts or essential truth.

It is important to note, that for a period after learning of the affair, I was in a state of emotional shock and unable to process information logically. I have written about these events as I experienced and perceived them in the moment.

Clarity came later. Many of the things I thought and experienced in the moment were not actually true. They were my reactions at the time. In the beginning, I had limited information and therefore a limited ability to fairly evaluate what was happening. This is universal among those who discover their mate has been unfaithful.

In reading this book, you, the reader, have the opportunity to learn the many truths that we did, but I have not spelled them out for you. I invite you to live through the experience with me and discover them for yourself. The conclusions you draw may even be different than our own.

It has not been easy to expose our hearts: the good, the bad, and the ugly. As human beings we often fall short of the ideals we set for ourselves. I concluded that we are probably not alone in some of the bad and some of the ugly, so I have laid it out here, at the risk of criticism and rejection, in the hopes that others will identify with our situation and be helped.

It is my sincere desire to play a part in ending the silence and shame around the topic of extramarital affairs, as well as clear up some of the misconceptions that are held by society as a whole. I do not condone affairs, but they happen, and I am committed to helping those who experience them understand, heal, and build greater lives on the other side.

I am also committed to helping those who have not endured this particular pain, to relinquish their misconceptions and judgmental attitudes about infidelity.

I hope that people will learn from our experience and be deterred from having an affair. It may at first appear to be a pleasant road, but it leads to pain and regret beyond description, and once it is embarked upon, one cannot turn around, retrace his or her steps, and undo the journey.

I cannot predict how likely it is that husbands and wives who find themselves tempted by an affair will be deterred by understanding the pain their actions will cause others. People in this position do not think of the beloved spouse they would be betraying, nor the painful realities and consequences, but only of the selfish pleasure they desire in the moment.

What can, however, be a deterrent to having an affair is learning to understand oneself, daring to look inside one's heart, facing the truth, and embarking on the road to spiritual growth. This road leads to a life suffused with indescribable pleasure and joy, a destination available only to those who have courage and are willing to do the work. For these people, there is a path that appears thorny in the beginning, but in the end leads to paradise.

Anne Bercht
Abbotsford, British Columbia
March 2004

P R O L O G U E

How can I tell my beautiful wife of eighteen years, with whom I make love almost nightly, that I am caught up in an affair? I'm not even sure how it happened. A few months ago I would have sworn I was not the unfaithful type. Now the woman I'm seeing has suddenly told her husband about us, and she's pressuring me to leave Anne and start a new life together.

The affair began when Helen asked me to lunch and told me about the struggles she was facing in her marriage. At the time, I actually believed that I would be able to help her by sharing some of the things that Anne and I do to keep our marriage fresh and strong. But I didn't tell Anne about that lunch.

Then, when Helen and I met alone for a second time, I felt a magnetic force drawing me to her. It was a force I chose not to resist – there was an emptiness in me that needed filling. Soon Helen and I shifted from being friends to lovers. Now we are facing a huge decision.

I constantly ask myself, why did I accept that first invitation? I still love Anne. How can I be doing this to her? I am confused and unsure what to do. But I do know I can no longer keep my affair a secret.

I have to tell Anne.

– Brian Bercht

CHAPTER I

cinderella ...Not

MONDAY, MAY 15, 2000

"Un-break my heart, say you'll love me again. Undo this hurt you caused when you walked out the door and walked outta my life. Un-cry these tears I cried so many nights. Un-break my heart, my heaaaarrt, oooooh."

The words of the Tony Braxton song blared from the radio, and I sang along with great gusto. I was enjoying every moment alone in the car, with no fear of my private karaoke being slightly off-key or just plain too loud. *Perfect song. Right in my range,* I thought to myself as I sang with passion. *The words are completely depressing, though. Boy, that would be awful. Good thing I have a great marriage. I feel sorry for people who have to go through that kind of pain.*

Commuting alone was a welcome diversion from my constant interaction with people. Don't get me wrong, I love people, but with three highly social teenagers, my home resembled a busy shopping mall more than a quiet place to escape from the outside world.

One of my biggest dreams at this stage in my life was to take a weekend and go to a cabin in the mountains all alone – without even my beloved husband Brian. I would eat chocolate and drink wine while reading a good book in front of the fireplace, totally uninterrupted. But there was no time in my life to make this dream a reality right now.

I swiftly rounded the corner, hit the left turn signal light and headed up the hill towards our home on a quiet residential street. Our place looked like all the other houses on the street. It was what's commonly referred to as a B.C. (British Columbia) box, in reference to its unoriginal floor plan.

I edged into our driveway, coming to an abrupt stop in front of the garage and simultaneously engaging the emergency break. I clicked off the blaring radio, switched off the headlights, grabbed the keys from the ignition, and hopped out of the car.

Swinging the door shut, I headed for the house with a bounce in my step. I had just come from music practice, where I was learning how to sing. I loved it! I had great friends there and singing was therapy for my soul. I opened the front door, feeling grateful for my life, grateful for Brian, and grateful for our marriage.

We'd been challenged in the past few months by my extra hours at work, the death of Brian's father, and the truly harrowing teenage episodes of our oldest daughter, Danielle, but I felt that we could make it through these problems. Brian and I were best friends and passionate lovers. He was a good provider, a hard-working, rough and tough kind of man's man, and I loved him beyond measure.

When I came in, I could see Brian standing in the kitchen. He turned and looked at me. He didn't look happy. I recalled what a grouch he'd been yesterday, which was Mother's Day.

He had complained that the kids didn't honor me in any way for the special occasion. Somehow this made me feel sad, guilty, and hurt all at the same time, as if it were my job to teach our children to honor their mother, not his. Brian had given me a pot of bright yellow geraniums, but it felt like they were given out of duty rather than love.

I forgave him, though. I knew the past few months had been hard on him. I was determined to be loving and supportive. In fact, I welcomed the opportunity to be strong for him when he needed me to. It made me feel like a good wife.

Now his eyes seemed to be filled with a strained and questioning sadness. I gave him a reassuring smile, and then he spoke.

"Anne, we need to get the kids off to bed so we can talk." Even though Brian's tone was serious, I felt excited. I really enjoyed talking with my husband and hoped that we could have a long overdue heart-to-heart. Over the past six months, I had wondered whether Brian was depressed. Something was wrong inside of him. I had made every effort to find out what was wrong, but he closed me off.

I suggested that I make coffee. He thought that would be fine. Coffee makes talking fun. It creates the mood.

When I had doctored up our coffees just the way each of us likes it, I entered the living room carrying two mugs. I handed Brian his, and curled up on the large chair next to the sofa where he was sitting.

"I need to talk with you about something," Brian said. I kept my mouth shut and waited. One thing I had learned from Brian is never to talk when you should be listening. Some people need long periods of silence before they can express themselves. His face looked strained. He looked into my eyes, then quickly looked away.

After a long silence, he said "I, um…" I continued to wait patiently and said nothing. I wanted to encourage him. I could see he was struggling intensely. I didn't know how to help him.

Whatever he was about to say, I wanted and needed to hear it. Still, a slow fear began creeping up my body, starting at my feet. I carefully placed my coffee mug on the table, having taken only one sip.

"This is really difficult," Brian said. "I don't know how to say this.

I don't know how to start. I really love you, Anne. I didn't mean for this to happen." After what seemed like an eternity had passed, he continued. "I'm involved with someone else."

———•———

When I was little, I decided I would *never* get married. If marriage was what my parents had, I didn't want any part of it, not the manipulation, the misunderstandings, the mind games or the pain, and especially not the divorce. Ever. But on Sept. 26, 1981, life dealt me a wild card. His name was Brian Bercht.

At the time, I was twenty and working as a draftsman trainee for an engineering company in Houston, Texas. My boss Tom was a man of character who was devoted to his wife and children. He was the first man to treat me with respect in the workplace. Tom was compassionate, wise, and an excellent mentor – which I needed.

I'd brought a mountain of personal problems with me to the job, like a snail carrying the weight of its house upon its back. I had money problems, relationship problems, self-esteem problems and, to top it all off, my seventeen-year-old brother was living with me, so that he could attend school in the United States. (Our Danish mother planned to join us as soon as she was able to sell her property in Europe.)

Six months of working with Tom had transformed my life into something I could be proud of. I felt like a truly free person. As a result, for the first time since I was thirteen, I was not only *not* dating anyone, I was completely uninterested in the whole dating game. Of course, this was the moment when my knight in shining armor decided to ride into town on his Yamaha 750.

Ironically, I met Brian while out on a blind date with someone else entirely. Tom set me up with a wealthy contractor named Dirk, a Canadian who was touring the U.S. by motorcycle with his buddy Brian.

Tom had fast-talked me into taking Dirk as my date to our company's annual outing, a baseball game at the Astrodome with luxury seats in a skybox. Dirk asked if he could bring his fellow biker along, which was fine with me. After all, I didn't want to be going on a date, remember? Brian was twenty-two.

The three of us had a great evening together, and over the course of the next two weeks I showed the two of them all the sights of Houston. When Brian asked me to go out with him alone, I said yes. Five nights – and five dates – later, Brian was over at my place watching me bake chocolate chip cookies for him. We were laughing, talking, and joking while I worked, thoroughly enjoying each other's company.

Something deeper was happening, too. When I looked into Brian's blue eyes that night, I felt something inside me passionately wanting to love this man, to be his companion and constant supporter. I suddenly knew I wanted to spend the rest of my life with him.

At precisely that moment, Brian blurted, "I can't ask you to marry me!"

"Why?" I responded.

"Because you are standing up!"

I strode out of the kitchen, headed straight for the living room sofa, and flung myself into a sitting position. Brian followed me, smiling with a sweetness rare among strong men. He got down on one knee, took my hand, and looked into my eyes.

"Anne, will you marry me?"

"Yes, yes, yes!" I responded with joy. It was that simple. And that right.

We hugged and we kissed and we wondered if we had both totally lost our minds. Less than three weeks had passed since the day we met.

The first thing we did was go to Tom for some sound advice. Neither of us wanted to make a decision that would end up hurting the other person. We were thrilled to hear Tom say he thought Brian and I were meant for each other. I had been raised without religious training, but had recently found meaning in life and values worth living for by including God and church in my life. Brian shared my new-found beliefs, and we thought our common values gave us a good foundation for building a marriage.

One evening, Brian and I had driven to the beach in Galveston, we decided to spend the night together there in my Pontiac Bonneville. Now, this is exactly what two young people intent on abstinence before marriage should not do.

That night in my car, Brian, in spite of his strong physical desire for me, stopped us at the heavy kissing stage and said, "You get in the back seat and stay there. I'll sleep here in the front. You are far too valuable a woman for me to sleep with before I've made a public promise to you for a lifetime."

As a teenager, desperately looking for the love that was lacking in my life, I had been promiscuous. My mother, with her Scandinavian ideals, encouraged me to enjoy and experience my sexuality. Waiting until one is married to have sex is not encouraged in Denmark. Unfortunately these early sexual encounters were not ful- filling for me. They made me feel used and cheapened, lowered my self-esteem and left me heartbroken. I wish I had been warned of the emotional consequences of such promiscuity.

Can you imagine then, how my heart melted that night at the beach in my car, when Brian told me that I was so special, so valu- able, that he wasn't going to sleep with me until he had married me! I accept no credit for the fact that our wedding night was our first night "together." That night in my car, I was overcome with desire and certainly would have given myself to him.

Our wedding was very small and hugely joyful. There were twenty people present: my guardians (who had made it possible for me to complete my schooling in the United States), my father, my best friend, Tom's close family, four coworkers, and five friends from my church. I wore a beautiful wedding dress I'd found in a Salvation Army thrift store, and I glowed from head to foot. It had been five weeks since the day we first met.

Much to the dismay of my father, who had offered to rent us a fancy car for the occasion, we chose to make our getaway aboard

Brian's motorcycle. We left in the pouring rain. It was the happiest day of my life. If I had it to do all over again, I would do only one thing differently. I would delay the wedding long enough to allow my mother time to travel from Europe. In my youthful state of self-centered bliss, it had not occurred to me that a mother should be given the opportunity to attend her only daughter's wedding, even if she were 5,000 miles away.

Our honeymoon consisted of finishing Brian's vacation, returning to Canada on his motorcycle, and including a detour to Vancouver so I could meet his family. We loved riding the motorcycle through the warm desert highways of New Mexico and Arizona, figuring out ways to kiss while wearing helmets and keeping our eyes on the road. Once Brian drove the motorcycle way out into the desert somewhere, and we made love in the sand near a cactus or two.

After spending a couple of weeks with Brian's family in Vancouver, we parked the motorcycle, a smart move when traveling through the Canadian Rockies in November, and booked a flight to Calgary, Alberta. When we stepped off the plane together it was -20°C – and me with my suitcase full of summery clothing that was suitable year-round in Houston. I had left behind all my other belongings for my new life in a small Alberta town with a man I was determined to love for the rest of my days.

So started my adventure, and had either Brian or I been able to see the snares that lay before us – including bankruptcy, infidelity, arson, suicide attempts and drunk driving convictions – I think we would have been too afraid to begin. But then we would have missed the blessings in disguise that the universe brings us all when we determine to live our lives with integrity and – no matter what happens – to never, never, never quit.

Life is not a straight and simple path, but I am convinced that each detour along the way holds a lesson uniquely designed to prepare us for our greater destiny, if we are only courageous enough to learn that lesson. As the saying goes, joy comes in the journey, not just in the final destination.

With Brian's confessions, it felt as though my journey was now blocked by an impassable boulder. I sat motionless, stunned. I had had no idea Brian was having an affair. I had never imagined there was anyone else. I had grown to trust him one hundred percent.

I knew these things could happen to couples and that's why I never took Brian for granted. That's why I worked so hard to learn and do all I could to be a great wife.

I felt as if my blood had stopped flowing through my veins. There was a sharp pain in my chest, as if someone was cutting apart the inside of my heart, turning and ripping a sharp knife into my flesh.

But I ignored the pain and the growing lump in my throat.

"I forgive you," I said placidly, as if this was a church play and I was a perfect little church mouse, performing according to script. My mind could not grasp what was happening.

"I knew you would say that," Brian snarled with frustration. "I wish you would just get mad and throw me out of the house. It would be so much easier!"

I explained that Brian would have to choose between us. It was her or me. I knew full well he would choose me. After all, the love we shared was genuine. Besides, I was desperate to get my Cinderella life back. After a long silence had elapsed, I realized that Brian actually wasn't sure who to choose. I was in a state of total disbelief.

Brian told me the rest of the story. He had known this other woman for six months. They met through work. She was one of the structural architects for the construction project Brian was working on. Their affair had taken place over the past two months during their lunch hours, in spite of our agreement that neither one of us would go for lunch alone with a member of the opposite sex. We had developed this policy precisely to protect our marriage from a situation like this.

The other woman was one year younger than myself, and according to Brian, she looked like me. She was also married and had one child, a six-year old girl. So there was not one, but there were two, families being broken up here. I didn't care to know her name yet, so I never asked. I was satisfied to be reassured that I had never met this woman. To me, she was a stranger and an enemy.

Brian and I sat in silence just staring, at nothing, for a long time. There was nothing more to say. Eventually he left the room and went to bed. I was unable to move from my chair.

So that was it. My husband was not only having an affair, but he had developed strong feelings for this other woman – feelings so strong, in fact, that when forced to choose, he wasn't sure who he wanted to spend the rest of his life with. I was not about to share my husband.

My marriage was hanging in the balance. My security was gone. My future had suddenly and without warning become unknown. Would he choose her or me?

I did not move from my chair all night. I sat frozen in place, staring into the darkness. This was the first night in eighteen years that Brian went to bed without kissing me goodnight. Even that felt surreal.

The pain was too great to bear. I was in a state of shock. It would have been much easier to deal with death than this betrayal by one so loved, so close, so trusted.

How could this be happening to me? Why were there no warning signs? If we had argued recently ... but we had been getting along wonderfully. If sex had been less exciting ... but we had been having great sex every night.

Well, maybe there were a few nights when I was too exhausted from a busy day. But whenever I didn't fall asleep the minute my head hit the pillow, we had sex. On a scale of one to ten, we had lots of tens – and a few what I call "regular sex" nights thrown in between.

I really thought I knew Brian. I was sure that I would have detected anything wrong in our relationship. The whole thing was so unfair, so utterly cruel. I hated the other woman.

For a fleeting moment, I imagined myself murdering her. I wanted to kill this horrible, awful human animal without morals who had come into my life and turned my perfect world upside down.

Then I was horrified. I couldn't believe that I had entertained a thought of killing someone. I saw that I had evil lurking within me, just below the surface. I saw inside myself and what I saw was ugly. I immediately forced the evil fantasies out of my thoughts and tried to think good thoughts. What would a good person do?

But for the first time in my life, I understood how one human being could take the life of another.

I thought about God and I was grateful that I had taken the time to develop a spiritual anchor to sustain me in my life's darkest hour.

"Even when walking through the dark valley of the shadow of death I will not be afraid, for you are close beside me, guarding, guiding all the way ... Your goodness and unfailing kindness shall be with me all of my life, and afterwards I will live with you forever in your home."

PSALM 23, THE LIVING BIBLE

The words I had once taken the time to memorize comforted me.

CHAPTER 2

Before *the* Affair

The first year of my marriage was the best year of my life. The whole year was like a honeymoon. In fact, we were married for eight months before we even had an argument.

Brian ran his own construction business, and I spent my days cleaning our small apartment, doing laundry, preparing meals and baking. It gave me lots of time to pursue the other activities I loved: reading, learning, walking, sports and friends. Brian and I also started working with local teenagers through our church, and found a real calling in organizing activities for them and inspiring them to reach for their highest destinies. The love Brian and I shared was truly special. When I compared notes with my girlfriends, I found that few other couples in our circle were experiencing marriage with the same level of intimacy. Many women I knew complained about their husbands, often insulting them, even in public. As I listened to their stories, I felt sorry for these women, but I also wondered if their marriages wouldn't have been better if they had encouraged their husbands more.

My motto was, "Treat a man as though he were what he ought to be, and he will become a better man." I tried to help Brian in everything he did. I admired him and believed in him wholeheartedly. He repeatedly proved himself to be wise, caring and kind. He also had a friendly personality and was well liked. I enjoyed showing up for social gatherings on his arm, just knowing I was the wife of Brian Bercht.

The two of us hadn't yet discussed whether we would have children, but in January, a little over a year after our wedding, I missed my monthly cycle. January gave way to February, and still no menstrual cycle.

"Maybe you should see a doctor," Brian said. Ten days later the doctor said, "Congratulations, Mrs. Bercht, you're pregnant."

Hearing this news, a sense of joy welled up so large within me I could scarcely take it in. Also, like many expectant mothers the world over, I could hardly wait! The love I felt for the tiny unknown human growing within me was already overwhelming. I busied myself eating the healthiest of foods, reading pregnancy and parenting books, and ensuring that I did everything to help that precious child grow healthy and strong inside me.

I clearly remember my first day at home with my new baby. Baby Danielle. Brian drove us from the hospital to our brand-new home which he had built for us. We had lunch and made love. Then, after a few hours, he went back to work. I waved from the living room window and watched his truck disappear down the snowy road.

Suddenly, I felt incredibly alone. It was just me and a tiny helpless child. My child. I knew nothing about babies, and I couldn't bear to fail this precious little person in any way. If the world was a fair place, each baby would come equipped like a doll from a store with a guarantee and an instruction booklet.

I held Danielle gently, securely, and affectionately in my arms. She was sleeping peacefully. Secretly I promised this new little person that I would always take care of her. I would never neglect her. I would do whatever it took to give her what she needed, not just physically, but emotionally as well. Then I felt afraid. It seemed too large a task, too big a responsibility, too much of a risk. I cried and longed for my own mother to take care of me.

During the four years that followed, Brian and I brought two more little people, Dustin and Tamara, into the world. Like Danielle, they were both unplanned, very wanted, and the product of deep love.

Danielle was a non-conformist child with unlimited energy. Not understanding much about children, I drew the false conclusion with her that I was simply inadequate as a parent.

I was thrilled when our son Dustin was born. Not only did we now have the son Brian and I wanted so much, but Dustin was a refreshing opposite to his older sister. He was so calm and quiet that other mothers used to ask me if I had given him a sedative. At the age of two on Christmas he was completely content with one matchbox car. We tried to encourage him to open his many other gifts, but he preferred to use the beautifully wrapped packages as a series of highways for the one small car, which he drove along while making a gentle *r-r-r-r-r-r-r-r-r-r* sound.

Throughout his years, Dustin has remained a deep thinking, calm and loyal individual. Once he embraces you as *friend,* you are his friend for life. If a person wrongs someone Dustin cares about, he defends that person no matter what the cost. Dustin is tolerant and patient, but once you cross the line, it's not so easy to obtain his forgiveness.

Tamara was my special gift. When I was pregnant with her, I had become very depressed, convinced that I was incapable of being the mother of three children. Throughout my pregnancy, I prayed for joy. Therefore when she was born, I gave her "Joy" for a middle name. Tamara Joy. Little did I realize how appropriate this was. I'll never forget when she was two years old. One day it was pouring rain and dark gray clouds covered the entire sky. She stood looking out the living room window disappointed that she couldn't play outside. Then she enthusiastically said to me, "It's raining, but soon it will be sunny!" I was amazed. I didn't realize there was such a thing as a born optimist. Tamara was always cheerful. She brought me constant joy. Imagine, God answered my prayer through the child I had been carrying.

I was privileged to be able to stay home and take care of them while Brian ran his construction company. With all my heart I wanted to be a good mother, second only to wanting to be a good wife. To me the greatest gift any mother could give her children would be to love their father and provide them with a home that had both a mom and a dad, something I never had.

I had eccentric parents and a very unusual childhood. My father had been a Captain in the British Army, an intellectual man who liked crisply ironed white shirts and believed a woman's place was in the home. My mother was physically a very beautiful woman, also very intelligent, outgoing, adventurous and impulsive. As a Dane, she was strongly influenced by liberal beliefs and women's lib. Opposites attract, but this match was nothing short of a war waiting to happen, and happen it did!

Born in Northern England, I made my first trip across the Atlantic when I was two weeks old. My father had secured employment in the United States as a high energy physicist, working at Chicago's Argonne National Laboratory. He was an unusually brilliant man, border line genius, who has made many significant scientific contributions to the world and given many talks in the White House. Unfortunately his achievements did not necessarily make him a good husband or a good father.

I spent my childhood moving back and forth across the Atlantic Ocean, because my mother was continuously getting angry and moving home to Denmark. The grass was always greener on the side we weren't living on.

I am the oldest child and only daughter with three younger brothers, two of them half brothers. When I was two, my first brother and I were bounced back and forth between countries and guardians as a result of custody disputes, which were dramatic for everyone and heart wrenching for my mother. During this time she lost so much weight that she was reduced to skin and bones. My mother never had anyone to help her through the trauma she suffered, which in many ways left her incapable of caring for her children, including me.

The first I ever remember being on time for school, I was in the second grade and it was the day in the fall when we turn back our clocks. I received a standing ovation from my class. I was so humiliated by the experience that from that moment forward I figured out how to set my own alarm clock and get to school by myself. I never had the right clothes or the right anything else and so I suffered constant ridicule and by the time I was in the fifth grade I hated school in spite of the fact that I was a straight "A" student. I had few friends at school throughout my twelve years at seven schools in four cities and two continents.

I love both my parents and tried hard to please them, but I always felt I failed. My father had a drinking problem which frightened me. He did try hard to be a good father. I visited him on weekends whenever we lived in the United States and he took me on special outings and to eat in fine restaurants, something my mother couldn't afford. My most positive memories with my father are walking in the arboretum listening to him whistle a tune, and when he used to read me poetry. His enchanting British accent contributed to his fascinating poetic rhythm and captivating voice.

My mother was often too busy working, being a single parent, to be my mother. She just wasn't able to be home much. But when she was home she used to tell me not to worry, that I was like the ugly duckling in Hans Christian Anderson's fairy tale and that really, I was a beautiful swan. It was just that the people around me couldn't appreciate me. That always encouraged me.

As a child, the only thing I ever wished for was a whole family, a mom and a dad together with me. I was always envious of the kids whose family lives seemed normal.

Now this gift above all gifts belonged to me. I finally had a family, and even if I had to be the mother and not the child, I was content to finally have fulfilled the desire hidden in the most secret place of my heart.

Brian turned out to be a very good father. In fact, he had an amazing ability to connect with children. He was also a good husband. And when it came to romance he was second to none.

One year when Brian had been putting in long hours at work, I had been complaining that he wasn't spending enough quality time with me. When Christmas time approached, I told him I didn't want a present. I just wanted his time. I'll never forget the thoughtful gift he gave me that year. It was a beautiful burgundy briefcase and inside was a matching daytimer. In the daytimer, he had already penciled in weekly date nights for the two of us. He kept them all!

I think my friends were envious. But I often found they were not as enthusiastic about sex as I was.

This was illustrated in a discussion I had with several of my girlfriends one evening. One friend had read somewhere that it might be a good idea to dance naked in front of your husband. She said she couldn't imagine herself doing that, and confessed that she felt shy about allowing her husband to see her naked at all. I encouraged my reluctant friends to feel free, have fun, and enjoy sex.

"After all, you don't want your husband to be tempted to go somewhere else to watch nude dancing, do you?" I asked. I would remember that remark twelve years later when I learned that having a great sex life is no guarantee your husband won't have an affair.

In 1993, Brian's business began to flag. Financial pressures mounted, and before we knew it, we found ourselves dangerously near bankruptcy. Then one Saturday morning while Brian was attending a seminar at the church, he received an urgent phone call. It was one of his staff members with bad news: more problems with customers and suppliers, more money lost.

When Brian hung up and returned to the meeting, the speaker was saying with authority, "It takes courage to face the reality of the situation. It takes courage to make a decision. It takes courage to do something about your problems."

Brian felt as if a ton of bricks had just landed on his head. *Yeah,* he thought, *the reality is that I have failed in my business and I've been refusing to face it.*

That afternoon Brian discussed the details of our dire situation with a close friend and spiritual advisor. Eventually they agreed that bankruptcy was inevitable and Brian would have to act fast. Otherwise, on Monday we would have to borrow even more money from the bank to appease suppliers, which would only make matters worse. They felt that leaving town, and relocating to the Vancouver area was our best option.

I felt resentful about being excluded from the decision-making process. I understood that bankruptcy was inevitable, but I didn't understand why we had to move to the West Coast. In my mind, there were many possibilities, including returning to Denmark, where I was raised and where most of my family still lived.

Brian's advisor, Pierre, said we should leave town as quickly as possible. Staying in town would mean no work for Brian, as well as mounting criticism and potentially volatile confrontations with debtors. Pierre suggested that losing the business would be hard enough. We didn't need to hang around for the hurtful gossip as well.

On Sunday night Brian made a plan. He would go to work in the morning, pretending everything was fine. I was to pack up the entire household into the large truck we owned for our business. At night Brian would collect his tools from his deserted construction sites and then come home. We would move out of our house by the end of the day, stay with friends for a couple of days while we took care of the legal paperwork with our bankruptcy trustee, and then drive the six hundred miles to Vancouver with no money and no real prospects.

On Monday morning I called one of my best friends, who sobbed in disbelief at the news of our plan. However, she also went into action, and by eleven that morning my living room was filled with empty cardboard boxes and twenty trustworthy women from our church. They had dropped their own plans for the day to work like bees and help me cope with my emergency.

The things that transpired in my home that day were a miracle, and a true reflection of how kind people can be in a crisis. Everything was taken care of. Someone looked after my children. Another person made a giant pot of chili and brought it over to feed everyone. Yet another friend put together a care package for my long drive. She included snacks and activities to entertain the children. She also packed encouraging cassette tapes, because she knew that once I stopped packing and started driving, I would begin to see the mess we were in and feel the pain of suddenly saying goodbye to virtually everyone I knew. I would need encouragement.

By midnight all the personal and household belongings that could be packed were loaded up. While some friends continued to move miscellaneous items from our basement, I was encouraged to go find the bed awaiting me at a friend's house. As I stepped out the door of the house into the crisp November air, it really hit me: I would never again cross this threshold and enter the house I'd called home for ten years.

That night a chapter in my life ended. Once again the future had become a great unknown. My pastor once said, "We may lose many battles along the way, but if we remain on the side of that which is good, in the end we win the war." I was shocked and saddened and afraid, but I was a warrior and I was going to win my war.

Rain was pouring down as we drove into Abbotsford, a small city thirty miles east of Vancouver and close to the Washington State border. With no place else to go we landed on Brian's mother's doorstep. Home is where they always let you in, no matter what you've just been through.

By May we had rented a house, and our life slowly began to settle into a new routine. I regret to say that it took me a couple of years to fully forgive Brian for not really including me in the decision-making process, and for moving me away from my close Alberta friends so suddenly. As it turned out though, Brian had made a very good choice. Abbotsford was a wonderful place for our family.

Overcoming bankruptcy proved to be both difficult and humiliating. It was not easy to go from driving new vehicles and having a nice home, to having one clunker work van and a rented house. I was quite sure that our new friends perceived us as a couple of really needy down-and-outers. People do judge by appearances.

As the years progressed after our bankruptcy, it seemed that life just continued to get busier and busier. We were working longer and longer hours, yet seemed to be enjoying fewer and fewer luxuries. Some years we couldn't afford to take any holidays at all. If Brian did manage to get time off from his construction business, our budget afforded us not more than a camping holiday. We rarely allowed ourselves the pleasure of eating out in a restaurant or going on a date.

Adding to our growing list of discouragements, Brian's father had just passed away. That was a story in itself. It didn't come as a shock. He had been in a near fatal accident some years previous that had left him in a wheelchair and with a serious head injury. The strange thing about his passing was that there was no funeral, so his grown children never had the opportunity to grieve the loss of their father. Two days after his father's passing, I asked Brian, "Are you really okay about losing your dad?"

"Yes," he answered, "I'm fine."

It was a Sunday afternoon, and I was tired, so I laid down for a nap. I awoke to find a barren wilderness, in place of my previous garden. Brian's decision to "trim" the shrubs had resulted in their complete disappearance. Fine, indeed!

While living in Alberta, I had been Brian's business partner, responsible for administration and accounting, something I could usually do from home or in the evenings, which allowed me time to raise my children and just be mom. Losing our business and the higher cost of living in British Columbia forced me to work outside the home, something I wasn't too eager to do.

Initially, I accepted a position in retail sales, which I didn't enjoy very much. But within a couple of years, I had landed an excellent full-time position working for a business consulting company. I started applying my skills in the role of office manager, and soon found myself assisting with seminars, sales and marketing and eventually teaching, developing curriculums and writing, roles I loved and excelled in naturally.

So this was the picture of our lives: a relatively normal middle-class Canadian family struggling to survive. Working hard, experiencing stress, doing all the things society expected us to do, and deep down … life was boring. Too much responsibility, not enough play. We were firmly planted on the treadmill of modern society, seemingly unable to disembark. Then came the new millennium, and with it our greatest storm, a year our family barely survived.

In February, Brian and I attended a leadership conference in Seattle, Washington. I was particularly inspired by a talk on never giving up. Brian seemed down during most of the conference, and on the evening of this particular talk he was feeling sick and had decided to rest in our hotel room.

The title of the talk was "It Ain't Over 'til it's Over," and the speaker discussed how often, when things look the bleakest, we are actually on the verge of one of our greatest personal victories. I believe I heard that message that night by divine appointment, although I was still unaware of the storm that was brewing in my life.

Everyone has a story to tell. Each and every individual on this earth is given a unique set of assets to enjoy and unique trials to endure in this life. At times when I hear another's story, I am awed that through no effort of my own, I have been spared their particular pain. But then I am given a trial that the next person is not. I ask myself, is it possible that the assets or strengths that I am given are the very ones I need in order to travel the particular journey that is mapped out ahead of me?

Part of my journey was raising my three children, including my exceptionally strong-willed daughter, Danielle. Danielle seemed to be born into this world with unlimited drive and energy, an unstoppable will, and a readiness to take on anyone who would in any way oppose her or stand in her way. There is not a doubt in my mind she is destined for some great success, but raising a child like this is no easy task.

As parents we believed a carefully administered "spanking" to be an appropriate form of discipline, and coupled with lots of love, understanding and age-appropriate guidance, a part of a healthy childhood. However, in Danielle's case, we quickly threw the theory away, as she would shout back at us, "Spank me harder, I'll do it more!" No amount of pain would ever deter Danielle from doing something she had determined to do. A different approach was always needed.

As the years passed, there were countless stories to tell regarding Danielle's dynamic personality. Some positive, some negative, some hilarious and entertaining, none boring and all dramatic. She is highly intelligent, extremely perceptive, and could persuade most people into pretty much anything. When she wants something, she will stop at nothing to get it.

As Danielle's mother I was living life on the edge. She won contests, was praised by her teachers, had accidents, went to the hospital, helped others, and helped the police with their inquiries. The only guarantee I had was that if some commotion was going on, Danielle would be there in one capacity or another. If I pulled up at the school and noticed any emergency vehicles, ambulance, police, fire, whatever, I would always drive up and quickly make my way to the center of the crowd. I knew without doubt that Danielle would be right in the middle of whatever was going on.

During the conference we were attending, Danielle had phoned us with a cheerful voice to say everything was going well, and she looked forward to talking to me when we got back. When we arrived home, she wanted to go out for coffee just her and me. I felt like a good mother. *My teenager wants to have coffee with her mom. What an open relationship we have,* I thought.

We sat down at a table in the small, cozy coffee shop, with a couple of fancy flavored lattés.

"Guess what?" Danielle said cheerfully, "I've decided to quit school." I was immediately onto her subtle ploy.

"Actually, Danielle," I said, "we are not going to have this conversation without your father here. Let's talk about something else now, and we'll talk about this big issue when we get home."

Danielle lost her cool and shouted profanities at me, creating an unpleasant scene in front of the other patrons. I got up and left the restaurant in silence as she shouted at me and people looked on in silent astonishment. I felt humiliated beyond description. Danielle followed me outside and demanded that I drive her to a friend's home. I left her in the coffee shop parking lot without saying another word.

Brian and I seemed to be on a teenage roller coaster ride whether we liked it or not. One conflict led to another, despite our efforts to deal with each situation with love and support. We had clear boundaries as to what was and wasn't acceptable behavior in our home, but Brian and I began to disagree about how to handle these conflicts, he leaning towards a hard line and me leaning towards love and support. Not easy disagreements to resolve when you are discussing someone you both love so much.

The stress began to take its toll. A month after Danielle started to act out, I came down with a very serious case of bronchitis that almost turned to pneumonia. The doctor ordered me to take a two week leave of absence from work. I coughed unceasingly as I lay alone on my bed.

Life was beginning to feel a little like one of those action films, where some guy (me, in this case) gets beat up and more bad guys keep coming from every direction.

After I recovered from my sickness, I decided to take an extended leave of absence from work to deal with the problems at home. During this time, I drew closer to my friends, and found more time for quiet and meditation.

I spent some of my down time at monthly gatherings with other women, where we shared personal stories to encourage each other. Often these brief presentations were about a major challenge and a corresponding victory.

In early May I sat contentedly in one of these meetings sipping coffee and listening to a young Japanese mother quietly share her story. When Mameha was a girl, she had been walking home with her sister one evening when a car came from behind and knocked the girl down. One moment they walked together hand-in-hand, the next moment her sister was lying dead in the street. A dozen of us sat stunned, eyes filled with tears as we listened to the effect this trauma had on Mameha, her family, and her future.

Mameha then told us in a low voice that her husband had had an affair and said he was leaving her for the other woman. Later he had decided to stay with her after all. Mahema said that despite having seen her sister run down, her husband's betrayal had been the most difficult experience of her life. "I don't even know why I shared that," she added, head bowed. "I wasn't going to tell you."

I felt so sorry for Mahema, believing that I would never have to go through such a terrible experience. I thanked God for Brian more than ever that night.

CHAPTER 3

suᴦviving
the fiᴦst Day

DAY ONE — TUESDAY, MAY 16, 2000

Footprints

One night a man had a dream. He dreamed he was walking along the beach with the Lord. Across the sky flashed scenes from his life. For each scene, he noticed two sets of footprints in the sand, one belonging to him, and the other to the Lord. When the last scene of his life flashed before him, he looked back at the footprints in the sand. He noticed that many times along the path of his life there was only one set of footprints. He also noticed that it happened at the very lowest and saddest times in his life. This really bothered him and he questioned the Lord about it.

"Lord, you said that once I decided to follow you, you'd walk with me all the way. But I have noticed that during the most troublesome times in my life, there is only one set of footprints. I don't understand why when I needed you the most you would leave me." The Lord replied, "My precious, precious child, I love you and I would never leave you. During your times of trial and suffering, when you see only one set of footprints, it was then that I carried you.

AUTHOR UNKNOWN

When the morning light began to fill the room, I was still in my chair and my coffee was still sitting on the table. Now cold and missing only one sip.

I looked around the room. It was full of flowers. I always loved flowers, but this morning the fragrant bouquets were more beautiful to me than they had ever been before. For some strange reason, I had received floral arrangements from all sorts of sources this Mother's Day.

It looked like a funeral had just taken place in my living room, and indeed it had. A part of me died the previous night.

I had always wondered why people sent flowers when someone died. It seemed a contradiction to me, as if a few bouquets would help to take the pain of grief away. Well they don't, but when your world is ugly and dark it helps to be reminded that there is still some beauty in the world. I looked at the flowers, they gave me a small comfort, and I was grateful for them.

Mustering all the strength within me, driven by an intense love for my children, I somehow pulled myself together just long enough to get the kids off to school. (Danielle was now sixteen, Dustin was fourteen and Tamara was twelve.)

Then, I took the next important step to get on with my life. I called a friend.

Lori, the wife of the pastor of my church was my first choice. I dialed her up after driving my kids to school. "Hello," she answered.

"Hi Lori. It's Anne. I'm coming over," I said. I didn't possess the capacity for the normal small talk.

"But Anne," she protested, "I'm not even dressed."

"That's why I'm calling you now," I said. "I'll be there in ten minutes, so you have ten minutes to get dressed."

I just had to make it to Lori's. I could make it that far, and at this moment that's all I required of myself. Only one small step.

I arrived at her home safely and felt that was an achievement. I walked up to the door, knocked and waited. When Lori opened the door, I just stood there trembling and began to sob. At last my body was able to give way to grief.

"What's wrong?" Lori cried. I was unable to speak, and continued shaking and sobbing in her doorway.

"What's wrong?" she repeated, shouting this time.

"Brian is leaving me for another woman." I finally got the words out. "Lori, he doesn't even know if he wants to be with me anymore."

Lori and I were relatively close friends. We had known each other for six years, and in her mind, Brian and I were a strong couple. We were known as a couple with strong moral convictions who had served others, given back to the community, and acted as role models for others. All now seemed shattered.

Lori and I sat at her kitchen table, and we both stared out blankly in disbelief. Neither of us spoke for a long time.

Finally Lori declared, "No, no, no. This is not going to happen. This mess is going to become a message." She spoke as one with authority, one without doubt. She then told me the story of another couple, whose marriage began as a total mess. But they had given their mess over to God. God helped transform their relationship into something beautiful. Then their mess became a message for others. The couple now has a television ministry.

For the moment, her words offered a small comfort. *Could it be that there was any hope at all for my future?*

"What are you going to do today?" Lori asked. "You have to have a plan."

This was the second right thing I did: I planned a survival strategy to live through the first day.

"Well," I said, "I was thinking about going to the mall."

I had always been a very modest person. I was careful with money and I didn't spend much on myself. I had never before used spending money as a way to comfort myself in a difficult time, but on this day, I thought I might buy a new outfit. On this day I didn't care about money. If Brian left me for another woman, they could begin their lovely relationship paying off credit card debt, I reasoned. If he returned home to me, we'd deal with it later. It was the least of my concerns.

"Great idea," Lori enthusiastically confirmed.

Next, I would go for a run. Since the New Year, I had taken up long distance running again. It's a sport I had enjoyed off and on since high school. Already I was running as far as seventeen miles in one stretch, but my usual routine was five miles, three times a week.

Then I would clean the house. A clean house always made me feel happier. Even though I didn't enjoy cleaning it, the good feeling of a clean environment was well worth the effort.

Lori was pleased with my plan, and I was grateful to have a friend to help me carry this burden. "One more thing," Lori said, "we are going to work on your appearance."

My appearance, I thought. *What's that got to do with it?*

"You know how men are," she said. "They are so visual."

I thought I looked good already, but over the next few days I followed her advice, by getting a new hairstyle, purchasing a tanning package and beginning electrolysis treatments.

Although there was some value in doing these things, the emphasis was wrong. Unfortunately, my presently unstable mind was hearing the words "Brian had an affair because you are not pretty enough." This vain imagination was having a significant impact, the future magnitude of which I was yet to experience.

The beauty treatments couldn't happen immediately, but shopping could. I entered the mall feeling numb and dazed. A constant sense of pain was my new companion. Yet I had mastered an attitude of determination. Lori's encouragement had worked, and I was going to conquer this great evil that was attempting to destroy my life, the lives of my children and ultimately Brian's life as well.

"Stay strong and be brave!" Lori had encouraged. "Also, give yourself time and permission to mourn. Something has been stolen from you. You can never get it back. You will never again be able to know that since your marriage, you are the only one your husband has been intimate with. The most important promise, a vow, has been broken. Life will never be the same again. And it's okay to cry about that."

I didn't feel like I could live through this, but it reminded me of childbirth. I wanted out really bad. But like a friend of mine who had actually jumped off the delivery table in the midst of childbirth and assertively announced to the doctors that she quit, I could not escape my situation.

Lori encouraged me to go to God for comfort and strength. Sometimes in life it feels as though things are so bad, that even God can't do anything or say anything to help. Those are the very times, when if we do go to Him, miracles take place and indeed He does carry us, when we cannot carry ourselves.

As I walked through the shopping mall, my mind was not on the shopping. It was on my marriage, my shattered self-esteem and my uncertain future.

I stayed clear of all the stores I normally liked to frequent and instead ventured into the youthful ones I would have shopped in as a teenager. Out with the career woman look and in with fun, easy and adventurous, an expression of my true self – or so I thought.

I bought a cute summer skirt and a white lace top, meant to be worn without a bra. I had been working on losing weight for a few months, and was delighted to discover I was one full dress size smaller than usual.

This small victory couldn't have happened on a better day. I was already blaming myself for the affair. After all, if I were really an attractive woman, this wouldn't have happened to me, right?

It felt good to walk out of the shopping mall with my lady-like parcels. The parcels didn't take away any of the pain I was feeling, but they did provide some comfort.

When I arrived home, I eagerly flung down the parcels and changed into my new clothes.

"Mom, that looks really cute. Did you just buy that?" asked Danielle with enthusiasm.

"Yeah," I said.

"Wow, that's different. I like that. Can I try it on?"

Danielle saw I was hesitating, so headed off to her closet to get something to offer me. She returned a few moments later with an adorable pair of jeans.

"Mom, do you like these?" Danielle asked. "Try them on. I think they might fit you." My sixteen-year-old daughter's denim fitting me? It seemed inconceivable that my thirty-eight-year-old body could fit inside these jeans. I looked at them inquisitively. They might fit.

"Okay, I'll try them on," I said.

Moments later I was spinning myself around almost breathlessly in front of our full-length mirror. I couldn't believe it. They fit! And I thought my posterior looked beautiful with just the right sexy curved shape.

I didn't want to take them off. I felt young and sexy again. This was definitely a good day for this miracle!

I let Danielle borrow my brand new outfit for the special outing she was going on with her girlfriends, and I remained dressed in her jeans with an adorable little top, which she selected for me. She even loaned me a pair of her white sandals and painted my toenails, insisting that this detail was essential for a great look. The new look was a bandage for my shattered self-esteem, and it helped me to live through the day.

All day, I busied myself thinking about what I could do to make myself simply irresistible to Brian. This whole thing was not going to happen. Lori's words earlier in the morning gave me a glimmer of hope, and I was going to fight.

Did this other woman actually think she could waltz into my life and walk off with my husband just like that? She didn't realize who she was messing with. I don't like to fight and make every effort to avoid conflict ninety-nine percent of the time, but this was the one time I was going to take on the battle, and when I fight, I fight to win. I'm not just shadow boxing or playing around!

This woman might have been having lunch, sex and companionship with Brian for two months, but I had been Brian's loving supportive wife for eighteen years. Together we had learned to make passionate love to each other like artists, perfecting a magnificent, unique and incomparable, musical piece through years of practice.

I raised our children almost completely alone, while he worked ridiculous long hours. I had supported him through the devastation of bankruptcy. And now after all the hard work I put into this relationship, should some other woman walk in and steal away the benefits and take away the man Brian had become? The man I had believed in, loved and forgiven many times? No way.

This other woman was going to lose the fight. I was the warrior and I was going to fight like Joan of Arc. I had purpose and passion, and I had pain.

I didn't eat all day. I had no interest in eating. My stomach would not even have been able to handle it. I couldn't fathom the thought of a cup of coffee, even though I was an addict. I had nothing but water all day.

I followed the plan I had made with Lori, and that helped me tremendously.

That evening our pastor contacted Brian, who agreed to at least meet with him. They spent three hours together and I had high hopes that this trained spiritual leader would have the wisdom to know how to talk some sense into Brian. The whole thing just didn't make any sense.

According to Pastor Dave, he spent at least two of their three hours together listening to Brian. And then he laid the facts on the line, in no uncertain terms. He told Brian what the Bible says about marriage and divorce, that he needed to break it off completely with the other woman and return to me and our kids where he belonged, that this whole affair fantasy was ridiculous and would cause everyone involved, including Brian, more pain than pleasure.

However, when Brian came home from this meeting, he said with great frustration: "Pastor Dave didn't listen to me at all. I'm sick of people telling me what to do and how to fix my life. Why doesn't anyone ask, 'Why? Why are these things happening? Why do you feel this way? Why do you want to do this?'"

I was discouraged with our spiritual leader. The church did not have the answer.

Brian: As hard as it seems to believe, the real purpose for my meeting with Dave that evening was to find at least one person who would be willing to listen to what I had to say without passing judgment. I was quite aware of the mess I had gotten myself into and was fully aware that what I was doing was wrong, yet somehow, I did not have the strength to do the right thing on my own.

I was looking for a friend who would stand by me and give me the support to make the right decision concerning my relationship with Helen. I knew what I should do (tell her that our relationship was over and that I never really wanted her), yet I felt that no one was able to hear the cry of my heart.

It is a truly frightening experience to be surrounded by people that care about you, only to find yourself with no one to hear you. I had made my situation in secret and now I was facing the consequences alone.

I knew what Dave would say. I agreed to meet with him as a friend only. He had to leave his pastor's hat at home. I was looking for a way out of this affair. Deep inside I knew I loved Anne and I did not want to leave her. I had hoped that Dave would listen to how I was feeling and the things that I was hurting about. I wanted him to understand the fear I had about hurting Helen. I didn't really want to spend my life with her, but wanted in my marriage some of that fun we had been sharing. I was hoping that Dave would see the scared man in front of him, who only needed a little support, belief and friendship in order to make the correct decisions concerning his own life.

I knew that if I told Helen that I was ending our relationship without having moral support from someone else, she would try to seduce me into being with her. I needed an anchor I could cling to when the persuasive charm tried to pull me out to sea.

After a few hours with Dave, I knew he did not hear what I was saying because he was still wearing his pastor's hat. I felt angry, alone and misunderstood.

I tried to control my thoughts that night, while lying in bed beside my emotionally distant husband, but they raced on out of control, like a racecar doing circles around a track with no finish line. I didn't sleep, but eventually it was morning anyway. My pain had not stopped the sun from rising again the next day. Brian left for work early as usual. Although I was awake, neither of us spoke as he got ready and left.

CHAPTER 4

forgiving the other woman

DAY TWO — WEDNESDAY, MAY 17, 2000

The difference between holding on to a hurt or releasing it with forgiveness is like the difference between laying your head down at night on a pillow filled with thorns or a pillow filled with rose petals.

LOREN FINCHER
MORE STORIES FROM THE HEART

After going without any food for over twenty-four hours, and without sleep for two days, I was dazed and weak. I got up and steadied myself against my bedroom wall. The dizziness left me after a few seconds. Unfortunately I wasn't just having a nightmare. Another woman had managed to have sex with the man who belonged to me and had been my lover for all these years.

Stepping on my weigh scale, I watched the needle steady itself. I had lost four pounds since yesterday. Good.

After using every ounce of energy within me to act normal and get my kids off to school, I came home.

What should I do with myself today? I was thinking. Read. I needed some encouragement. Pray, because I needed help from a Super Power.

The phone interrupted my thoughts.

"Anne, how are you today?" It was Lori. "Would you like to get together and talk? Do you want to go for a walk, and then we can exercise too?"

It felt good to have a friend who cared. We arranged to meet three hours later at a local park for a walk. Then I went to the kitchen to get a glass of water in place of my regular cup of coffee, I returned to my bedroom, and started reading my Bible.

Although I read for half an hour or so, the words on the pages seemed devoid of meaning. I put the Bible down, prayed for help and strength, and then sat in silent meditation. Restlessness was stirring within me, so I rose to my feet and began pacing my bedroom floor, talking to myself and perhaps also to God, trying to get a grip on my feelings, trying to understand, trying to figure out what I should do.

What kind of a woman could do this to someone? I thought to myself. *How could Brian do this to me? Didn't either of them care? How could they be so selfish?*

But Brian was a good man. I didn't want to think of him as bad, so I thought of her as bad instead. No, I thought of her as worse than bad. I thought of her as evil.

I contemplated how women can be so incredibly cruel to each other, how when they decide to pour on their seductive charms and go after a man, they can be almost irresistible. Unprincipled women can be subtle and manipulative in their approach, playing the part of a nice person, and considering themselves to be nice, all the while maintaining an agenda of selfish ambition.

I was finding false comfort in my vain reasoning as it continued to gain negative momentum, moving me deceptively towards a place where peace was not.

My raging thoughts continued on. *I suppose in reality these are the women, who for whatever reasons, have been incapable of finding a man of their own to truly love them. Perhaps they have married someone who is unable to give them the love they long for. Perhaps they are unable to behave as women who deserve that love. So they reason to themselves that they'll just steal a man who belongs to someone else, and I'm sure they feel justified, like an animal killing in the jungle to satisfy its most basic of needs.*

I imagined this woman pouring on her charm, all the while smiling and joking, giving Brian the impression she could give him something he didn't already have at home. *How did she do it?* I wondered. *What did she look like? Was she prettier than I was? Was she a better lover?*

In my mind I saw my husband naked with another woman, enjoying her embrace, and I winced. The thought that the most intimate part of my life had been betrayed made me feel exposed and ashamed. As my anger intensified, I began to pace my bedroom floor, back and forth, faster and faster. What did she look like, I kept wondering, unsure if I dared to find out? *If only this woman didn't exist, that would fix my problem.* Rational reasoning was leaving me completely now.

I wondered how I could kill her, how I could annihilate her from my life forever. Maybe I could do it with a gun. After all, all I would have to do is pull the trigger. Just one quick pull, like pushing a button.

I knew I didn't have the ability to do anything too gory. I couldn't stab her. It would have to be more immediate than that. But where could I get a gun? I didn't know anything about guns. I didn't know where or how to buy one, but I guessed I could find out.

Was I capable? My palms were cold and clammy. I wrenched my fists together tightly, tensing the muscles in my arms as tight as I could, while I bit my lower lip. I tried with all my might to keep from screaming.

I closed my eyes and was motionless, as if in a trance, and I tried to picture myself standing in front of this woman who had stolen the affections of my husband from me. I pictured her to be beautiful with long, dark hair. I saw her as young and slim with flawless features and large breasts, yet with evil clearly visible within her eyes.

I pictured her laughing at me, and I could see straight through her mask of goodness even though Brian had not. He had been deluded, and I needed to save him from the regret he would experience with this deceitful woman.

Brian is in danger, I thought. *Like an ox on the way to the slaughterhouse and like a bird flying into a snare, not knowing the fate awaiting him there.*[1]

I pictured the gun in my hand, hidden. I saw myself saying, "I hope making love to my husband was really good, because you are never going to experience pleasure again. Have fun in hell."

Then I imagined the fear in her eyes in the split second just before I pulled the trigger, and I took pleasure in seeing her suffer for a moment. I wished I could make her suffer more, but I knew I wasn't capable of inflicting prolonged pain. I had to be fast and I had to make sure I didn't miss. I was angry enough to do it.

Oh God. What was I thinking? It was as if I had just awoken from a terrible dream, and I trembled, feeling frightened of myself.

"God help me," I said out loud, as the war between good and evil raged within me. I then reasoned that God probably understood me. For a moment, I tried to stop my thoughts and get a grip. Then I thought, maybe I didn't care about God anymore. Why had He allowed this to happen to me? I felt desperate. I would have to be very careful to kill without getting caught ... *How would I get rid of the body,* I wondered? I thought about how smart the police were at solving crimes, and I thought about what a lousy liar I was.

What if I spent the rest of my life in prison? Would killing her have been worth it? It didn't seem to me that being a good person mattered anymore. Maybe I could get someone else to kill her. I wondered how I could meet someone who didn't care about killing and could do it for me. Maybe I could visit a prison, and talk to the inmates, and learn more from them. I wondered what I might have to offer someone in exchange for the deed. What might I have that was worth the price of a life? Maybe I could just throw this woman off a bridge.

Every time I thought of her, I refused to think of her name. Helen. I knew her name, but I didn't like using it. I didn't think she was a valuable enough human being to be worthy of having a name.

I thought about what I might have done if I had walked in on Brian and his lover while they were having sex. There would probably have been enough adrenaline in me to make me physically stronger than both of them in that moment. I saw myself throwing this woman out naked into the street, taking delight in her humiliation, and functioning with such fury that even Brian was afraid of me.

What's the point of trying to be a good person, I thought, *if you just end up with nothing for all your years of hard work and doing the "right" things? What were the "right" things?* I didn't feel sure I knew anymore. Black seemed white and white seemed black. I didn't care about myself anymore. I didn't care whether I lived or died. I didn't have anything to live for.

Then I remembered my children. I did have something to live for. *I have to be smart for them,* I thought to myself. *I have to keep living, so I can take care of them. They need me. I have to protect my babies and make sure they never get hurt. I have to live and fight for them.*

I just wanted to get rid of Helen. I wanted to make the whole thing go away and get my life back.

I started to calm myself down a bit. The futility and evil of my thoughts was coming into perspective. Two wrongs don't make a right. I couldn't kill someone, but certainly now, for the first time in my life, I understood how someone could. If I allowed myself to react drastically, I knew I would destroy my own future and self.

Brian wouldn't want me anymore if he ever found out that I had lowered myself to killing. There must be a better way to get revenge, a sly and subtle way. Maybe I could do it without doing anything illegal. I wanted to win Brian's affections back, and I wanted to hurt the other woman. I wanted to make her pay for stealing from me, the one thing she could never give back, purity in my marriage.

Then, as if a voice was speaking to me, I heard the words, "You have to forgive her." I don't think they were audible words, just words somewhere in my mind. Yet not my own words, for they seemed to interrupt my own thoughts.

Tears began to pour down my cheeks. I knew the words were true and their truth seemed to penetrate the very center of my being. I wanted to do the right things, but I didn't know how I possibly could.

A long time before learning of Brian's affair, I had done a lot of studying about what it means to really forgive and why we should do it. Forgiveness interested me because I have always had a tremendous amount of forgiving to do in my life. And, quite honestly, it has always been one of my weaker areas. If ever anyone was a master of hanging on to even small offenses for years, it was me. And this hanging on had contributed to a great weight of sadness throughout my life, hindering my ability to experience true joy.

When I became aware of this negative root in my life, I decided to learn what it really means to forgive someone and how to do it. On this day that I wanted to kill Helen, my understanding of forgiveness was invaluable. I understood that the only person who suffers from not forgiving is the offended person, not the person who has committed the offense. I also remembered that the only person who really benefits from forgiveness is the offended person, not the offender.

I could not yet acknowledge Brian's part of the guilt. I viewed him as "friend" and her as "enemy."

Finally, I crumbled to my knees and screamed out, "Oh God,

where are you? Help me. I don't know how to live through this." It felt as if there was an ocean of pain and tears inside of me so huge, that even if I cried all day, I would barely have made a dent in releasing its storming waves of grief.

Yet as I cried out in desperation, I realized that the laws of the universe could not work on my behalf while I myself was harboring hatred within my heart. I had to understand what was true and right, right now.

"And you will know the truth and the truth will set you free," the voice inside my head was saying.

What was truth right now? The truth was my marriage was probably over. The truth was my husband had developed strong feelings for another woman and this truth seemed too cruel a reality to bear. I wanted to run away from the truth, yet I needed to be strong and brave.

Willfully forcing myself to try and think with understanding, I asked myself what was the truth about this woman who had won the affections of my husband? Could it be that she was just a hurting individual, who had reached out and done what she needed to do to meet her own deepest needs? If I had lived her life, would I be capable of the same thing she had done? I didn't know.

I began to think of the times in my life when I had done wrong things, and caused pain to others. I thought of how wonderful it was to be forgiven, and how everyone has a place of kindness in their heart, no matter what they've done in the past.

Was I a better, more deserving individual than her, that I deserved a better life? I knew I wasn't. I was frail and weak like her. I didn't want to admit it, but the Bible taught that all human beings were my brothers and my sisters. In that context Helen was my "sister" too.

"Lord," I was decisively forcing myself to pray for my own benefit, not to benefit the woman who was ruining my life. It reminded me of the same will and resolve I had used many years ago, when I used to jump out of airplanes "for fun." I had been underage at the time, and in order to have permission, I had to persuade my mother to sign a release waiver. When she said to me, "I'll sign this paper, because I know once you get in the door of that airplane, you'll never jump," one thing had been determined with unbending certainty: dead or alive, I would not be landing with the airplane. When the moment came for me to willfully throw myself out of the plane, I remembered her words and my decision. I was frightened beyond description, but when my brain gave the muscles in my body the commands to move, they obeyed. I always had a choice. Not a choice over what would happen to me, but rather a choice over how I would react to it.

While wrestling with myself to pray and to forgive Helen, I thought about Corrie ten Boom's remarkable story, *The Hiding Place,* her account of surviving unthinkable atrocities at the hands of the Germans during World War II. Both her beloved father and sister were killed. Years after the injustices had taken place she had been speaking in a church. There in the audience was the guard who had killed her own dear sister, in a very cruel and inhumane way. After the service, she spoke to the man and forgave him. If she could forgive, I could too.

I thought of forgiveness as an inner decision. I understood that it wouldn't make my pain go away, and I understood that forgiveness didn't mean I wouldn't remember it anymore. What it did mean was that I was making a decision to release my feelings of anger and resentment towards the person who had wronged me.

These thoughts helped me to continue.

"Lord, please forgive my sister for the pain she has caused in my life," I prayed on my knees on the floor beside my unmade bed. My head rested on rumpled quilts I'd made wet with my tears. I trembled and I sobbed.

The pain was so great that I wondered if I was bleeding. It felt as if there were one hundred pounds balancing on top of my head, yet with each word my load seemed to lighten.

"Forgive her for her wrong in stealing my husband's affections from me. God, I know I need to forgive her, but in myself I cannot, yet it is my choice." I willed myself on because I understood it was the key to my own freedom. "I choose to forgive her," I continued forcing myself. "Please help me to do that. Please bless her in her life and meet her needs, but not through my husband. Please help Brian to see the wrong he is doing, and please restore our marriage, if you can."

I believed it was my responsibility to take one step in the right direction and that God would walk beside me, helping me to take the rest. That was faith.

As I ended my prayer, an inexplicable peace filled the room and I collapsed upon my floor exhausted. I felt like a soldier, just finished fighting the battle for my own freedom. I had been a prisoner to my thoughts of anger, hatred, murder and revenge. They had been destroying me from the inside out, threatening my very future. The war with my enmity towards Helen was not yet over, but the first battle had been won and for the moment the vexation was at rest.

At this moment, I encountered a special connectedness to God, which is difficult to describe. I sensed God's presence and power in my life far stronger now, after discovering this betrayal, than ever before and ever since. Yet in the moment, I didn't even recognize it. I was merely surviving. It was later when the strong presence left me that I missed it and recognized that it had been there. I believe this is where the forgiveness came from. I merely yielded to it.

There was an hour and a half left until my walking date with Lori, but I wished it were now. I needed to talk to someone, now.

I didn't feel like it, but I forced myself to get ready for the day. I chose an attractive, but casual outfit to wear, and fixed my hair and makeup. As I prepared to go out, my pain at times felt so intense, that I would stop, hold onto a wall and wait while the tears flowed down my face. Then when they stopped I would wipe my eyes and keep going.

When I finished getting ready, I looked in the mirror and I

thought I looked nice. I could hide behind my appearance. No one would know what was happening to me, although part of me wanted to tell the whole world how hurt I was.

Lori had convinced me the day before that I should be very cautious about who I told, because most people would not be able to handle the news and might hurt me with the information later.

"Also for Brian's sake," she told me. "In the event that you do work out your relationship it may be very difficult for Brian if everyone knows about his failure."

I followed her advice, just in case I later would agree with it, although at the moment I did not. *When Brian could go out and betray me, willingly causing me this much pain, should I now be protecting him? If he could do such a thing, should I now have to keep it a secret, so he doesn't get hurt?*

Every time I shared the truth with someone the pain felt a little diminished, but I was expected to keep this pain to myself rather than experience the relief of sharing. I didn't want to remain sworn to this code of secrecy, but I decided to err on the side of caution. To keep the pain to myself, I avoided people altogether.

By the time I finished getting dressed, there was still half an hour until I would meet Lori. I was really looking forward to our meeting. It was the only thing that was keeping me going at this moment.

I decided I had just the right amount of time to go to the tanning salon. Before yesterday, I had never been to one in my life. Going in had actually felt intimidating, but once inside, the staff had been very friendly.

It was good to lie there, feeling the warmth of the light penetrating my being, listening to music, and enjoying the fragrance of the tanning lotion. When I had finished my session, a clean white towel was awaiting me, with a tempting mint on top.

It looked inviting. *Should I eat it?* I decided not. I was fasting now, completely fasting. The last thing my body needed, I reasoned, was the equivalent of a spoonful of sugar. I did not allow myself to eat the mint. I left it behind.

Lori and I parked our vehicles side by side in the parking lot, and as I got out of my car, she said, "Anne, you look beautiful today. You are a beautiful and kind woman." The words were so simple, but exactly what I needed to hear.

Lori and I walked fast as we talked, which helped to diffuse some of the feelings of anger. Lori did a lot of listening. She told me I was amazing, and she couldn't believe how strong I was, and how well I was handling it. She expressed her pride in me for just carrying on about my life, and keeping busy instead of wallowing in self-pity.

These words of encouragement were like vitamins for my soul. I really needed to hear them, and they strengthened me. Lori was a busy woman, carrying the responsibility of attending to the spiritual needs of many, while supporting her husband in his ministry. Yet she was taking time out of her day to be with me, and she made a commitment to do it every day until I felt I would be alright on my own. Not only that but she was also fasting and praying for my marriage to be restored and healed! This support gave me strength.

Sharing with Lori what had transpired in my time of meditation that morning, the fact that I had chosen to forgive Helen, solidified my decision. I knew I would continue to wrestle with my feelings of anger towards her for some time. That was normal, but fantasies of murdering her were no longer going to be allowed a place in my mind.

I even confessed to Lori that I had felt like killing Helen, but I wasn't comfortable with sharing any of the details. Some places within our hearts feel too dark and too evil to ever risk sharing with anyone.

Reflecting on my decision to forgive, I knew that I could not control what Helen or Brian or anyone else would chose to do in their lives. However, I did have the ability to control my own thoughts.

I decided I was going to live through this, and I was going to do it well. Two wrongs never make a right even in little things, and they certainly don't in big things. Brian and this woman may have done what was wrong, but that didn't mean I should respond by doing what was wrong. I was going to fight evil with good, even in my thoughts.

After I left Lori that day, I decided to take serious action concerning my lack of sleep. I drove back to the shopping mall, and headed for a cosmetics counter, where I spent about thirty dollars on lavender scented luxury bath supplies, which were supposed to be calming. There was definitely a need for "calming" in my life right now.

I went home, with a couple of hours left before my kids came home from school.

I lit "calming" candles in my bathroom, played "calming" music on the stereo, and drained an entire bottle of the lavender bubble bath into the tub. As the lavender fragrance filled the bathroom, I submersed myself in the soothing waters, and for the first time in two days, I started to feel my muscles relax. Half an hour later, I lay down in bed, soothed and relaxed, and at last I fell asleep.

When I woke up an hour and a half later, I felt a little stronger. After spending a little quality time with my kids, I cleaned the house and made supper. I wanted everything about our home to be as inviting as possible, sending a strong message to Brian, "This is where you belong. This is your home. This is where you want to be."

Before Brian came home, Danielle questioned me privately, "Mom, are you having problems?"

Knowing I was never able to hide things from her very well, I answered honestly, "Yes." I hoped she wouldn't ask any more questions.

"Problems with Dad? Are you and Dad having problems?"

"Yes," I said. "But don't worry, honey. We will be all right." I felt that I was lying now, and hoped she was finished asking questions.

"Thanks, Mom, for telling the truth," she said, seeming content with my answers.

As I walked down the hallway, I passed the slightly open door to our office. I stepped inside and peered at the mess that confronted me. The mess reminded me that I'd neglected the bookkeeping for Brian's business because of all the stress I'd been under. This was a task I was expected to do just because I was his wife. I had not completed his fiscal year end or filed the business tax returns. Brian had asked if his papers were filed before he told me of his affair and I had answered evasively, making him think they were done when they weren't.

I sighed as I contemplated the hours of boring, tedious and detailed accounting work. There was no way I was capable of concentrating on this job in my traumatized mental state, and I didn't care anymore anyway. It was the least of my concerns. I wondered how good Helen's accounting skills were. Well, if Brian was going to leave me for her, they would be getting a large box, with all the pieces of paper which currently made a mess of the office. They would just have to find out, *wouldn't they?* As far as the filing of Brian's business returns was concerned, my contribution was complete.

My thoughts then turned towards my next battle: a dozen people were coming to our house for Bible study that evening.

I had to make it through some of these regular life commitments and routines, I thought, so no one would suspect anything was wrong. I was quite sure I could do it. All I had to do was make coffee, tea and juice, and act normal for two hours. Luckily someone else was already committed to bringing the cake.

Before the guests arrived, I dressed myself in a beautiful Oriental outfit made of a floral print on brown silk. I wanted to look as beautiful as possible for Brian.

The guests arrived, each one an authentic character with a unique personality. First Fred, an older gentleman, whose wife had recently passed away. He bore an unbelievable resemblance to the cartoon character, Fred Flintstone, which he was very aware of, so he inspired laughter by saying "Yabadabadooo" at any opportunity.

I served Fred a cup of coffee and listened to him say again how wonderful his wife was, and how lonely he was without her. On previous occasions, I had felt tremendous compassion for Fred, but on this day I didn't want to hear about his pain.

Do I have to sit here and listen to him? I thought. *He should only know how much pain I feel right now.*

Yet, I was almost wishing he were my husband tonight, the way he spoke so highly of his wife. He didn't look like much, he wasn't too ambitious, and he struggled with a gambling addiction, but, oh, how I longed for Brian to speak about me the way Fred spoke of his wife.

Then John arrived, the former drug addict. I wondered if the effect of those drugs would ever completely wear off. He always seemed hyper as if he was on speed. As he entered, he looked up at me and said, with unrestrained expression "Wow, you look amazing tonight. You look like a queen. I can't handle being single. It's not fair."

Normally a compliment from John didn't mean much, but tonight his attention gently stroked my damaged ego.

The next one to arrive was Eleanor, a quiet woman in her early forties, who had endured unspeakable abuse in her childhood, the effects of which were still clearly visible. She took a seat in a chair and watched the others talk, but said nothing herself.

Next Jerry and Mary arrived, the leaders of our group, along with their three adorable children. Jerry was a serious man who loved to study and lacked in humor. Mary was a calm sweet lady, who never had any trouble getting along with anyone.

There was no sign of Brian, so I made excuses about his having to work late unexpectedly. We opened our session with a prayer, led by Jerry, and I was relieved to hide behind my closed eyes for a few moments. I was careful not to think too much for fear that I would start to cry.

Yet this moment in corporate prayer was still precious to me. I became aware of the presence of God in the room, and while we prayed, I felt as if I were on a temporary vacation to a land far away called Peace.

Next on the agenda for the evening was the singing. Since I had always enjoyed singing, and since I had a reasonably good voice, I found singing to be therapeutic. Fortunately, tonight we were singing a brief assortment of very familiar tunes, which allowed me the precious chance to close my eyes and escape from my present world of pain into a place of beauty, wonder and peace.

As if the music had been selected solely for my own benefit, we ended our worship time with a particular favorite, the words of which suddenly seemed to intensify in their meaning, the melody gentle, yet powerfully moving.

Faithful one, so unchanging
Ageless one you're my rock of peace,
Lord of all, I depend on you
I cry unto you … again and again
You are my rock in times of trouble
You lift me up, when I fall down
All through the storm, your love is the anchor
My hope is in you alone.

"FAITHFUL ONE" MUSIC AND LYRICS BY BRIAN DOERKSEN
WWW.BRIANDOERKSEN.COM

At this moment I was comforted to embrace the concept of a faithful God who never changed, even when my personal world was crashing all around me.

Jerry read from the scriptures and at that moment, I found myself staring out blankly as if in another world. Where the prayer and music had been helpful, the words from the Bible seemed irritating and irrelevant. Didn't anyone understand how much pain I was in? As the biblical discussion continued that evening, I found myself wondering how much longer I would have to endure what seemed like nothing but a bunch of philosophical gibberish.

Jerry shared how he had once lost his job, and the fears he went through wondering how he would provide for the needs of his family. As I listened to him speak, I thought he sounded like an idiot. Did he not think he had enough skills to secure other employment?

Mary shared how difficult it was for her to deal with the constant disorganization and disruptions in her home caused by three small children. How irritating! As if it really mattered in light of the suffering in the world.

Fred rambled on about how he should have treated his wife better while she was still alive. I wished he would shut up.

John was shouting about the importance of telling everyone the good news of salvation. He spoke with the intensity of a raving lunatic. I kept Eleanor company in her silence.

Normally, I had many things to say and share, but tonight this social gathering felt more like an Iron Man competition in enduring stupid people, than a time of encouragement and inspiration.

Relief swept over me, when at last the meeting was closed with a prayer, bringing me almost to the end of my charade. I successfully avoided cake, coffee and tea, sticking to my fast without anyone noticing.

As the others carried on with the usual small talk, I was restless, fidgety and irritated. The things that were being discussed seemed trivial and boring. These friends seemed shallow as they wasted their time talking with enthusiasm and passion about what color they decorated their bathroom, that they felt a cold coming on, or that someone at their work forgot to praise their accomplishments.

I'm sure I rushed my guests out of the house that night. I worried about Brian's whereabouts. Maybe I wouldn't even see him tonight. Maybe all my effort to look nice, clean the house, and create a pleasant atmosphere was all for naught.

When Brian did come home that night he was cold and aloof. He was purposely late, unwilling to face the group of friends and acquaintances.

We did sleep on the same bed that night, a good two feet between us though. And again he refused to kiss me, which was overwhelmingly painful. I still could not grasp my new reality.

How could he go from loving me to not having enough compassion to reach out to me with even a small kiss when I was suffering so much? I wanted to reach out and grab him and make love to him, like we had so many nights before. Maybe tomorrow we would wake up, he would change his mind and everything would be fine again. With that thought in mind, I managed to fall asleep.

---

1. Proverbs 7:22-23

C H A P T E R   5

It's over

DAY THREE — THURSDAY, MAY 18, 2000

Lay a whisper on my pillow,
Leave the winter on the ground.
I wake up lonely,
There's air of silence in the bedroom and all around.
Touch me now, I close my eyes and dream away.
It must have been love but it's over now.
It must have been good but I lost it somehow.
It must have been love but it's over now.
From the moment we touched 'til the time had run out.
Make-believing we're together that I'm sheltered by your heart.
But in and outside I've turned to water like a tear drop in your palm.
And it's a hard winter's day, I dream away.
It must have been love but it's over now,
It was all that I wanted, now I'm living without.
It must have been love but it's over now,
It's where the water flows, it's where the wind blows.

"IT MUST HAVE BEEN LOVE," BY ROXETTE

Weight: 153 pounds. I had now lost five pounds in two days and fifteen pounds since January. I was still fasting and planned to continue to exercise as well.

As I dressed in my running shorts to get ready for the day's run, Danielle asked if she could join me. I welcomed the opportunity to spend some time with her that wouldn't require me to talk much.

As we set off at a comfortable pace, we picked a route that started with several minutes of running uphill.

I was really struggling this morning. Clearly I did not have the energy I was accustomed to. I ran silently, trying to ignore the protest my body was making, but within five minutes, I was forced to slow to a walk. Danielle looked at me in astonishment.

"What's wrong with you?"

I confessed that I was fasting.

"Why?" she asked, as if that was about the stupidest idea anyone could ever have.

"For spiritual reasons," I replied.

It was half true. Lori suggested that there was a powerful spiritual connection that takes place when you combine fasting with prayer, which I was also engaging in daily. This appealed to me.

But also I was fasting because the thought of food turned my stomach. Besides, I was afraid that maybe Brian was leaving me because I was too fat. I didn't have much to lose. For a woman of my height, 145 pounds would be a normal weight.

I tried to keep running, but it became impossible. We turned around and went home after walking and running only one mile.

At this point I realized that I wasn't going to be able to continue to function at all with my current fast, so I decided to allow myself a small amount of fruit juice everyday from now on.

Later that day, I was expected to attend a school sports day to watch my younger daughter, Tamara, compete. Again, Danielle had asked to join me. Looking back now, I'm not sure why she wanted to be with me so much, but I imagine she sensed that something was seriously wrong, and she wanted to find some way to protect me.

I was afraid to be close to her. I didn't feel it was my job to tell the kids about Brian. After all, maybe he would come to his senses soon and it wouldn't be necessary to tell them at all. I didn't want Danielle to feel rejected in any way, so I told her I would be happy to have her join me. She sensed my reluctance.

At the stadium, I chose to stand and watch the races close to the track rather than sitting in the stands with the majority of parents. I was making every effort to avoid everyone who didn't know. Lori and Pastor Dave had decided to tell the leaders in the church, just a few trustworthy individuals, and I was glad for the extra support that provided.

Danielle was talking to me now, but I wasn't really listening. Nothing mattered, it seemed. I couldn't think properly. I was just trying to make it through the next hour without breaking into sobs in front of everyone. *Don't cry, don't cry,* I repeated to myself silently in my head.

"I don't think they should call it fasting and prayer," I heard Danielle blurt out.

"Why?" I looked at her incredulously.

"They should call it fast and *****," she said.

The words cut me like a sword.

"Because that's all you are, since you've been doing this," she said. "You're just acting like a *****. I think you should just eat and be happy."

I would have given anything to leave the planet at that moment. Surely I did not have the stamina to deal with that level of confrontation. I remained quiet, and somewhat horrified.

I thought I was covering up my pain. I thought I was acting happy.

Couldn't she see that I was smiling? *Maybe I'm not smiling*, I worried. I stared straight ahead at the race, and with serious concentration, I made every effort to configure my face into a genuine smile. When I felt confident I had a good smile on, I decided to check. I turned to Danielle.

"Danielle, does it look like I'm smiling?"

She turned and looked at me very analytically for a few seconds.

"You look like your smiling on the outside," she said with an evil tone, "but you're about to kill someone on the inside. That looks like a Gary Morrow smile," she added.

"Who the heck is Gary Morrow?"

"Oh, he's our manager at the restaurant, and whenever he wants to yell at us behind the counter where the customers can see, but not hear, he makes this giant smile, and swears at us and tells us to work faster."

Well, at least I knew exactly how I was presenting myself. Avoiding people was definitely important, I reasoned, and perhaps avoiding Miss Perceptive would be helpful as well.

Brian came home again that evening, and I had done everything within my power to create a pleasant atmosphere within the home and look like a million dollars.

I still could not comprehend the situation, and the ramifications it was going to have. Somehow, I reasoned, if Brian would just break off with the other woman, I could just forget about the whole thing and my happy life would be back again.

I suggested we go for a walk after dinner, so we could talk privately. After all it had now been three days since he told me of his affair and in all that time we hadn't had another opportunity to talk. I wanted to know where I stood, now. I couldn't take this uncertainty about our future anymore. Brian accepted my invitation and suggested we go out for coffee as well.

We walked towards the busy streets of downtown, instead of through our local park. This was a compromise we had worked out in our marriage years ago. I liked to walk. He liked to be in the midst of noise and commotion, where everything was happening. We had always walked hand-in-hand, but tonight he would not hold my hand. That was very painful.

"What are you going to do?" I demanded. "You have to make up your mind, Brian. It's her or me. I refuse to share you with another woman." He didn't want to make a decision.

"Brian, I can't understand it. If you love me how could you do this to me? Don't you realize how cruel you are being?" The conversation was uncomfortable and strained. There was sorrow in his eyes.

"Everyone is always trying to tell me what to do." He said, "No one really cares about me. No one cares enough to ask why."

"Why then, Brian, why?" I pleaded.

"Because I want to," he retorted, and the words struck a painful blow deep into my injured soul.

As we walked, the street seemed surreal. There wasn't much traffic, there weren't many people, and there was a warm sunshine glowing down upon us.

"Brian, if you're not going to break up with Helen, does that mean you have decided to leave me?"

"Well I guess I have" he said, exasperated by my persistence.

"But Brian, what about our wedding vows?" I questioned. "You promised you were going to stay with me for a lifetime. You promised to be faithful to me. Me and only me."

"That was then and this is now," was his reply. His words pierced my broken heart. We walked on in silence for what seemed like a long time. There didn't seem to be more to say. That was it. It was over. My marriage had ended. Just like that.

"So that's it then?" I said.

"Yeah, I guess so," came his reply. "Would you still like that cup of coffee?" he then asked.

"Okay." It seemed strange, but I guessed I could. At this point he seemed oddly kind to me.

When we settled down in the coffee shop, he asked me what my plans were, as if I might have prepared for this day in advance. Of course I hadn't, yet I said the first thing that came to mind. "I'm going to live in Denmark," I replied.

"But I won't be able to see the kids?" he protested, yet with gentleness. It was clear that he was not going to stop me from pursuing what I wanted. It seemed, somehow, in spite of the choice he was making, that he still wanted me to find happiness in my future.

"That's kind of a decision you made," I told him. "There's nothing holding me in Canada if I don't have you," I replied. "This isn't my country. I don't belong here without you." He choked on my decision, yet accepted it and understood.

"I want you to know you are never going to have to go without money," he promised. "I'm going to make sure you are always well taken care of financially." His kindness seemed incomprehensible in contrast to the cruelty of what he was actually doing. Nonetheless, any kindness was welcomed, and I never forgot his tenderness in that moment.

When we returned from the walk, I was restless. I couldn't stand to be in the house, and I didn't want to be near Brian. So, even though it was ten o'clock at night, I drove over to Lori's.

She welcomed me with open arms, and hugged me for a moment. I wanted to stay and hide and cry like a baby in a mother's arms.

"It's no use, Lori. It's all over," I said. "He told me he's leaving. We might as well quit fasting and eat."

She was visibly angry about the whole situation. It was great to have someone to be angry together with.

"Fine, we'll eat," she said in disgust. "How about watermelon? I just bought it, and it won't be too heavy on our empty stomachs."

As the large knife came down in the center of the melon with extreme force, Lori looked like an executioner letting down the blade of a guillotine, as she took out her anger on the innocent fruit. *Boom*, came the sharp sound as the blade hit the wood and two halves of melon went flying in opposite directions across the counter.

We sat in her outdoor hot tub eating the watermelon and enjoying the darkness and stars in the pleasant country atmosphere of her property, as I relayed the details of the day.

Later Dave came home from his meetings and we repeated the information, as he listened with astonishment and compassion, feeling a sense of responsibility to provide answers to a situation that didn't have any.

"Anne," he said, "You can do what you want in this situation. You can leave if you want and go to Denmark and no one would ever blame you. Everyone would understand and you have every right to do that under the circumstances. But I just have a feeling it's not over between you and Brian. You guys are a strong couple and you are both wonderful people. Ever since I have known you, I have admired you both, and even though I don't understand, I still believe Brian loves you. I really encourage you to hold on. Just don't react too quickly. If you take off for Denmark right away there will be such finality to the whole situation. Why don't you wait a while, maybe three months at least? Give Brian a chance to change his mind."

I didn't really like what I heard. It meant hanging in the balance and not knowing what to do with my life. Yet, I saw value in his words and considered them.

Dave then proceeded to tell me that the other woman might be pregnant with Brian's child. That thought horrified me.

"They only had sex a few times, and some couples can spend months trying to get pregnant before they are successful," I protested.

"It only takes one time," he insisted, "and you need to be prepared."

The thought was overwhelming. I didn't want to hurt an innocent child, but I just didn't see how I could possibly stand Brian being tied to this horrible woman through a baby, who would be a half sibling to my own babies. It would mean he would have to be forever tied to this woman whom I considered to be a whore. It would mean I would have to deal with her, and deal with her child who, although innocent, would stand as a permanent reminder to the most painful experience in my life.

It wasn't fair.

"If she is pregnant, Brian will have to contribute financially to the child," Dave was now saying. I choked on the lump that was growing in my throat, and did not answer him. "That will significantly impact your financial situation as a family. As Christians it's important that we take responsibility for things like this."

I felt like throwing up. I wasn't interested in being a Christian right now, yet I believed in God, and I dared not throw away my faith at a time when I knew I needed God more than ever. I thought I might have to leave Brian for sure, if there were a child to deal with.

During this period of trauma and shock, I was not able to process many things logically. Two months passed before I remembered that Brian had had a vasectomy, and that I myself had not needed birth control for over thirteen years! I suffered this extra worry and anxiety for nothing.

Dave also told me that I should be prepared to be poor now. That made me really angry, but as usual, I held a lot of the real emotion I was feeling inside. I told Dave it wasn't true, and that Brian had promised to take care of me financially, but both Lori and Dave were quite sure my replacement wouldn't allow that for very long.

That, I thought, they were probably right about. But what they had underestimated was my own ability to create wealth. How dare Dave say that I was going to be poor, he who preached that all people had the ability to succeed!

Yet, I respected Dave, so I pondered his words and his advice. Maybe he was right and I was just unwilling to face another painful reality.

I was somewhat aware of my own inability to make rational decisions right now. I knew I was merely fighting to survive, trying to live through my days, one moment at a time. I didn't want to have to make decisions. I was afraid of making decisions. What if I was wrong? What if my life became worse?

Part of me wanted someone else to tell me what to do, the other part of me knew that this was my life, and only I would live with the outcome of the decisions I made. Therefore, I knew I must make them myself. Here I was with two wonderful, giving people, giving up their time to help me in my time of need, yet I was still feeling alone and afraid.

I saw the error of my ways, allowing my husband to be my sole provider for most of our lives together. Sure, I had now worked outside the home and independent of Brian's business for a few years, but I was only creating a small supplemental income. It was far from something I could live on independently.

Never again would I allow myself to rely on another person to provide for my financial needs. I felt that it would be impossible and perhaps irrational to ever trust again.

A strong belief system had been permanently altered. It wasn't true, that if you spent all your energy ensuring you were a great wife, your husband would stay. There is no such thing as "happily ever after," I concluded.

I had believed what I had been taught in my church, that my life should be about pleasing my husband. He was to be the financial provider. My job was to support him. If I was a good wife, my husband would love me. I believed that because we were "good" people, we would never go through something like this. I learned that no one knows the future, and no one can know all of the decisions another person will make during the course of their lifetime. No matter how great your marriage, how strong your faith, and how good you are, you cannot know your future. To me it was now clear that it is unwise for anyone to be unprepared to support themselves financially. This would never happen to me again.

"Hey, I just got an idea," said Dave. "You might not like it, but it might impact Brian, and cause him to change his mind."

"What idea?" Lori asked.

"Tell him you want him to tell the children with the other woman there." Lori and I stared wide-eyed. "Tell him that you think it's only fair. Your children have a right to meet the woman who is better for their father than their own mother is."

"He won't do that," I said.

"It doesn't matter," said Dave. "The mental picture will cause him to think about the reality of what he's doing."

It was a shocking proposal, but it warranted consideration. Only what if Brian decided to do it? It would be too difficult, perhaps even cruel, for the children to meet this woman at the same time as learning about the affair. Yet, I supposed if it came to this, in the last minute, it might stop Brian from actually leaving. The thought of Helen squirming in her chair in front of my children appealed to me.

Brian had told me that Helen was a thoughtful and caring individual like me. Yuck! To me, the way she was hurting my family proved she was the opposite and only thinking of her own selfish desires. I thought it would be good for Helen to personally witness the pain she was causing my children. I wondered if she would still think she was a good person when she saw their pain as she stole their father.

Lori thought this whole idea might be going a bit too far. She was a good balance for Dave's "say it like it is" approach to people's problems. We discussed the pros and cons for a while.

Ultimately, like everything else, it was my decision.

CHAPTER 6

when Life Doesn't Make any sense

DAY FOUR — FRIDAY, MAY 19, 2000

Even before the gift of life was yours, it was tainted by the schemes of the Spoiler — for his intent is to spoil all that's good. He sends rains of sorrow and floods of defeat, but the Gift Giver will not have His purposes thwarted. For through the storms of life, the Savior's voice is heard more clearly than before, and His presence is felt with intense reality. Through the blinding rain, the Life Giver extends His nail-scarred hand and takes your trembling hand firmly in His own.

FROM *HUGS FOR THE HURTING*
JOHN SMITH

Weight: 151 pounds. Thirteen years ago to this day, I had given birth to Tamara Joy, a precious treasure of a girl. A gentle, caring soul, who brought harmony and peace wherever she went, a child who was truly a gift from heaven.

Now, how was I going to make sure she had a great thirteenth birthday, when in fact I wasn't even sure how I myself would survive another day? I was glad she had school all day. I was glad we were only having a small family gathering to celebrate, and I was glad Danielle and her boyfriend were going to be making her feel special, by surprising her with cupcakes and singing at her school.

My father phoned me from Chicago this morning to wish Tamara a happy birthday, but she was already off to school, so he had missed her. He asked me how things were going, and since Lori had advised me not to tell anyone about Brian's affair, I lied through the entire conversation.

Part of me desperately wanted to tell my father how hurt I was. This was my own father. Even if we didn't always get along so well, I wanted to tell him. But maybe it was true, I reasoned with myself, maybe I would one day forgive Brian, but my father might not be able to. Then it would make our already strained in-law relationships even worse. I wondered if my father couldn't hear the trembling in my voice.

Here Brian had gone out and done the wrong thing, leaving me in desperate pain, yet I was expected to keep the secret, and by so doing increase my own pain, because talking about my situation made me feel better. I had to lie, because he had an affair! Was there such a thing as rights and wrongs anymore?

I was lying, to save Brian from dealing with the consequences of his own choices. I was lying to our daughter. I was lying to my father. How many people would I be required to lie to? I must be the one who is in the wrong, if I am required to cover up like this. Is it because I haven't been a good enough wife? Surely, I must have done something shameful, if I must keep it hush-hush. The secrecy made me feel dirty and ashamed.

—————•———

In the afternoon, I went to the mall with Danielle. We had to buy an appropriate purse for her to use in a week, when she would be accompanying her boyfriend to his graduation ceremonies.

This was about the last thing in the world I felt like doing on this day, but I loved Danielle, and I was dedicated to helping her have a memorable evening, no matter how difficult it was for me to help her while I was in so much pain.

As we looked in one store after another, there didn't seem to be anything we could use. I was so tired and disoriented, I felt like a foot soldier lost in the jungle without my compass and without food. Perhaps we'd left making this purchase too late. It was mid-May and the graduation supplies were well picked over.

Finally, we found a perfect handbag at a large department store. The purse was exactly what Danielle wanted. It was small, decorated with white pearls and complete with a long, gold chain strap. A wave of relief swept over me until I realized there was not a single sales associate in sight.

We walked swiftly down the center aisles, passing one abandoned till after the other, but found no one to help us. A young lady looked forlorn, as she waited at the abandoned cosmetics counter. And a couple of women shuffled through racks in ladies' wear, but where was the staff? *Have they all taken lunch at the same time?* I wondered.

Time seemed to pass in slow motion. A minute felt like an hour. I wanted to get out of that store so badly.

What the heck did they expect us to do! I just wanted the damn bag, and I didn't want to steal it. My frustration level was rising at a disturbingly quick rate, so contrary to my nature. I felt like I was going to die if I didn't get out of that store fast.

We continued striding through the aisles, my eyes searching like spot lights for someone wearing a name tag. Where were they?

Finally, I spotted a clerk and headed for her like a cruise missile locked in on its intended target, which now had no chance of escape.

She was a middle aged woman with a sensible and matronly disposition, who seemed to be going about some work with a certain level of seriousness, but that seriousness did not involve serving the public at this moment. Upon interception, I confronted her and demanded that she locate a supervisor immediately. I was beyond accepting a mere cashier to take my money at this point. Someone was going to hear about my pain.

I told the manager, a small thin man with glasses, in no uncertain terms that this was completely unacceptable for a retail store. I suggested that they hang signs around saying *Please steal everything because we're too cheap to hire staff.*

In desperation, we purchased the handbag, because it was the only suitable one we had found in the entire mall. But when I was done, I told the manager I would never in my life set foot in his store again. Danielle couldn't believe how angry I was. She had never seen me behave this way. I never had.

Later that day, I was relaying the incident to Lori, and she told me about her similar experience, on the same day, at a restaurant with her mother and sister. She had complained about the food, sent it back to the kitchen, and refused to eat.

We laughed at our similar experiences, our irrational outbursts, and I saw that Lori was really carrying my load with me. Interestingly enough, we both had continued to fast, even though the night before we both had agreed to start eating.

Brian's mother arrived as planned around dinnertime, with her load of gifts for Tamara. She always gave the children handcrafted gift bags, which she made herself and filled with candies, small gifts and other intriguing craft items. It was very thoughtful, and she was very talented in this way.

I had prepared a light and easy birthday dinner that evening.

When food was served, I encouraged everyone to sit down and begin eating without me. During dinner I managed to keep myself busy serving the others.

No one seemed to notice that I myself was not eating. That was good. It was easy for me not to eat. This was my fourth day without food, and I had lost my appetite completely. Throughout the evening, whenever I looked at Brian, I noticed that he looked sad and much older than he was. I was sure he had aged ten years in the last four days. His face appeared tired and strained.

I never saw him look at me once during the evening, as we both did our best to go through the motions of this paradoxical celebration. I worried that our problems would ruin Tamara's special day. My sadness was overwhelming, and I was on the verge of tears throughout the traditional birthday proceedings. I knew the slightest upset would send me sobbing. Were we really pulling this off successfully, I wondered?

Did Tamara not notice? She didn't.

Did Brian's mother not notice? What would she say? I was not close to her. We were from two different worlds. I felt misunderstood by her. I would never start mending my husband's socks, when I could buy a package of six at Wal-Mart for $3.99, and therefore I thought I would never win her approval. God knows I had tried.

I wondered if Brian's mother would care about my feelings if she knew what her son had done. I imagined she would be unsympathetic. Raised during the war and having lived a difficult life, she was a tough and strong person.

After dinner, I brought out the store-bought cake with thirteen lit candles, and we all sang to Tamara. It made me smile to see a gentle sparkle in this kind soul's eye. I loved her more than words could ever tell. I had managed to protect her from some pain, and for that I felt a moment of happiness.

I had purchased an ensemble of summer clothing for her birthday that year, and as always Tamara Joy received them with a grateful heart. I wanted to hug her and give her the world, yet I felt afraid to let her too close. I had to protect her from my pain and the truth that she could be losing her father.

I was overwhelmed with grief that I had not been a good enough wife to keep her father for her. I blamed myself. I was so sorry and so sad. I wanted to die, but I didn't want to die, because I knew she needed me.

Making it through the dinner and cake that night was one of the hardest things I ever did. The heaviness in our home was thick. Brian had agreed to stay at our house until after Tamara's birthday.

"You can't let her forever associate her birthday with the day her dad left her," I told him.

Luckily Grandma didn't stay too long, and after dinner Tamara and Dustin went off to attend the church youth group, while Danielle left with her boyfriend. It gave us a break from trying to act like everything was normal.

Again, Brian and I sat alone in our living room, the same place where the nightmare began for me, four days earlier. We talked cordially. I asked him about his day and he answered me like a monotone recording. He asked me about my day and I said it was fine, when of course it wasn't.

We both wanted to talk, but what was there to say? He had made his decision.

I asked him about practical details. Brian planned on staying in a hotel until he and Helen had set up their own home together. I asked if he had met her daughter, and what she thought of the whole thing. He said that she was fine, that she liked him. It didn't surprise me. Brian was great with kids.

I winced when I thought of him taking his limited energy from his own children to raise the children of a stranger. Helen's daughter was six, and suffered with diabetes.

He must really love this woman to leave all he had with me and start raising a young family all over again, I thought. Who was this man sitting across from me, whom I had shared eighteen years of my life with, who only four days ago had been my best friend, and now was leaving me?

The awkwardness of this surreal situation was interrupted by the sound of our phone ringing in the kitchen. I got up and answered it, because Brian didn't look like he was in the mood to talk to anyone who could be phoning our house.

"Hello, this is the Bercht residence, Anne speaking."

"Did you say this is the Bercht's?" a man asked, as if that was exactly who he was trying to reach.

"Yes," I replied. And with that the caller hung up. I stood there holding the receiver stunned, wondering what that was all about.

Returning to the living room, I told Brian what had happened.

"Dial *69," he replied. So I did, and after writing down the number, I repeated it to him.

"Shoot! That's Helen's number," he said. "Her husband must've been phoning to see if I was home. I bet he's coming over here to beat me up."

"You've got to be kidding me!" I said as I watched Brian begin to shake, a look of fear growing in his eyes.

"Surely, he wouldn't go to that extreme," I said. "What kind of low class people have you been associating with?"

Brian looked at me but didn't answer.

"Brian, I wouldn't worry about it, you're a strong guy. Even if he does come over, you can handle yourself," I encouraged.

"No. He's way bigger than me," Brian responded, without a moment's hesitation.

So we began to wait hopelessly for this moment of truth. What could we do? Part of me was afraid too, of seeing my husband getting beaten physically. I was sure glad the kids weren't home. Part of me thought maybe this wasn't so bad. *Maybe he deserves to get beaten up. Maybe this will be good for him.*

I decided to relax. It wasn't my problem. Whatever was going to happen to Brian was going to happen, and he probably deserved it. It came into perspective for me, just how many people were being hurt here, by the selfish acts of two inconsiderate people.

Brian paced back and forth in the living room of our home, while I watched him. He was sweating, and every two laps across the length of the room, he peeked through the closed draperies and watched the cars on the street. I had never seen my husband act this way. It was useless to try and talk with him right now. His mind was preoccupied.

I wondered what to do with myself. I didn't feel like doing anything. I was in suspense about what was going to transpire this evening in my formerly peaceful, happy home. Picking up a book, I attempted to read.

"There he is," Brian said suddenly, after thirty minutes of his pacing routine, as he peered through the curtains on one of his surveillance passes. I looked at him and said nothing. I was scared. Silently to myself, I prayed for God's help. Brian clenched his fists and seemed to be preparing to meet his assailant head on. I wondered if I was safe. I wondered if our home was safe. I was completely unaccustomed to physical confrontations.

We waited. But for what? I wasn't sure, the door bell? A long minute passed. Nothing happened. Brian walked back over to the window, and carefully peered through the side of the curtain once again.

"He's gone!" Brian said.

False alarm, I thought, *he's paranoid. Oh well it's good for him. He deserves it for acting like such a jerk. What on earth is he thinking? What is Helen thinking? Devastate two spouses, break up two families and we're all just going to live happily ever after?*

Brian decided he must have made a mistake and resumed pacing the living room. After a while, with no more false alarms, he went downstairs to our rec room, although I sensed he was still very much distracted and very tense. Our expected offender never showed up. Or had he indeed shown up, but changed his mind because he also was scared? Had he perhaps turned around after my prayer? Were we still in danger? Danielle came home around nine o'clock. Brian joined me in the living room and told me that he wanted to tell Danielle tonight about his affair and his decision to move out.

"Sit down, Danielle. I have something to tell you." He spoke without emotion. "Yeah. So I've had an affair on your mother and I'm going to be moving out."

I sat beside Danielle on the sofa and held her, trying to offer some comfort. She sobbed big heaving sobs, while wrestling with this over-whelming information. In her mind it was not her mother he was leaving. It was her personally. Although she was sixteen years old, she was still a young child, and there was really no other way for her to process this information.

I glanced at Brian sitting across from us, and to my astonishment, saw that he was also crying. This was the first time I had ever seen my husband cry. He was raised in a home where it was seen as a weakness to cry. Anger was frequently expressed in his family, but that was the only emotion he was allowed to reveal.

Brian did not cry when he lost his business. He did not cry when his father died. He did not cry when he failed to live up to his own ideals as a husband and a father. Yet tonight he cried.

What was really going on inside my husband's head? I wondered. I really didn't understand how he could be willing to cause his own pain. Why didn't he just break it off with the other woman, and stay with his family where he belonged, when I was offering to forgive him for his moral failure? It didn't make any sense.

Unable to cope any longer, Brian retreated to our bedroom, grabbed his gym bag, and packed his things, including the hair gel

I now hated. He had told me recently after getting a hair cut, that the stylist had sold him this new and great hair gel that women were supposed to find irresistible. "Cougar bait" she had called it. I was mad. The stupid stuff worked! *How dare he purchase "cougar bait" hair gel?* I thought.

It didn't seem like he packed very thoroughly or thoughtfully, he just seemed in a hurry to escape from the painful realities he faced in our home.

I stayed in the living room while he threw these items together, yet I knew full well what he was doing. I couldn't bear to see, hear or experience any more. I was on an overdose of pain. I sat numb in my chair, staring as I had on the first night, but now I stared with my arm around my devastated teenager.

There were no words that fit the situation. Our usual non-stop talking was replaced with an eerie silence. The only sound that broke that silence was Danielle's gentle sobbing.

Brian emerged from the hall looking like an old, worn-out man. He seemed ashamed and desperate. I longed to reach out and comfort him, as I had so many times before, but now he was rejecting me.

"Bye," he said to the two of us in a factual and numbing way, as if he were merely heading to the corner store for milk. We didn't answer him. How are you supposed to say good-bye to someone you love, when life doesn't make any sense, and there is no plausible explanation for the events at hand?

Danielle and I watched his van disappear down the street. With the finality of the moment, her tears subsided. She seemed to be pulling herself together with inner resolve, building a wall around her heart and leaving her father, the one person who had meant more to her than anyone else, shut out on the other side.

I held her hand as we stood and watched the ending of our lives as we had known it. I wasn't crying. I was trying to be strong, nonetheless I felt a tear trickle down my cheek. Gone was her father, and gone was my husband. We felt abandoned. Permanently.

Danielle: The moment I came home that evening and entered my living room where my parents were seated, I knew something was different. The air in the room felt thick and chilling cold as if you could cut it with a knife, and intuitively I knew it was as if my mother was entertaining a stranger that evening, a man inside my father's body, but a man we did not know. Up until this day, I had always known that my father loved me, more so than I knew my mother loved me. When I was bad, and that was often, my father always addressed me with a lot of emotion, emotion that told me he loved me. He yelled at me, and I yelled back at him, but that was okay, both of us could relate to that. I always knew the yelling was about love, his love for me. My mother on the other hand dealt with me with unbending calmness. She kept her emotions under control. A lot of the time it seemed that she was operating without emotion, just with facts. No matter how much I argued and provoked my mother, she would not give in, she would not bend. Dealing with my mother felt like dealing with an inanimate brick wall. The lack of emotion made me feel less loved. I always waited for my father to come home, then I knew I could get a response, and usually I could get what I wanted. Not with my mom.

Tonight the stranger who occupied my father's body spoke without emotion. That's how I knew it was not my father. His eyes were blank. He said "Sit down I have something to tell you," as if he were merely a reporter reporting on facts that didn't matter to me at all. "Yeah, so I've had an affair on your mother, and I'm going to be moving out." The way he said the words so matter of fact, made me think he was just joking. I was waiting for him to say "just kidding" like he had so many times before. My real father was always telling jokes. When I looked into my father's eyes as he spoke tonight, I felt an evil presence and for a moment I thought I was looking straight at the Devil. I was gripped with fear, and I felt hatred towards this presence inside my father's body. I wanted to kill. I felt completely neglected, abandoned and despised. What had the last sixteen years been? A big joke! How can you love someone and then just walk out on them?

As soon as the stranger wearing my father's body left, I phoned my boyfriend. "You have to come and get me," I said. He told me that he couldn't because he had to work early the next morning. "Come and get me," I repeated. The answer "no" was not an option.

When my boyfriend picked me up, we drove around in his truck, and I unloaded the whole mess on his shoulders. We drove to a freeway overpass, up on a hill, which sported a view of the entire valley, and we made plans to kill this stupid woman my father thought he needed to live with. We planned to shoot her. First we were going to harass her, and do it in a way where she never would be able to find out who it was. We wanted to drive by and throw rocks through her windows. We wanted to rob her. We wanted to take sharp metal objects and scrape up her car at night. We wanted to follow her, and accidentally trip her in shopping malls. We wanted to spill burning coffee on her. We wanted to make her life a living nightmare, after all that's what she was doing to mine.

It comforted me, to talk about plans for justice to be delivered.

Never once in all our talking did I ever think of how hurt my mother must be. I was consumed by my own pain.

C H A P T E R   7

The VISION

DAY FIVE — SATURDAY, MAY 20, 2000

Now faith is the substance of things hoped for,
The evidence of things not seen.

HEBREWS 11:1, THE BIBLE, KJV

On this day, I started a journal.

Journal entry, May 20, 2000:
This is going to be the story of how our marriage went through
death and was restored. I make this statement by faith at a time
when it seems like it's over. But it ain't over 'til it's over. This message
was preached at the vision conference in Seattle in February, and
Brian should have been there to hear it. He was sick that night and
stayed at the hotel while I attended the meeting alone. Today God
laid restoration in my heart.

This journal keeping became a way to sort my thoughts, in a time when sanity and rational thinking were hard to find. It provided a measure of therapy in the midst of my desolation.

My mother phoned. Again, as with my father, I attempted to hide everything by covering up with lies.

"Everything's fine, Mom. I'm doing really well," I said. "Yes, the family is doing great. I'm very happy."

But she was too perceptive

"Anne, there is something seriously wrong over there. I can tell. What is it? I demand to know. What is wrong with you today?" It was useless trying to hide this from her, so I confessed the truth. To my surprise, she was not only compassionate towards me, but she seemed compassionate towards Brian, as well. This was amazing, in light of the strained relationship between them. She told me she understood how tremendously painful it must be for me, yet encouraged me that I was not alone.

"Very few men are actually faithful to their wives for a lifetime," she comforted. I expected her to encourage me to leave Brian. She was a firm believer in women not tolerating injustices at the hands of any men. Yet now, she spoke with wisdom in place of hate.

She said I should consider things such as: has he been a good husband, is he a good father, and is he a good provider?

"Maybe you can work through it, and maybe he is worth keeping," she suggested.

Every time I had the chance to share my struggle with a willing and sensible listener, I gained a little extra strength.

Perceptive in more ways than one, my mother asked about what I had eaten since hearing the devastating news. When she found out about my fast, she was understanding and wise. She recounted a traumatic experience from her own life, where she also had been unable to eat, and she encouraged me that now, more than ever, I must have basic nutritional requirements met. This was necessary for survival, and also for the mental energy needed to make sound decisions.

She understood that I was incapable of eating normal food, so she encouraged me to have meal replacement drinks, and take nutritional supplements. I followed her advice, and found my new partial fast helped my body cope with the shock and pain it was enduring.

In the early afternoon Lori phoned me, eager to share some news. She told me that she had had a vision. She had been to a marriage reaffirmation ceremony earlier that day, for another couple, who had once also stood on the brink of divorce, yet had rebuilt a beautiful relationship together.

While my marriage now seemed finished forever, this couple stood celebrating a new and better marriage with each other.

"Anne, as I watched Andrea and Bill, standing before the minister, renewing their marriage vows, I cried, but I wasn't crying for Andrea and Bill. I was crying for you and Brian, and I was crying in a happy way, because I didn't see Andrea and Bill. I saw only Brian and Anne," she said. "Anne, I know with certainty, even though you stand now in your darkest hour, one day that will be you and Brian, celebrating your rebuilt relationship and great love for each other. I believe what I saw this morning was a vision from God for you. I saw you and Brian in your reaffirmation ceremony clearly in my mind."

I wrote Lori's words in my journal and clung to them like a welfare recipient to a lottery ticket. It seemed highly unlikely that they were true, but I hoped they were.

CHAPTER 8

friendship *in* Adversity

DAY SIX – SUNDAY, MAY 21, 2000

Crisis breeds camaraderie. It turns total strangers into cherished confidants. We're relieved to discover someone whose experience bears a striking resemblance to our own. It gladdens us to know we're not alone. We will always enjoy our childhood friends – the ones we lived next door to or met on the playground in second grade. But when we grow up, our needs change and God provides friends of a different kind – friends who are formed in the School of Hard Knocks, companions who've come from the classroom of life.

FROM *HUGS FOR FRIENDS*
G.A. MEYERS

I woke up in my empty bed, the beautiful canopy bed my carpenter husband had built for us, with the solid oak posts and mahogany stain. But there was no more Brian in our bed.

Usually on Sunday mornings, Brian would make me a cup of coffee and join me in bed and we would talk. But on this day there was no Brian, no coffee and no talking. I thought about what to do.

For eighteen years I had attended church on Sundays with Brian, and we were well-known there. I wanted to go again this morning, because I always found the services refreshing and encouraging, but how would I deal with the people?

If only I could sneak in unseen, like a ghost. How could I avoid everybody in that limited circle of church goers, who knew me so well? What would I tell them when they asked me where Brian was?

I felt less fragile on this morning. I was growing accustomed to the ever-present feeling of sadness. I was also regaining some sense of physical strength, even though I had ingested only one liquid meal in five days. Weight: 150 pounds.

I thought about my two younger children. Of course I would have to go to church for their sake, I didn't want them to know anything was wrong or that their father had left them. They still thought Dad was just working long hours and I still hoped he would change his mind, and they would never need to be hurt.

I timed my arrival at church strategically five minutes late, to ensure I would not have to make small talk with anyone. My children joined the other teenagers at the back of the church, while I walked forward bravely and took a seat in the center pews. I was as alone as I could be and felt as if I were attending my own funeral.

One of our church leaders, a woman and a friend, intuitively moved from her own seat and took a seat beside me, carefully flowing with the situation, and not drawing any unusual attention to it. She hugged me from the side and smiled at me compassionately. Her action warmed me from the inside, and a sense of relief swept over me. She was like my body guard. Should I be asked a question I could not answer, she was there to protect me.

As the worship service proceeded, we sang one new song after another. Although I loved singing, I was in no mood to learn something new. How I longed to sing something familiar, so I could just close my eyes and hide in the beautiful words of familiar church songs.

Our pastor's desire to be cutting edge and exciting with his music selections was not appreciated by me at all that morning. However, his preaching provided me with a meal for my soul, and I furtively left as the closing prayer was being uttered and waited for my children in the car.

Later that afternoon, Danielle and I had opportunity to sit and sort through some of our initial feelings about Brian's departure.

"I'm going to get that woman's phone number," Danielle said. "I want to hurt her back for what she's doing to our family."

"Danielle," I responded, "Don't let this woman get you in trouble. It's not going to help you if you get involved and get charged with a crime."

"Oh, I won't get caught," she said. "I'm going to find that woman's phone number."

"I already have it," I said, remembering the strange call from her husband.

"You do?" Danielle said, impressed.

"Yes, I do."

"Can I have it?"

After Danielle promised me she wouldn't do anything extreme, I gave her Helen's phone number. I wasn't sure what she might do with it, but I felt she was entitled to something to comfort her, and if this phone number helped then I thought she could have it. Besides, Danielle would get what she wanted somehow anyway. It's not that hard to find a phone number.

"What are you going to do Mom?"

She wanted to know and it was a fair question. I probably shouldn't have been talking to my daughter about my feelings, but being evasive would only have contributed to her sense of insecurity.

I told her how I felt. That I hoped Dad would come to his senses and come home where he belonged. I told her that I didn't understand why this was happening. And I told her that whatever happened in the future, that I was no dummy and was perfectly capable of taking care of this family by myself. I told her I wanted to go and live in Denmark, that I thought it would be good for our family to experience something new, that I thought it would be helpful to have the support of my family.

She didn't like my Denmark idea at all. She didn't want to leave her friends and comfort zone behind. It saddened me, but I reasoned to myself that I could overcome these objections with time.

Danielle wanted to know if I wanted to get back at the other woman. I confessed that I did, but that I had thought the situation through and decided the most effective way to get to her might actually be through kindness. I quoted the bible verse:

If your enemy is hungry, give him food to eat; if he is thirsty, give him water to drink. In doing this, you will heap burning coals on his head, and the Lord will reward you.

"I'm not going to let her control me," I told Danielle, "and I'm not going to let her win by turning me into an evil person."

We sat and discussed if there might be a way to cause Helen some pain without getting too out of hand. Something subtle. Nothing illegal.

Did we not desire to inflict pain on Brian also for his part in hurting us? No, not yet. We loved Brian, and we were not ready to let go of our image of him as a good person. It was much easier to direct all of the blame and anger towards a person we didn't know and certainly didn't love.

We discussed all kinds of things like breaking into Helen's home, telling her off, humiliating her at work and beating her up. Although we knew these things weren't really options, it felt good to talk about them. We were on the same side, and talking together was easing the pain for both of us.

It's amazing how a traumatic experience can lead you to consider things you normally never would. Six days ago, I would not have been able to comprehend another betrayed person's intense desire for revenge, nor their need to grieve. I would probably have given them lame advice about forgiveness and doing the "right" things, instead of comforting them in the same way I would if their loved one had died.

As Danielle and I continued to discuss our options, we came up with a plan that offered complete satisfaction to our strong and very human desire to retaliate. Our eyes lit up and regained a sparkle, as this master plan unfolded before us.

It was simple, yet marvelous. We were going to pay Helen a "visit," equipped with well-chewed chewing gum in our mouths. We would ensure that we got really close before we would swiftly and "accidentally" drop our gum into her hair, right on top at the roots. One of us would hold her while the other proficiently mashed it well into her bangs.

The plan was flawless! Helen would not actually be injured, but the incident would necessitate baldness on the top of her head. For the first time in six days we were laughing hysterically with delight. If Brian was going to leave us for another woman, let him have a bald woman!

Were Danielle and I serious? Yes and no. What if she got us back? The last thing we wanted to deal with was forced baldness. Or what if she got us back in some worse way? It was a struggle. I had made a decision to forgive, yet I still found myself waffling between doing the right thing and wanting to punish her for causing my family so much grief.

In the evening I found myself alone at home, and it was almost unbearable. I could not be alone with my thoughts. I had to find someone to talk to. Part of me didn't want to see anyone, but another part of me couldn't stand to be alone. An uncontrollable feeling of restlessness was overtaking me.

I elected to spread out my support a bit and phoned another couple, also leaders in our church, who knew about the affair. When I dialed up Vincent and Alexandra, I actually asked if I could come over. This was out of character for me, since it's not proper to ask to be invited to someone's home. Yet I was desperate, and hoped they would understand. They were happy to help and welcomed me over. I parked in the driveway of their immaculate, upper class home. Everything about it was inviting: the beautiful flowers, the attractive ornaments, the flawless paint, and the calming color combinations. As their door opened, both Vincent and Alexandra greeted me with a warm flow of kindness.

Alexandra was holding a tiny, baby dachshund, which barked excitedly. It was the latest addition to their family, and another precious treasure to Alexandra. Alexandra loved animals.

"This is Rusty," she said, as she ushered me to come in. I petted the small, loving creature in Alexandra's arms as I entered the doorway, commenting on how cute it was.

Somehow touching the animal was comforting me, as it seemed to love me instantly and was doing its tiny best to lavish me with affection, licking me enthusiastically on my neck, face, hands and wherever else it could reach.

"Can I hold it?" I asked, reaching out to take the small creature from Alexandra. I held tight as it squirmed about.

"Careful, careful," Alexandra said.

Before I could even comprehend what was happening I dropped the dog and it landed squarely on its head. We all scrambled to pick it up. I felt like crying. Not only had I hurt the dog, but I knew it was upsetting for Alexandra.

"It's okay," Vincent said. "The dog can handle it."

I stood before them like a fragile reed, which could be broken at the slightest force, too weak even to hold onto a puppy.

They invited me into their living room and encouraged me to sit down, bringing me a glass of water since I refused everything else.

Alexandra was a fitness instructor and well attuned to the common symptoms of someone whose spouse has had an affair. She saw all the eating disorders and appearance obsessions regularly at her workplace.

When Alexandra learned that I was fasting, she was concerned for my health. She did not feel fasting was a good idea at the best of times, much less in a time of crisis.

She had made a beautiful homemade borscht that evening, but I refused to eat it. She encouraged me to take some home in case I wanted to eat it later. I accepted, and, later at home that night, I did actually eat it. The soup tasted good and made me feel a little stronger, yet as I ate it, I worried about my weight and whether or not I was doing the wrong thing spiritually by not staying completely true to my fast.

Journal entry, May 21, 2000:
Vincent and Alexandra were an awesome encouragement to me.

It was not that anything profound had taken place during our time together, it was the fact that we were together. I knew they were successful, busy people, but they had put their own schedules on hold to be with me when I needed them, and the fact that they would do this communicated to me that I had value. When your spouse is tossing you aside for another, like a well-worn garment being replaced by a new one, one feels as if one has no worth remaining, like a piece of garbage (something that had value at one time), but now the only thought towards it is how can I get rid of it with the least cost and inconvenience to myself. By being available, Vincent and Alexandra had also saved me from myself. They had given me a chance to talk about my feelings, and every time I shared my story with someone my pain was slightly diminished. They didn't talk much that evening. I did most of the talking, but in what they did say they offered compassion, understanding and perspective. I had felt safe sharing with them, because although I wanted to talk about how Brian's actions were hurting me, at the same time I didn't want anyone to think badly of him, and I knew that they wouldn't. They sought to understand.

DAY SEVEN – MONDAY, MAY 22, 2000

I woke up at half past four. This was far too early, but a chance to attend the 6:00 AM prayer meeting at our church, attended mostly by businessmen before they went to work.

I showed up and lucky for me, the only others there were leaders who knew of my situation. They asked me how they should pray for me, and for an update on what was happening between Brian and me. I gave them a raging, excited, non-stop venting of my feelings.

I was unaware of my lack of self control, as the words spewed out like soda from a shaken can. I got a sense of my wild state though, when they stared back at me wide-eyed, as if I were some sort of crazy woman. Their eyes showed compassion, but also confusion. What do we do with this out-of-control female? I don't know how they felt when it was all said and done, but I definitely felt better.

Brian came home unexpectedly around three o'clock that afternoon. Danielle had now become my partner in the crazy win-back-Dad-at-any-cost routine. The other kids still believed that Dad was just working a lot. Danielle and I were keeping the home immaculate "just in case," and ensuring that all laundry was always done.

When Brian arrived home, he was treated like royalty, with undivided attention, in spite of the hurtful and distant behavior he was displaying. Danielle and I ignored his behavior. The truth was, we were afraid.

My identity was thoroughly shaken, and I really didn't know who I was or who I should be anymore. All I knew was whoever I had been hadn't been good enough. I had to try harder, work harder and be something else.

Brian had told me that one of the main things that he found attractive in the other woman was that she liked sports. I hated team sports and I hated the way Brian was hypnotized by the television set when he was watching them. I criticized him for what I called "wasting" time watching sports.

For the first two years of our marriage, Brian and I watched television together every night. I felt this got in the way of enjoying quality communication time. Eventually I had grown so dissatisfied with the situation, that I had persuaded Brian to get rid of the television altogether. In a relatively short period of time, we filled the gap by reading books, engaging each other in the stimulating conversation we had been missing, and enjoying quality visits with friends. It had been a great change, yet tonight I regretted it.

Tonight, in my endeavor to win Brian's affections back, I rented a sports movie.

What a devious plot, I thought to myself as I envisioned Helen "pretending" to like sports just because she knew she could steal someone else's husband that way. I couldn't comprehend a woman actually enjoying watching sports. I didn't get it. *Why watch someone else live life?* I thought. *Wouldn't you rather be involved in spending your time doing something rather than just watching someone else really live?* But then I thought maybe I was wrong. I wanted Brian so badly. From now on, I decided that my new identity included a love of sports.

I watched the movie that night with determination to enjoy it, and neurotic determination to be better than Helen in *every* way, but Brian remained grumpy and closed off. I found it very difficult to be around him and not be kissed, not hold his hand and not even have him be willing to sit beside me like he always had in the past.

That evening Brian and I talked privately before we went to sleep. It turned out that the reason he had come home that night was to tell the other two kids he was moving out, however I had successfully stalled him and since it was now late he decided to spend the night at home instead of returning to his hotel. I used the opportunity to ask him if he would be kind enough to grant me one last favor before he left me for good. I told him he would then be completely free to leave and I would not make it difficult for him. So he promised me my favor, without knowing what it was.

I then spelled out my final request: that he tell the other two children he was leaving, and that he do it with Helen there.

"Anne, surely you can't be serious?" he asked, appalled by my request.

"Brian, you're walking out on me, and you are walking out on your responsibility as a father. Our children are going to be severely hurt by this however they find out and they are going to need some way of coping emotionally. I'm convinced that meeting the other woman, who is better for their father than their own mother is, will help them to be able to process this." I didn't mean what I was saying, but I wanted Brian to face the reality of the situation.

"When they see what a kind person she is and how willing she is to be good to them, it will be much easier. Otherwise they will have no choice but to view her as some sort of evil person who is just out there. You just promised me this one last request," I reinforced. "It's the least you can do now that you've decided to walk out on us after all these years."

"Okay, I'll do it," he said, reluctantly.

I wasn't sure that I had made the right move, but then I wasn't sure of anything anymore. Not even sure of who I was, and definitely not sure about right and wrong.

Brian slept at home that night and I viewed it as an opportunity to lure him back, glad to have him in my territory rather than Helen's. I had a strange sense of sexual arousal going on, a feeling of needing to prove something, combined with an overwhelming feeling of love for him.

I was losing my lover of eighteen years and I wanted him back at any cost. As we got ready for bed that night, I thought carefully about how to approach him. Normally we slept in the bed naked together. *Should I be naked tonight under these circumstances?* If I wore some of my alluring lingerie, it would be too obvious.

Brian resented it when I purposely tried to seduce him if we weren't getting along. Unlike many men, Brian attached a lot of emotion to lovemaking, and didn't like to have sex unless we had resolved issues between us. Yet sometimes when he saw me naked, he would get aroused and give in. This I viewed as a good thing, because he was never angry with me after we made love. Sex seemed like the ultimate cure all for discord between us. In the past, we could never stay angry with each other for very long, because the desire for sex always brought us back together.

I opted for the strictly naked approach to seduction this evening and purposely walked around wearing nothing but my jewelry while I brushed my teeth and got ready for bed. I ensured that Brian saw me as I did so, yet acted as if I were innocently going about my business, unaware of any effect this might be having on him.

He did look. Then I climbed into our bed beside him. He was keeping well to his side of the bed with his back turned towards me, although he was also in the nude, as always before.

"Brian, I still really love you," I said to him softly.

He didn't respond. I reached towards his back, stroking it gently with my finger tips the way I knew he loved, but he quickly twisted himself around in the blankets, cutting himself off from me, making it so that I could not touch him. His rejection reinforced my assumption that I was not physically attractive, and, really, it was cruel.

DAY EIGHT — TUESDAY, MAY 23, 2000

I had now lived through one week of my nightmare. I had lost ten pounds so far, but was starting to experience the second wind typical in a prolonged fast.

I was also still dedicated to lengthy periods of spiritual meditation. On this particular morning, as I closed my eyes, I saw myself as a beautiful, strong goddess in white flowing robes. Behind me stood all the forces of goodness in this world. Then I saw Helen opposing me in black and crunched over, fearful and weak.

The army of darkness that stood behind her looked small and powerless, and they knew they were no match for the forces of good.

I may have been imagining what I wanted to see in my head,

nonetheless, I began to feel strong and powerful. I had a sense of renewed energy and spirit flooding my soul, and for the first time in a week, I felt confident about my own future.

Somewhere deep inside, I knew that if I did not lower myself by doing wrong, but allowed the forces of good in this world to work on my behalf, I would eventually win, whatever winning looked like.

That night, I sought out Mameha, the young Japanese mother who had shared her own story regarding her husband's affair a few weeks earlier. I needed someone to talk to who could identify with my experience. Now we knew why she had shared that part of her story. It was to encourage and prepare me. I didn't relate to Mameha in many ways. She was a very different person than I, still she understood my pain and it was very helpful to talk to someone who had been there. Those who haven't, try as they might, truly don't understand.

Mameha shared with me how she had met the other woman, whom her husband had not only had an affair with, but had planned to start his life over with. I focused all of my energy and attention on Mameha, listening intently to every word she spoke. I did not want to miss the slightest detail of her experience, which might offer some insight into my own. How did it feel to meet her, I asked? Did you feel intimidated by her? What did you say to her? Was she nice to you? I flooded Mameha with questions and she answered every one, honestly and compassionately. Clearly Mameha was no longer hurting over this situation. I wondered how she ever could have gotten past it.

"It was very important for me to meet the other woman," Mameha told me. "It somehow helped me to put things into perspective. I could see that she was just a person, somehow not really that different from me." *Not different from her! How could Mameha be so accepting of this woman who was willing to destroy her home, and steal the father of her children,* I wondered?

"It also helped me to see that she wasn't as pretty as I imagined her to be. That really helped me," Mameha was saying. I continued to listen spellbound. "I think it's very important in this situation to meet the other woman. Anyone going through it should do it." Mameha told me. I was now inspired. I had a new goal. After all, I had the phone number. Tomorrow, I would phone Helen.

CHAPTER 9

crazy
making

DAY NINE – WEDNESDAY, MAY 24, 2000

What if?

What if I had listened to my instincts?

What if I were younger?

What if I didn't have issues?

What if I had shaved my legs more often?

What if I had put your needs first?

What if I had maintained the status quo?

What if I hadn't looked for answers?

What if I had never found out?

What if I were more like her?

What if I didn't have to be right?

What if I chose to be dysfunctional?

What if I had never met you?

What if there was no such thing as regret?

What if I were dead?

What if the sun shines for you tomorrow?

What if it never shines for me again?

DEIDRA ROBERTSON, A PERSONAL FRIEND
FIRST TIME PUBLISHED

Another morning, another day. Another day I didn't want to live through. I sat in my bed drinking grapefruit juice, staring at the white walls of our bedroom. Our landlord wouldn't allow us to change the colors in this rental house, and the lack of décor served as a subtle but constant reminder of our past financial failure, and the fact that we still couldn't afford to buy our own home. The blinds on my window were closed, yet the daylight was seeping through the cracks reminding me that I would not be able to hide from reality for very long. The shadows in the room reflected the darkness in my heart.

I opened the Bible on my night table and read, searching for an answer, searching for hope, and searching for someone to love me.

Once again tears found their way down my cheeks, as I thought about Brian's deceiving me with lies, being intimate with Helen, and not loving me anymore. Closing the Bible, I returned it to its home on the night table. I could not see the words anyway. My tears obstructed my view.

"Dear God, I need your help and your strength," I began to pray. Sliding sideways off the edge of my bed, I landed on my knees and continued. "I don't know what to do. I feel so alone. All my life I tried to be good. I tried to be a good wife. I tried to be a good mother. Why is life so hard for me? Why can't I do this? Why have I failed? Why doesn't Brian love me anymore? What have I done wrong? I don't understand."

As I voiced my inner heart to the silence of the room, I began to feel a little stronger. I was slowly gaining clarity. *I am a wonderful, beautiful person. I will make it through this.*

I rose to my feet and began to pace the room, remembering some powerful prayers from a book given to me by a friend. These prayers were like formulas for fighting evil. And here I was fighting for my life, my children, my marriage. Pacing around, I began to feel like a warrior, fighting a war, like the leader of an army, leading the troops out to battle.

With my hands on my heart, feeling the vibration and energy inside me as I spoke, I began to voice out loud the things I wanted. I claimed my husband's affections back. I was going to fight for my marriage. I was not going to lie down like a doormat and let some woman walk off with my man. I was the marriage warrior.

When I looked at the old brown clock radio that had followed us around since Brian's bachelor days, I saw that an hour had passed. Helen's number lay beside the telephone on the night table I had nothing more to lose. It was time to call.

Still I stalled. I got dressed. I rehearsed in my head what I would say. *Hello, Helen. This is Anne Bercht. I understand you want to marry my husband. I thought it might be a good idea if we met.* No. Lame.

I cleaned up the kitchen, continuing to stall. Maybe I didn't have to plan my dialogue before I phoned. Maybe the right words would come to me in the moment. I had a clear goal. I wanted to get her to agree to meet with me. I would trust my instincts and I would not stall any longer.

Carefully I dialed the number. Time seemed to stretch into slow motion as the phone rang. Once. Twice.

"Hello," a man answered.

"Hello. Is Helen there?" I asked.

"No she's not. Can I ask who's calling?"

"Yes. This is Anne Bercht, the woman whose husband Helen has been sleeping with," I said. "Is this Helen's husband?"

"Yes, it is. My name is Richard." Silence. I waited for a signal, not sure what to say next. "I'm glad you called."

He sounded nice, not like the jerk Helen had painted him out to be when talking with Brian. Brian told me that during his first lunch with Helen, his intentions were simply to help Helen with her marriage, since Brian and I had considered ourselves quite knowledgeable in the area of making relationships work.

Brian had told me how horrible Helen claimed her husband to be. This had somehow, in his mind, justified his actions. Now I was speaking to this "horrible" man, and he sounded quite sensible.

We discussed our common pain, when and how we found out, and how we were coping. We shared information about the times we knew our spouses had been together. Richard told me how he felt sick when he thought of his wife having sex with another man in his own bed where they had had sex together so many times.

We talked about how Helen had invited Brian to have lunch at her place, which was close to Brian's building site. All this while her husband was away at his own job, and her daughter had been in school. At least the stories Richard and I had been told matched! I could understand how the two of them having sex together in Richard and Helen's bedroom had made Richard feel even more violated, than had it been a neutral location.

Since we lived so far away from Brian's work, Brian and Helen had not had sex in our bed, and I was grateful for that. If they had, I knew we would have to sell our bed, even if it was the beautiful handcrafted bed that Brian had designed and built just for us. I would not have been able to sleep, much less have sex, in that same bed again.

Richard and I talked about how awful it was that our spouses lied as they had.

He shared how heartbroken he was when he heard his daughter talk about how wonderful someone named Brian was, only to discover his wife was sleeping with that man. When I told Richard it wasn't surprising that his daughter liked Brian, because Brian was great with kids, it made him feel worse.

Richard told me also how hurtful it was to discover that Helen and Brian had spent a weekend together in a small city only a four hour drive away. Helen had taken Brian there to visit relatives, and she introduced Brian as the man she would soon be marrying. She said that she and Richard had not been getting along and were getting a divorce.

I was shocked. *My own husband is going around making wedding plans with another woman, and I don't even know he's having an affair! I must be the stupidest person alive.* I felt humiliated beyond description!

What kind of people were Helen and Brian? Did these relatives know Brian was already married to someone else? Or had he just pretended to be single?

When I realized the timing of their romantic getaway, I felt outraged. I remembered feeling lucky to have such a loving husband when Brian had offered to give me a break (just after my sick bout with bronchitis) and take Tamara to her volleyball tournament himself. I had felt delighted seeing him so excited to pack his clothes, feeling blessed that my children had such a wonderful father. Because Brian had not revealed this important detail when he had disclosed his affair, I felt betrayed all over again. Learning the truth from a stranger made me feel even more embarrassed, foolish and ashamed. *Why had trusting my husband been the wrong thing to do?*

Richard said he would like to meet me in person and talk with me more. I agreed, but said that there would have to be other people present. I would not meet him one on one, making the same mistake our spouses had made.

Richard promised to let Helen know that I had called, and that I would like to meet with her in a civilized way, that I thought it would be mutually beneficial. I thanked him for the talk, and didn't question him about his call to us a few nights earlier. I understood. He probably had intended to assault Brian or at least confront him, but had changed his mind, I reasoned. Hanging up the phone, I realized we had talked for forty-five minutes.

The conversation left me feeling a little better, but wondering how to spend the rest of my day. I thought about Brian. Perhaps I should show up unexpectedly at his work at lunch time, and see if he would take me out for lunch on the spur of the moment. Brian loved surprises. At least he used to.

There didn't seem to be much animosity between us, despite the heartbreaking situation we were in. Maybe he would see how sweet I was, and remember the fun times we shared, and it would make him want to come home. Maybe I didn't have to be a reminder of his responsibilities anymore. Helen was becoming his responsibility, the very thing he was trying to escape from with me. I knew that one of the things that had made being with Helen fun for Brian was the fact that they weren't doing "life" together. No problems with kids, worry about bills or tiredness after a long day, just fun. But now that they were planning their lives together and she seemed to be replacing me as "wife," I reasoned that I could take on the role of the fun one providing the escape from reality.

As I thought further about this possible surprise rendezvous, I thought I could dress like an absolutely irresistible babe. I would turn on my feminine seductive powers full blast. I had the power to be irresistible to Brian when I wanted to be.

It was a risk, no doubt, but I had nothing to lose. I had already lost it all. I stood only to gain. With only a short hour to spare, I made my decision. I would do it.

Starting with a quick bath, I shaved my legs to a satin smooth finish. After drying off, I started getting dressed by putting on a sexy white thong. Pulling out my new skirt and top purchased nine days earlier, I got dressed and examined myself closely in the mirror. Having lost ten pounds in nine days, and twenty since January, I felt sexier and younger than I had in some time. My striking dark brown hair waved past my shoulders in gentle curls. The fake sun tan I had been working on since Day One gave me a healthy glow. I gave myself a quick manicure and pedicure, choosing a full bodied red color to accent my look. Men always seemed to prefer red nail polish. To finish off, I added subtle, but definitive make up, creating a natural yet alluring presence. I had one goal alone. To turn every head on that construction site, and when I left, I wanted the other workers to ask Brian, "Who was the absolute babe?"

The one-hour drive was along a pleasant country road, and it was a beautiful summer day. The drive gave me some time to think, but also time to be anxious. Brian had finished the project where he and Helen met, so there was no risk of running into her, unless of course they were having lunch together.

Driving my car into the construction zone, bumping along the unpaved dirt, I parked by the other vehicles and headed towards a mobile office trailer, using my limited acting skills to appear confident, like I belonged there.

A couple of guys working off in the distance saw me and looked up from their work, indicating that I was meeting my goal. My presence there had not gone unnoticed.

I found Brian alone in the office, leaning over a set of architectural drawings. It was 11:55 AM. Perfect.

"Hi," I greeted him cheerfully as I walked in the door. "I thought I would surprise you and take you out for lunch."

"Well, I've already had lunch. I had lunch early today," he said, looking unimpressed by my arrival. "If you wanted to have lunch with me you should have phoned in advance, so I could make plans."

I felt condemned already and found myself apologizing. The disappointment in my eyes pierced him, as I stood not knowing what to say next.

"Well, we can talk here for a while if you like," he said, switching to a merciful tone of kindness.

He offered me a bottle of drinking water, my normal lunch these days.

"Are you still fasting?" he asked.

"Yes. I can't really eat anyway. The thought of food turns my stomach."

He looked concerned. My eyes surveyed the well-organized but dusty office. There were blueprints and stacks of paper all over. The trailer actually had two windows, which, although dirty, brightened things up considerably. On one wall there hung a large calendar with all sorts of writing on it, but no pictures. On another wall there was a bulletin board, full of schedules and people's business cards, but again no pictures.

Brian always ran a respectable jobsite. He didn't allow the workers on his jobs to pin up pictures of scantily clad – or not clad – women anywhere on site. Some of his workers teased him for his Christian faith and moral convictions, but Brian always stood his ground.

Even though he worked in construction, Brian took pride in appearing clean and neat – never a hair out of place. The only thing that hinted at the fact that he worked hard physically was his extremely muscular, lean and attractive physique, especially his big arms and broad shoulders.

"So what do you want to talk about?" he asked.

"I don't know. I thought perhaps we could just have a nice time together."

"You didn't seem too concerned about having nice times together two weeks ago," he said.

"Brian, how could you say that? I've always wanted to have good times together," I said. "You are the most important person in my life. Times have been hard lately, with Danielle acting out and everything. I can't help that."

"See, that's the problem with you. You're always thinking about yourself," he said. "You don't care about me. You never ask me how I'm feeling. All you care about is your own hard time. Why don't you ever ask me why I say that? Because you don't care."

"Brian, I do care," I protested. "Why then, Brian? Why do you say that you don't think I'm concerned about having nice times together?"

"Why should I tell you? It's too late now. Obviously you don't care," he said.

"Obviously, I do care. That's why I'm here." I argued. "Brian, why are you doing this to me? I don't understand. Don't you see that this is a mistake? Think of all the good times we've had. Whatever the problem is, we can work it through. We can fix it."

"Well, I've been trying to fix it, but you don't listen," Brian said. "You never listen to me."

I had always considered myself an excellent listener. "Brian, what do you mean I don't listen to you? Of course I listen to you."

"No, you don't. And you're not listening now."

"Yes, I am. You're saying that I don't listen to you when you talk," I said.

"That's right. But it's too late now," he said. "I've made my decision."

"Brian, it's not too late. You can change your mind. We can work things out."

"Look, Anne, I'm making a mistake," Brian said. "I'm making the biggest mistake of my life. And I want you to leave me alone and let me make it. If I'm making this mistake, I want to make it really big."

As I heard the nonsensical words he was saying, I could hold the tears back no longer. He was acknowledging that his actions were a mistake, yet he was choosing to make a mistake consciously. Did he not understand that the bigger he made the mistake the more painful it became for me? I felt as if I was not even speaking with a sane individual.

"I hear you tried to phone Helen today," he said.

We sat facing each other on stools in his cluttered office. My skirt had creased up to about the middle of my thigh, revealing most of my smoothly shaved legs. I crossed them in a sexy manner. I needed him to notice me, to remember who I was.

"Yes, that's right," I replied, changing my posture to confidence, strength and defense. He was evidently picking a fight.

"Well, you're not allowed to contact her without going through me first," he said. "If there is going to be any talking between you and Helen, I am going to know about it and you are going to do it through me." he said with authority, as if he were the President of the United States, giving war orders to the national defense. Now, I was mad. Timidity and caution left me.

"If I want to talk with Helen, I will talk with Helen," I said, raising my voice. "I will not arrange it through you, and I do not have to tell you about it. You have been meeting Helen behind my back for two months. You have been sleeping with Helen. Now you dare to tell me that if I want to speak with her I have to do it through you and tell you about it! Forget it. Yes, I want to talk with Helen, and, no, I won't do it through you. I'll do it myself, thank you very much."

Brian was left speechless. I think he understood his hypocrisy.

Before either of us had a chance to say anything else the door flew open. In walked a thin, dark haired man in coveralls, letting Brian know about a problem on the site. Brian told me he had to get back to work. I understood.

"Well, thanks for the talk and the water," I said, holding back the majority of tears. Attempting a smile, I reached towards him out of habit for a hug. He gently put out his hand, resisting me. There was no hug. Again I was rejected.

Aware of his eyes following, I made my way back to my car. I stole one quick glance back at him before I got in. He was still looking, and if I wasn't mistaken, it was a look of attraction. The outfit had done its job. I continued looking at him, but didn't wave. He did the same.

Reflecting on the conversation as I retraced the road back home, I felt it had been a positive step forward. At least he had talked to me, and I had actually gained some insight. His feeling that I didn't listen to him was a major issue – apparently worth leaving me for. I just didn't understand why he felt this way? Could it not be fixed? I played over his words in my head: *Leave me alone and let me make this mistake. If I'm going to make a mistake, I want to make it really big.* When I arrived home, I was worn out from sobbing.

The afternoon necessitated dealing with some of the regular duties of living life, including a trip to the grocery store. Still dressed in the same clothes that I had on during my meeting with Brian earlier, I headed out on my errand. Walking past the parked cars towards the waiting shopping carts at the entrance, I felt confident. I hadn't dressed this way for years, and it made me feel sexy, as I became aware of the fact that the construction site was not the only place where I was turning heads.

After choosing the items I needed, while waiting in line at the till, I noticed Lenora Unger in another line. She was Suzie Homemaker *extraordinaire*, and one of the last people I wanted to run into by chance. She had a "perfect" life or so I thought. I didn't think I could tolerate even a brief conversation with her. What would we talk about? Her bathroom décor? I looked away. *Careful, careful, avoid eye contact, don't look that way*, I coached myself.

Then, I looked right at her, and she looked right back at me. I was standing there with my new hairstyle, new clothes, twenty pounds lighter than she last had seen me, my eyes covered with dark sunglasses. As I looked, and she looked, I realized, she couldn't even recognize me. This amused me. What a timely disguise! At this moment, I realized I had nothing to fear in public. My appearance had changed so drastically in the past nine days that I was unrecognizable to acquaintances. This fact provided me with a mild sense of pleasure and amusement, making me feel like a famous Hollywood movie star, avoiding the onslaught of unwanted publicity, as I hid my face in public with a sleek scarf and dark glasses.

Again, it was Wednesday, and I could not get out of my regular Bible study hosting commitment without drawing unwanted attention to myself. So again, I gathered inner resolve to make it through a social event for a couple of hours.

Pastor Dave was a welcome addition to our group that night. I felt safer with him there, knowing he would be sensitive to my pain and needs this night.

In my church, we believed the Bible is divinely inspired, and is therefore true and relevant to our lives today. My Christian friends and I also believed that some people, including Pastor Dave, have a special prophetic ability. That evening Dave spoke these words:

A thousand years is like a day to the Lord, and a day is like one thousand years. To God time is not. You live your lives in a sequence of time, one event following the other, but in eternity all things that will be, have already been. In eternity there is no time. All has been done already. There is no in between. I knew every day of your life before any of them came into existence. Do not doubt your future, for I hold your future in my hands. I have not forgotten you. Don't doubt. Don't doubt.

I received the words as a divine and personal encouragement.

CHAPTER   10

small
Miracles

DAY TEN – THURSDAY, MAY 25, 2000

There are parched and barren fields in our lives.
There is autumn in our existence.
But these are the grounds of our growth,
The seedbeds of our miracles.
In these fields we will someday blossom ...
And the innocence of the world
Will return with our own.

RICHARD CANIELL
FROM *WHAT THE ROAD PASSES BY*
JONES/HUGGINS

I woke up and embarked on my new routine, with my new companion pain securely at my side.

Weight: 146 pounds. I felt encouraged that I had lost twelve pounds in nine days. I recorded my weight in a journal, where I also kept track of the items I allowed myself to consume. Whether I should have been encouraged by my weight loss, or whether I should have been concerned about my health, I do not know.

After returning from driving my kids to school, I poured a glass of fruit juice and retreated to my bedroom for a time of spiritual meditation, reading, and prayer. Sometimes sitting in my bed, sometimes pacing my floor, sometimes loud and sometimes quiet, but always with the blinds drawn. Always hiding from the world outside. It was my private and personal time.

When I was finished, I would force myself to dress attractively, fix my hair, and put my makeup on, no matter how much I felt like giving up and staying alone in my bed to cry all day. Daily I fought the forces that sought to lure my life to the bottomless depths of despair.

Lori phoned. "Anne, you need to come to the ladies' meeting this morning," she said. "Otherwise people are going to be wondering what's going on with you. It will probably be good for you."

I had been in the habit of meeting with a small group of women from our church, committed to helping the teenagers in our community in practical and tangible ways. This morning, I did not want to go. But I willed myself there anyway.

Since the weather was so nice, we met in a park instead of someone's home. Only three other women were there this morning: Lori, Mameha and Gloria Neufeld. I liked Gloria, but she was someone I was not supposed to tell. Pastor Dave and Lori had encouraged me not to tell anyone except the leaders in our church, and Gloria was not one of our church leaders. (Neither was Mameha, but I told her anyway for obvious reasons.)

We sat around a picnic table, trees in bloom, birds chirping. A beautiful moment, but I felt as though I was in a dungeon, carrying a ball and chain around my ankle.

I did not want to be there. I did not want to keep quiet. I thought of nothing but my broken family, my endless unanswered questions and how inadequate I was as a woman.

Gloria told us about her life with the many teenagers in her family. She had five biological children and had adopted a sixth. But while she described her children's interests and the activities they did as a family, I found that I didn't care.

My head hung down and I looked at the picnic table. I felt as if I might die talking about these seemingly trivial things, so I spoke only when a question was directed at me. Otherwise I was silent, on the verge of tears. I did not have it together this morning.

When we finally closed with a traditional prayer, I closed my eyes, bowed my head, and lost it. Tears flowed and sobs came. Gloria put her arm around me, offering comfort. I longed to tell her the truth, but a lie came out instead.

"It's okay. I'm just having a bad day," I said. "I had a fight with Danielle yesterday." Danielle had become an easy scapegoat for me, and everyone bought it. "Don't worry about me. I just need to get home."

Shortly after arriving home, my peace was disturbed by the ringing telephone.

"Hello," I said. Gone was the formal telephone greeting. Whatever I had done before, I wasn't doing anymore. Everything was changing: my attitudes, my routines, my beliefs about what was important.

"Hi. This is Helen. Is this Anne?"

"Yes, it is." *Thump, thump.* My heart was beating fast and loud. I was sure I could hear it beating within me.

"I understand you would like to meet me," Helen said.

"Yes, I would," I replied. "Thank you for returning my call."

"Well, I think that's a good idea," she said.

Good, good, I thought, scared to death.

We made plans to meet the following week at her house. This way I could see the setting where Brian had been having many of his secret rendezvous lunches. I wondered if I could find a way to see the bed, where they had made love. I wanted to know every detail about

Brian and Helen's relationship. I wanted answers to my many questions. To me the most painful part of their affair was the secrecy and the lies they told, not the fact that they had sex together. I didn't want another woman to have any more secrets with my husband.

After we arranged our meeting time, Helen carried on the phone conversation.

"Brian is very special," Helen said. "He's not just an average carpenter."

"Yes, I know he's not an average carpenter." I thought of what an amazing man Brian was. He not only did exceptional work in terms of quality, service and speed, but he was also a very friendly, kind, well-liked and trustworthy human being. "I've been married to Brian for eighteen years, and I know him much better than you do. I think very highly of him and I've never once thought of my wonderful husband as average. I don't think I need you to tell me my husband is not average. It never once occurred to me to think of him that way."

I didn't mean to sound aggressive, but what did she think? That I needed her to tell me what kind of man my husband was? That I didn't think he was a great man? I think it surprised her to hear that I had no anger or animosity towards him.

"Brian and I are soul mates," Helen said next, beginning to ramble a little nervously. "Brian and I are planning our future together, and I hope this can go as smoothly as possible. Brian tells me you are a loving caring person, and I am too. I want to have a positive impact in your children's lives as well."

"No. You and Brian are not soul mates," I said. "Brian is my soul mate."

"Look, Helen," I continued. "I know this will be hard for you to understand, because you do not believe in God, as Brian and I do, but when you have a faith like Brian does, you cannot just walk away from it and still feel good about yourself."

"I'm aware of Brian's religious convictions," she said. "But I think

Brian has been questioning these beliefs for quite some time."

I realized, at this point, that my attempt to reason with Helen was somewhat pointless. Bringing up Brian's spirituality under these circumstances was futile.

"I know you are really fighting this," Helen said. "But Brian is the one who will decide who he wants to spend the rest of his life with."

"Yes, he is," I agreed.

I didn't like it, but it was true.

"I'm tall and slim," was the next thing I remember her saying. Was she trying to scare me off, intimidate me, or get me to quit trying? Were tall and slim the most desirable qualities in a female? Or was she worried I might not recognize her when she opened the door to her home for me on Monday morning? I thought she was ridiculous.

Finally, she told me how to find her house and our conversation was finished.

Hanging up the phone, I realized the term soul mate had just taken on a new and negative connotation for me. I now hated that phrase. It seemed that I hated a lot of things these days. *How dare this woman say to me she was my husband's soul mate?* I thought she sounded like a stupid bimbo. I groaned just thinking about it.

Then there was her comment about wanting to have a positive impact in the lives of my children. What was wrong with this woman? Was my husband not enough? Now she wanted my children as well? Over my dead body would she have a positive impact in the lives of my children.

I wondered what I could do to stop it, but I realized I wouldn't need to stop it. My children would not be interested in the woman who replaced their mother to their father, under these circumstances. Helen was living a fantasy.

For the next couple of hours I busied myself around my home, taking care of necessary domestic tasks. Again my day was interrupted by the intrusive telephone. When I answered this time, to my surprise, it was one of my coworkers, Susan Shanahan.

She was a beautiful individual, with distinctive class, character and reasonable financial resources. At times Susan was perceived by others as being a bit of a snob. In reality, she was a down-to-earth, caring, compassionate and sensitive individual. Yet for the most part we were little more than acquaintances, our paths rarely crossing beyond the realm of our work.

"Anne, I don't know what it is," she started, "but this past week, I have not been able to stop thinking about you. You have been really heavy on my heart all week. I have been praying for you steadily. Finally, since I can't stop thinking about you, I decided to just give you a call. I'm wondering, are you okay?"

Susan had never phoned me unexpectedly at home before. The timing and accuracy were amazing. There was only one way she could have sensed something was up with me, and that way involved something beyond the walls of the five senses. This was a small miracle, and it provided me with a jolt of encouragement. Not so much because she called and cared, but because I recognized her as a messenger, carrying a message from Someone greater than this world, and that Someone apparently cared about me.

The message was *I am taking care of you. I have not forgotten you.* Sensing this phone call was a divine appointment for my benefit, I confided in Susan the truth, even though I was not supposed to.

I told her everything, and once again, I felt so much better for the opportunity to define my emotions out loud.

"Oh Anne! Your entire world is turned upside down isn't it?" she said.

Her words comforted me. I felt understood, and for a moment I sensed the tension in my muscles ease.

But as I continued to unload my burden, I wound myself right back up again.

"He likes the other woman better because she likes sports," I told

Susan. "I always complained when Brian watched sports. I didn't know how much they meant to him. I wish I had understood this. But sports aren't that bad. I'm going to like sports from now on too."

She was a wise lady. She immediately caught the unhealthy behavior pattern, the ridiculous obsession and the error in my thinking, and carefully nipped it in the bud.

"Anne, it's fine for you to take an interest in sports for the sake of your husband, but do not lose sight of your own identity," she said. "You do not need to change who you are to win Brian's affections back. You are a wonderful person as you are. I'm sure the other woman's interest in hockey is not the real reason why he is leaving you. That's just what he is saying right now. You don't leave a marriage after eighteen years because your spouse doesn't like hockey."

Don't lose sight of your own identity. You do not need to change who you are to win Brian's affections back. Her words carried a significant impact, and I pondered them often, as I walked my personal journey to healing in the days and months ahead.

———•———

While driving the short distance to the park, where I was meeting Lori for an afternoon walk, I listened to a CD titled *Hillsongs from Australia*. The following song accompanied me on my drive:

My Heart Will Trust

I'll walk closer now on the higher way,
Through the darkest night will you hold my hand,
Jesus, guide my way.
For you mourn with me and you dance with me
For my heart of hearts is bound to you.
Though I walk through valleys low,
I will fear no evil
Like the water stills my soul
My heart will trust in you.
For you counsel me, and you comfort me
When I cannot see, you light my path. †

The words comforted me, and, again, tears flowed, tears which carried the poison of pain out of my body.

As we walked, Lori and I discussed my upcoming meeting with Helen. First of all, I intended to fight Helen with kindness. I would even give her a friendship card.

I told Lori that I had no real purpose in my meeting with Helen, other than to meet her, see what she looked like, and put an end to the mystery and my own vain imaginations. Perhaps my forgiveness would be easier when I saw that she was not a devil-horned temptress out to ruin the lives of others, but rather another woman, another real human being with needs and hurts, just like me.

I also planned to bring along something I'd once seen at a conference about relationships. It was a prop, really, a teaching aid that illustrated the effect of broken relationships on people.

Lori thought it was a great idea, and as we concluded our walk, reminded me that she would be praying for me, and that she thought I was handling everything very well.

———•———

In an effort to continue to care for my family, I had placed a chicken in the oven to roast for dinner. Brian told me he would be home after work to tell the children he was leaving. Still, I was outdoing myself trying to create a pleasant and inviting atmosphere, hoping he would change his mind.

I continued to avoid food, believing that fasting and prayer might save my marriage. During the past ten days, I had four meal replacement drinks, an occasional piece of fruit and one bowl of borscht.

At 6:00 PM, with Brian not home yet, I decided to proceed with dinner without him. I lifted the lovely and aromatic roast chicken from the oven and began to carve it up for my children. I looked at it longingly. It was the first time I had been tempted by substantial food in over a week. I stood there, now almost in a trance, contemplating eating a piece of the succulent meat.

Chicken would be good for me, I was thinking, *and it's not fattening.* I was nearly ready to have a bite right out of a leg, when a voice broke the silence.

"Don't eat it, Mom." The voice caught me by surprise. It was Tamara. She had picked up that I was fasting, but didn't know why and certainly had no idea what was going on between Brian and I. I asked Tamara if she was pleased that I was fasting and she said she was. Upon hearing this confession, I returned the chicken leg to its place on the serving platter and served dinner to my children, but ate nothing myself.

———•———

The supper hour gave way to bed time, and there was still no sign of Brian.

Returning to my darkened bedroom, my life broken and torn, I wondered how I could make it through yet another night. I felt so alone, so frail and so helpless.

When I became a Christian eighteen years earlier a particular verse in the Bible stood out as being meaningful and personal for me.

Delight thyself also in the Lord;
And he shall give thee the desires of thine heart.

PSALM 37:4

The only real desire I had ever really owned in my heart was the desire to be part of a family. I wanted to belong somewhere and to someone. As a child, I never knew this. I grew up alone most of the time, my single parent mother struggling to survive life herself, in a time when mothers and fathers generally still stayed together and single parents were shunned. Not very many friends were allowed to come to my home. We were the bad people. And the fact that we moved across the Atlantic Ocean so often made it nearly impossible to keep friends, fit in, be normal or acquire nice things. Each time we moved, I had to leave most of my belongings behind.

But all of that had been okay, because at the age of twenty, I had become a Christian, and then God had given me the only thing I ever really wanted: a family. Sure, I didn't get to be the kid, but I got to be the mom, and that was okay with me. I often encouraged others by sharing my personal story, and whenever I did, I concluded by sharing the verse, Psalm 37:4.

Psalm 37:4 isn't true. God lied. I cried to myself as I thought these thoughts. I would never again be able to share my story, I thought, because it was no longer true. The desire of my heart, a family, had been taken way.

As I sat desperate and devastated in my bedroom that night, the silence was disturbed again by the telephone.

This time it was my friend Andrea, the wife of one of the leaders in the church who knew about our situation.

"I just wanted to phone to encourage you," she said, "but I don't really know what to say."

So I did the talking, told her about the recent events in my life and the fears I had for my family's future. Although I shared with her, I kept my darkest feeling to myself. I didn't want to reveal my weak side.

"Before I go," Andrea said. "I have a scripture to share with you, which I believe the Lord has laid on my heart for you. It's Psalm 37:4. *Delight yourself in the Lord, and he will grant you the desires of your heart.*"

I nearly dropped the telephone receiver. Andrea couldn't have known what that verse meant to me, and she certainly had no insight into my private thoughts of the past hour.

It was another small miracle!

I was not alone, and I was not forgotten.

CHAPTER 11

Danielle
calls
the other
woman

DAY ELEVEN – FRIDAY, MAY 26, 2000

The Reckoning

Time has got a little bill – get wise while yet you may,
For the debit side's increasing in a most alarming way;
The things you had no right to do, the things you should have done,
They're all put down; it's up to you to pay for every one.
So eat, drink and be merry, have a good time if you will,
But God help you when the time comes, and you
Foot the bill.

ROBERT SERVICE

The doorbell rang, announcing the arrival of the cable man. He was here to hook me up to the world of sports. I was determined to outdo Helen in everything, including television viewing skills.

When the cable was hooked up, I settled into a comfy chair with the remote in hand. I could love sports just like Helen did. I would figure out what it was that was so great about them. Hockey was supposed to be a big deal right now. The NHL playoffs were in progress.

But as I flipped through the channels, I couldn't find any sports to watch. I turned off the TV and made a mental note to purchase a *TV Guide* during the course of the day.

Later, while I was cleaning the house so it would be perfect "just in case" Brian came home, Brian phoned.

"Hi," he said. "I thought I'd let you know that I'm going to come home tonight. I'm gonna deal with this thing and tell the kids. We've stalled long enough. And by the way, I'm not bringing Helen. That's my final decision."

I was relieved about the Helen issue, although I didn't tell Brian. I figured that the request had likely already served its purpose.

"Brian, you can't tell the kids tonight," I said. "This is the night Tamara celebrates her birthday with her friends. She's having a big sleepover."

It was the truth, yet I sensed Brian's frustration as we went from one important event to the other that hindered him from telling our other two children he was leaving. I thought maybe it was destiny, still hoping he would change his mind.

"Our cable television just got hooked up," I offered lamely. I was trying to sound upbeat, hoping to lure him home.

"So what?" he said. "Don't you think it's a little late?"

"It's not too late, Brian," I said. "I'm sorry I said I didn't like watching TV. I can learn to like watching sports on television. I'm really going to try."

"You'll never like watching sports, Anne," he said. "You're kidding yourself."

"I will like sports on television. Just you watch me," I said. "If it's important to you, it's important to me."

"I wish you had put this effort in before. Now it's too late. I'm leaving," he said. "Well, I gotta go, good-bye."

"Bye, I love you," I said out of habit.

Anne, you sounded pathetic, I scolded myself after hanging up the phone. *But you're wearing him down. Yes, he's going to come home soon. Think of all those little encouragements you've had, especially with Andrea quoting your favorite scripture.*

Delight thyself in the Lord, and He will grant you the desires of your heart.

Brian: For the past twenty minutes I had found temporary peace while driving from the jobsite to my latest "home" in a motel. The drive provided me with an escape from all the work-related and personal problems that I now faced.

These new living quarters of mine were a far cry from the lovely home that I had just left behind. I made my way to the second floor of the motel and inserted the key into door #214. Noticing how easily the door opened and recognizing that the lock had been broken, I immediately reported the damage to the manager so the lock could be fixed.

"Did you see your friend?" asked the older, tired-looking man in charge. "He waited around for a long time for you this afternoon, but eventually he left."

That was strange. No one except Helen knew where I was staying. While making my way back to my room, I wondered if it had been Richard, Helen's husband, who had broken in.

Well nothing appeared to be missing, so I tried to put that concern out of my mind.

About ten minutes into an old rerun of a classic boxing match, and before I had a chance to shower up from my hard day at work,

Helen was knocking on my door.

"Hi, can I come in?" she asked. "I told Richard that I had to run a few errands before supper, so I can't stay long."

"I'd like to offer you something to eat or drink," I said, "but as you can see the selection is rather minimal."

"That's OK. Maybe this would be more fun," she said, as she began to remove her clothes.

"So do you like what you see?" Helen asked.

But even before I could mumble anything in response, she was fondling and kissing me, and only moments after her entrance, we were fully engaged in sex.

So much for the warming up theory about women! This was not the first time we had skipped foreplay entirely.

While we were both lying naked on the bed, enjoying the post-orgasmic relaxation, the phone rang.

"Hello" I said.

"Is this Brian Bercht?"

"Yes. Who is this?"

"This is Karl Stennerson, Helen's father. I would like to talk with you right away," he said. "Would that be possible?"

"Sure, when?" I asked

"In about ten minutes."

"OK, I will see you then."

"Who was that?" Helen asked.

"It was your dad," I said. "He is coming over here to talk with me right away."

"Where was he? Was he downstairs? How long before he gets here?" Helen asked frantically.

I observed fear in her eyes and a slight terror in her voice. Helen was afraid of disappointing her parents, and saw them as her only seemingly secure source of financial stability, with Richard out of the picture. As rapidly as the clothing had been removed, so it was now returned to our bodies. Hardly two minutes passed from the phone call until Helen was scurrying out the door, like a teenager escaping out the window of her lover's room, as the footsteps of angry parents approached.

I knew that Helen's father was a man of considerable means and influence, something that he used generously to help his only daughter. I knew that what Helen and I were doing would not meet with any type of approval from her parents, who she said were more concerned about outward appearances than inward happiness.

I also knew that it was Helen's father that had introduced her to Richard ten years earlier, when Richard first began working for Mr. Stennerson's company.

I had time to tidy up the bed and get dressed into something cleaner than my work clothes before Karl arrived. I was also able to catch the last rounds of the fight that I'd been watching before. I was happy to see that George Foreman was still victorious, even fifteen years after his infamous fight.

The knocking on my door triggered many thoughts: *If Karl was violent would I be able to handle him? Would he be alone? Would he threaten me?*

But all these things were about to be revealed.

Before me stood a well-groomed, healthy looking man with gray hair parted to one side. He was a few inches taller than me, and also about twenty pounds heavier. Obviously retirement was treating him well.

"I'm Karl Stennerson. Helen's father." He spoke authoritatively, like one who has habitually used intimidation to get what he wants.

I reached out my hand to greet him and said as firmly as he had,

"Brian Bercht." I offered him a seat on the sofa while I took my seat in a chair opposing him.

"Mr. Bercht, this is not the way we do things in the Stennerson family," Karl began in a condescending tone, as if I were the only guilty party in this affair. "I am not going to tolerate this relationship between you and my daughter. I want you to get your sorry *** home were it belongs and leave my daughter alone. My family is disgusted with the behavior of you two and we are not going to put up with it."

I thought that it was a bit strange that this man was trying to control the life of his thirty-seven-year-old daughter.

"I know that Richard and Helen have had some problems but those problems stay in the family. We don't need any outsiders meddling with that," he said. "Do I make myself clear, Mr. Bercht?"

"Well, if you are that concerned about the welfare of your daughter and about the marriage problems that you know she is having, why haven't you done something about it sooner?" I asked. "Helen has been quite unhappy for some time now, and it seems that if you are such a caring father as you say that you are, waiting until now seems like a pretty weak gesture for a father. Why haven't you done something sooner?"

Karl was noticeably agitated.

"Look Mr. Bercht, I'm here to tell you to leave my daughter alone."

"What are you going to say to Helen?" I replied.

"Never mind, I will deal with her myself," he said. "I am a man of considerable means, and I have the necessary connections to make life very difficult for you," he continued. "If you don't bugger off, you will be very sorry."

He rose to his feet and so did I.

"Well, I am glad that you said what you had to," I said. "I will give thought to those things and weigh them carefully."

I reached out my hand in an attempt to be civil. We shook hands and he was gone. I refocused my mind on the immediate tasks ahead of me, showering, dressing and looking for a place to eat my supper. ALONE!

———•———

Danielle: The night before grad my boyfriend Jason took me out for dinner at a family restaurant. It didn't really matter to me where we went. It was just fun being together. We were both in an awesome mood that night, eating nachos and drinking coffee while talking about our friends, who was going to be at grad, who was going with who, and the big party afterwards.

Jason wanted to call his friend, Steve, so he asked me if I had Steve's number stored in my cell phone. I was using well over a thousand minutes a month and had nearly a hundred phone numbers stored in it. I'd programmed my phone to say "Hi Sexy" on the display whenever I turned it on, which I thought was pretty cool. I flashed the greeting at Jason and raised my eyebrows at him a couple of times just to make him laugh. Then I started to flip through the phone numbers quickly in alphabetical order looking for Steve's number.

My mood changed instantly when I came across a phone number to which I had attached a swear word in place of the person's name. All this anger started to rise up inside me. *****face was the best I could do to give a name to the phone number of the women who was screwing my dad. I thought of her as worse than a whore because she wanted to break up my family. At least whores don't try to break up families. I wanted to call that woman up and give her a piece of my mind. I wanted to hurt her for the way that she was hurting me.

I was so mad at that moment that I told Jason I was going to call that *******- *****! Jason looked pretty worried. I don't think he thought that I should call her. He asked me what I would say. I said "I'm going to ******* tell her, I'm going to ******* kill her!" And then I just went for it. I hit the "send" button and waited. I could just feel my adrenaline pumping, heart pounding. I looked at the display on my phone. It read "calling *****face." It rang once. Twice. Jason, who was Asian, looked pale like a white man about now.

A man's voice answered "Hello." I had a pretty good idea it was Helen's husband. The next thing I knew the words; "I'd like to speak with the *******-***** who's ******* my dad," came out of my mouth. There was a pause on the other end, then I heard the man say (not to me), "Honey, there is someone on the phone who would like to speak with the *******-***** who's ******* their dad."

Wow! He repeated the words exactly as I said them. Helen deserved it for what she was doing to me, trying to steal my father. She refused to get on the phone and that made me even madder. "Look, tell that ******* whore she better get on the ******** phone and talk to me. I'm going to make her pay for what she's doing to my family," I yelled into the phone.

Helen's husband told me that he understood how I felt, that he agreed that it was wrong what his wife and my dad had done and he told me that he was really hurt by it too. The way he didn't try to tell me I was wrong and didn't yell back at me helped me to calm down. He asked if I was okay and if I had been doing drugs. I told him that I hadn't which was true. He even asked if I needed help and offered to come and get me and to drive me home! I had to reassure him several times that I was fine before he believed me. His kindness, calmness and understanding helped me to relax and by the time I finished talking to him, I actually felt much better.

When I hung up the phone, I was shaking, but Jason encouraged me. I don't know what I would have done without him. We ordered more nachos and coffee and talked about my family for quite a while. When we were done I called my mom for a ride home (something I rarely did), so that maybe I could have some time alone to talk with her.

Dedicated as I was, I went to pick up my daughter when called, and as usual Danielle asked if I minded if she drove. No problem, I didn't really mind. We drove through the blackness of the night. Rain poured down heavily. It was late.

When her phone rang, she answered it in her standard, almost overly sweet voice. "Hey, this is Danielle."

She listened for a moment.

"No, no. You're the one who is wrong," she said, each new syllable blurted out with more volume and intensity than the last. "Don't you ******* tell me what to do." Whoever she was talking to was getting a serious tongue lashing. "No, now you listen to me ... You're the one who is a jerk."

As the conversation continued, I felt sickened by her choice of language and uncontrolled anger. I didn't know what to do, but unless it got completely out of hand, I thought it was best to leave the verbal tantrum left unchallenged. Besides, whoever was receiving this tongue lashing had the option of just hanging up.

All the way home the verbal assault continued. I tried to figure out who she could be so mad at and what it was all about, but the angry words offered no clues.

Whoever was on the other end was either not getting the opportunity to speak, or was shouting back with equal volume, because from my end it was clear that Danielle was not listening. She was giving someone a piece of her mind and it wasn't good.

As we pulled into the driveway, Danielle continued shouting into the phone, "No, I'm not going to let you talk to her. Don't even bother phoning the house." She hung up and ran into our home.

Inside the home phone rang, and Danielle answered it before it could ring a second time.

The yelling and intensity continued. Apparently the caller was not finished with Danielle yet either. I tried to listen in on the conversation but as soon as Danielle noticed me lingering around the corner, she went out the kitchen door onto the sundeck at the back of the house. She shut the door and continued her argument in privacy, undaunted by the rain.

Before long Danielle came inside and gave me the phone.

"Hello?" I said, curiously.

"Hi," said Brian. I couldn't believe it. Had this been my daughter's opponent for the past twenty minutes?

"Listen," he said, "Danielle phoned Helen this evening and swore at her. This behavior is totally unacceptable. You need to get *your* children under control." I was outraged. In the past, Brian had always referred to our children as *our* children, even when they misbehaved.

"This is not how my children are allowed to behave," he continued. "I want you to do something. You get your daughter under control. She is not allowed to phone Helen and she is certainly not allowed to talk like that to anyone."

"Listen," I said. "I have no idea about Danielle phoning Helen, but if it's true that she did, then I can imagine what kind of language she might have used, and I want you to know that I'm not going to do a thing about it. I suggest that you get the log out of your own eye, before you go around worrying about the speck in your children's.[2] Our children shall not be required to behave at a standard higher than that which their own father requires of himself."

"Anne, this is different …" Brian began.

I cut his objection short. "No, it's actually not one bit different. I'm not going to do a thing about it. If Danielle felt she needed to talk to the woman her father is leaving her mother for, so be it. She has every right," I said. "My decision is final. I'm not changing my mind. Good-bye."

I slammed down the phone. I had never spoken so assertively to my husband, and it felt rather good. I could feel my heart pounding, as if I'd just delivered a sermon on human rights to the Ku Klux Klan. I was sure I was right, and I was rather impressed with my rebuttal. A man walks out on his family, and then expects them to exemplify characters on *Little House on the Prairie?* Guess again. Every action comes with a price.

---

2. Biblical reference to Mathew 7: 3-5

C H A P T E R   1 2

our children

DAY TWELVE — SATURDAY, MAY 27, 2000

The Child

I am a person beginning my life
Starting my journey to grow.
Absorbing all your nourishment
To teach me what to know.
I listen and your voice shows me
The way I should speak my mind.
Will you teach me to yell and criticize
Or to be respectful and kind?
I reach for your hand to lead me
Into a world full of hatred and love.
Will you teach me to touch with gentleness
Or react with a punch and a shove?
I crave the knowledge inside your brain
It's much more vast than mine.
Will you encourage me to want to learn
Or make my desire benign?
I feel what your heart is saying
Even though it's not said aloud.

You cannot hide your thoughts from me
I know when you're disgusted or proud.
For I am a child living in your world
And each thing you do impresses me
That's why I watch each move you make
For what you do, is what I'll be!

AUTHOR UNKNOWN

On Day Twelve I awoke to an already hustling and bustling household. It was a special day: Danielle would be attending graduation ceremonies with her boyfriend Jason. This was the day she could show off her soft lilac silk gown and white beaded purse.

Danielle had a tendency to panic under stressful conditions of this nature and I was already feeling too weak to deal with the slightest additional stress, so although part of me hoped more than anything that I could help Danielle have a great day, another part of me was afraid to face it.

Brian and I were invited to a pre-ceremonies get-together with Jason's parents around six o'clock. I was stressed about that because I had no idea whether Brian planned to show up or not, whether he cared or what I was going to say to Jason's parents. I would have given anything to find some tactful way of getting out of this engagement.

In the afternoon, Danielle had an appointment with a hairdresser, to have her hair done in an expensive and elaborate do for the special occasion. At about half past four, I watched Danielle's hair receive its finishing touches at the beauty salon.

Suddenly she blurted out, "Quit staring at me mom!" It was rude. I felt embarrassed and humiliated. Attempting not to make matters worse, I took a seat that faced a different direction. It was obvious that Danielle was once again on the brink of exploding.

On the way home Danielle was saying that she didn't like her hair, and it wasn't what she expected. I reassured her that she looked beautiful (which she did), but it didn't help, and inwardly I agreed that it wasn't the best style for her, yet I dared not say so.

Upon arrival home, Danielle ran to her room, looked in her mirror and started to sob. "You look beautiful," I offered trying to comfort her. "No, I don't. I look like Curly Sue!" she shouted. I stared, feeling sorry for her, wanting to help her, yet not having the slightest idea how.

"I'm not going," she announced. Seconds later I could hear her on the phone scolding her innocent date, telling him she wasn't going and offering no explanation.

The stress was overwhelming. It seemed impossible to encourage her.

At this moment Brian came home. I greeted him cautiously doing my best to appear happy. I prepared him a plate of food, serving it to him in front of our newly hooked up television, where he was already sitting staring at a hockey game. Then I sat down on the sofa beside him. He kept watching and eating, but said nothing to me.

Moments later Danielle was peering down the stairs, seemingly having gathered herself together, "Mom, can I talk to you privately for a minute." I headed back upstairs hoping I could handle whatever was about to happen next and wishing I had Brian's emotional support on this high stress day, but I didn't.

"I'm going to the grad after all," she told me. "Jason talked me into it. I just love him." The female teenage roller coaster was in operation at full speed! At this moment we seemed to be back on top. I went back downstairs to ask Brian if he would still be coming with me to meet Jason's family as promised two weeks ago. "No," was his answer.

I wanted to cry. *How could I now be emotionally so far away from my husband?* I wondered. *If only Brian would kiss me. If only he would reassure me. If only he cared about what I was going through.* Instead he was distant, uncaring and aloof. *How could he leave me to deal with this alone? What was I going to tell Jason's parents?*

I thought about not going, but reasoned that would be worse. Hopefully, I wouldn't have to be there for very long. I wished I could understand why Brian didn't want to be married to me anymore, but at this point the only explanation I had been given was that it was because I didn't like sports.

"Time to go," Danielle announced from down the hallway in her bedroom. We headed for the car.

"Isn't Dad coming?" She questioned.

"No, I guess he's not."

"What are we going to say Mom?"

"Don't worry, Danielle. It'll be alright. We'll apologize and explain that he had to work." She looked sad. "Danielle, this is your special day. You go and have a great time, and don't worry about your father. Don't let your dad spoil this day for you." She smiled as if resolutely closing a door to a part of her life, and then swinging open a different door that hopefully would lead to a better place. I was proud of her.

Jason's parents greeted us kindly. They complimented Danielle on her appearance and I complimented Jason on his. He was a nice young man and well-mannered. Danielle's stunning appearance and confident, outgoing personality no doubt won her a lot of grace from the many young men who were interested in dating her.

"Where is your husband?" Jason's mother questioned.

"Oh, he was so sorry he couldn't be here. He had to work," I lied.

I was ushered to a seat on a black leather sofa, where hors d'oeuvres and sweets were pushed eagerly upon me in the name of hospitality. "No thank you," was not going to be an acceptable answer. I took one small plate, and on it allowed a lone piece of cheese, a stick of celery and a small dainty cookie, attempting to appear delighted.

"Take some more," Jason's mother urged.

"This looks delicious," I lied again, "but really I have a very small appetite."

Jason's mother looked puzzled, but put the trays down and

helped herself to a generous portion. I was glad the teenagers were eating so at least it appeared that someone was enjoying the hard work that had gone into creating such a beautiful array of goodies.

I had to explain how my husband was self-employed and sometimes you just couldn't leave a job until it was finished. They looked skeptical. They were not impressed by his absence, but continued the visit politely. When Danielle had captivated everyone's attention by telling one of her entertaining tales of adventure, one by one I placed the three items on my plate into my mouth and politely chewed, smiling. As Danielle continued on in her usual animated and expressive story-telling style, I snuck off to the restroom, where I got rid of the food by spitting it in the toilet.

At last the time came for Jason, Danielle and Jason's family to head off to the ceremony, and I was free to go. I had won another small battle in my personal war to survive.

Returning home I felt extremely fatigued. I sat with Brian in the rec room watching sports and the news. Several times I tried to initiate some small talk, but he was in no talking mood.

Eventually we went to bed. He told me that he came home to tell the children he was leaving. I was out of excuses and delays. The children were going to have to know. I couldn't keep living in a lie with our children, and it seemed that Brian really was going to leave us. It was best he told them himself. Yet I wasn't going to encourage him.

It didn't happen that evening.

Brian: Deep inside I was hesitating, wrestling with my decision, afraid of hurting my children. I didn't know how to tell them, had no idea what to say or how I could explain my behavior so that they would understand the truth, and still respect me.

I wore an elegant satin night gown to bed that night, something which, in the past, had been used strictly as evening lounge wear. I didn't want to expose myself to Brian. His plan to tell the children he was no longer willing to be their full-time father was just too painful for me. Sleep was hard to come by – so was clarity concerning our situation.

DAY THIRTEEN – SUNDAY, MAY 28, 2000

On Sunday morning, while my two youngest children and I got dressed up for church, Brian pulled on his jeans. He had no intention of attending church. Instead, he gathered us into the living room.

I knew what was coming and could feel the unavoidable grief deep in the pit of my stomach. But I could not force this man to live with us, if he had chosen otherwise. I knew I had done everything within my power and understanding to make things different. It was over.

Brian sat in a chair alone. I was in the middle of the sofa with Tamara on one side and Dustin on the other. Danielle was over at a friend's house. I put an arm around each of these two precious souls, and drew them into myself in an attempt to protect them. We sat directly across from Brian, facing him like two opposing teams, mother and kids versus father.

There was a moment of silence and anticipation, yet these two younger teenagers had no idea what they were about to hear.

"There is something I have to tell you kids," Brian started. "It's not very easy for me to say this."

The kids listened attentively, curious.

"I want you to know that I love you very much and this has nothing to do with you kids, but your mother and I are getting a divorce," he said. "I have been having an affair with another woman, and I am moving out and going to live with her."

The kids looked at me, searching for my reaction, searching for reassurance.

"I'm so sorry, kids," I said. "I'm very hurt too. Your father has made up his mind. I have encouraged him to change his mind and give me a second chance, but he won't."

"I will still be your father and try to see you as often as possible. I just can't live here anymore," Brian said lamely, as if that would help them to understand.

"But Dad, don't you love us anymore?" asked Dustin. "Yes, I love you," Brian said. "Isn't mom good enough?" Dustin asked. "Can't you just be with her?"

"It's complicated, son." Brian was once again offering a response that didn't come close to the explanation our son was searching for.

Dustin remained quiet, sullen and composed, much like he had following a fight Brian and I had when he was only ten. After that fight, Dustin had said to Brian, "Well, I certainly don't appreciate the way you spoke to my mother!" Dustin then displayed his loyalty to me, his desire to protect me. Brian and I had both been astounded by the impact our arguing clearly had on our son.

Now four years later, it was my arm that tightened around Dustin, reassuring him of my faithfulness, confidence and loyalty towards him. I knew I could never under any circumstances abandon my children. I was steadfast like Dustin. You would have to kill me to separate me from my kids.

"Can't you just be friends with this woman and stay with mom?" Tamara asked in childlike innocence.

Brian searched my eyes. I knew he was looking for an answer. I bailed him out.

"No, Tamara. That is one thing Mom can't allow," I said. "Dad cannot have two women in his life. He is not "just friends" with this other woman. He wants to be with her now and he doesn't want to be with me anymore. I am not willing to share your father with this other woman. Either he is devoted to me and to us, or he cannot live here."

Tears were streaming down her face, desperation and disillusionment evident in her eyes. I pulled her in tighter with my free arm. "Mom will always be with you," I said, "I will never leave you." Tears came down my cheeks as well.

Brian gathered up his things and left without another word. The children and I were still sitting on the sofa when we heard the front door close behind him.

After comforting the kids as best I could, it was clear that we had to get on with our day. Lori, whose two children were close with mine, offered to take Dustin and Tamara for the afternoon. She would let her children know what was going on so mine could have some peer support. In the meantime, I sought out Brian's friend Darrell Barnes, who I hoped would be able talk to Brian and offer him advice and support. Helen was setting Brian up to get advice from someone she knew. I thought I could do better by hooking Brian up with Darrell.

Darrell and his wife Jeanette were friends we'd met a few years ago through our church. They were quality people, with a sincere desire to help others. They were also very real people, who did not try to put on a phony front to impress others. Most importantly, I knew Brian had respect for Darrell. Perhaps Darrell could understand Brian and be the friend he needed at this difficult time. Perhaps Darrell could help Brian to make the right decision concerning his life.

I rang them up on the phone. "Jeanette," I started, "I have a big problem, and I think you and Darrell can help me. I was wondering if I could come over this afternoon and talk to you both about it."

She welcomed me over so I headed straight there, relieved, but a little nervous.

When I arrived, they couldn't believe how different I looked and how much weight I had lost. They were generous with their compliments.

They offered me something to drink, but I declined, telling them about my thirteen-day fast. The story of my fast gave way to my real story: Brian's departure.

I explained the details and then told them how Brian needed a man to talk to. I told them how Helen was encouraging Brian to talk to her friend who had been divorced twice. I told Darrell how Brian had always respected him, and asked Darrell if he would consider contacting Brian to offer his friendship during this confusing time.

"Will he listen to me?" Darrell asked. "What will he say? Will he be angry when he finds out that you asked me to contact him?"

I told Darrell there was no need to lie, to just be honest and tell Brian that I told him everything and had asked him to call. I explained how Brian kept complaining that no one would listen to him and that all Darrell needed to be was a friend with a listening ear. I told Darrell that I didn't have any magical expectations about their time together, but thought it was worth a try. So Darrell agreed.

As I drove home, I was feeling strong, almost invincible, strengthened once again by the act of verbalizing my story to willing listeners and encouraged by their friendship. I thought about my meeting with Helen tomorrow. I was scared, but I was feeling like a brave warrior. I trusted that I would be able to say the right things and have a positive impact on her life, and that impact would involve helping her to see that a future with my husband was not going to bring her the happiness she was missing in her own life. I trusted that I would be able to speak the truth in love and although I was still feeling an almost unbearable sense of pain, at the same time I felt as though I were enveloped in an extraordinary and unexplainable peace.

Later that night, when I tucked Tamara into bed, I struggled to answer her difficult questions. "If Dad still loves me, why is he leaving me?" At this point I couldn't understand it either. I tried to explain that her father would always be her father, no matter where he lived or who with.

"Mom?" she asked, as I started to leave her room.

"Yes, Tamara."

"I wish we still lived in the bible times." *Bible times, bible times, what did she mean bible times? I was thinking as fast as I could. What was so special about those days?*

"Why?" I asked.

"Because then Dad could just have two wives," she said. "He could marry the other woman and still keep you."

I was stunned by the innocent logic of a child. I didn't know what to say. I had always wondered how women in these cultures coped emotionally with sharing their husbands.

I walked back to her bed, smiled into her eyes, and kissed her one more time.

"Yes. Perhaps it would be better if we lived in Bible times," I said.

As I closed her door behind me, I wondered why my child had to go through this. She was searching for any solution to keep Brian and I together. *Why do grown-ups have to go around screwing things up for children,* I wondered?

CHAPTER 13

Meeting
the other
woman

DAY FOURTEEN – MONDAY, MAY 29, 2000

I will go down with this ship.
I won't put my hands up and surrender.
There will be no white flag
above my door.
I'm in love
and always will be.

CHORUS FROM
"WHITE FLAG" BY DIDO

When the sun rose, its gentle rays penetrated the cracks of my window blinds and gently woke me up, reminding me that, regardless of my changing world, Mother Nature was still constant.

I awoke full of sadness, and feeling tired of fighting. This was the day I was supposed to meet Helen, and I didn't want to go anymore. I lay in bed without moving.

What if Helen is prettier than me? What if she is better than me? What if I do something stupid? Say something stupid? I didn't want to face the truth.

I wanted to hide from my life, stay cocooned up in my dark bedroom and never see anyone again. I felt as though I was dead, but still breathing. Tears fell down my cheeks, dampening the sheets, but I didn't even make the effort to wipe them away.

I felt like giving up, hanging the white flag of surrender outside my bedroom door, and saying to my enemy, "You win – just go now and leave me alone." *I can't go anyway,* I thought, *because I forgot to buy the construction paper and glue for my presentation.*

I had just decided not to meet Helen when the doorbell pulled me out of my thoughts and out of bed.

Lori stood on my doorstep. In her hands was a small bag containing construction paper and glue.

"I knew you would be chickening out this morning," Lori said. (I wondered how she knew, when I myself had been fully convinced I was going yesterday.)

"You're right," I confessed. "I just decided not to go."

"Well, I just wanted to encourage you. I believe you are doing the right thing," she said. "You go, girl! I feel like I'm living through this with you, and I'm so proud of you. You are doing an amazing job, and you can do this."

I smiled and welcomed her in. Her friendship and praise made me feel better.

"No, I just came to bring you these supplies and to encourage you to go. You don't have much time to get ready, so you go," she said. "I'll be praying for you."

Lori gave me a hug and was on her way. I stood watching her go. There I was with my construction paper and glue, and no more excuses.

I started to get ready.

What would I wear? I had to look very attractive, even sexy, yet it had to look natural, not like something I had put special effort into. Honestly, I did desire to intimidate Helen, yet another part of me desired to do the right thing.

I chose a new pair of jeans, which complimented my slimming figure and a tight fitting tank top in a light blue color. The top was slightly low cut, and revealed a subtle amount of cleavage.

I fixed my hair and makeup in my usual manner, taking a careful and long look at myself in the mirror when I was finished. I examined myself from every angle and practiced smiling in different ways, tweaking and rearranging my hair again and again, until I was completely satisfied with my ensemble of intimidation.

Afterwards, I turned my attention to the bag Lori had provided for me. *How cute!* I thought. *And how thoughtful of her.* Of course I couldn't just show up with construction paper and Elmer's glue tucked up under my arm, and Lori had thought of that – the presentation was all prepared for me. Lori had also included a greeting card in the bag, because I had said I was going to write Helen a nice card.

The front of the card had a picture of a Victorian girl walking through a flower garden. It was blank on the inside, leaving me room for my message.

I didn't have much time. *What was I going to write?* I practiced on a scratch paper first:

Dear Helen, If only we had had the opportunity to meet under different circumstances. I am sure you are a wonderful person, for my husband to consider his future with you …

I stopped and stared at what I had written. I wasn't going to say my husband was considering his future with her. I started over.

I wanted to write *There is no way my husband is going to spend his life with you,* but I thought this would make me sound insecure. No. I wanted to write something neutral, and I wanted to rise above the situation and my own feelings and write something kind. I wrote:

Dear Helen,

You have hurt me more than words could ever tell. Yet, I am sure you are a wonderful person. I want you to know that I have forgiven you for what you have done and I wish you the best in your future. I also want you to know that God loves you very much and he has a wonderful plan for your life, but that plan does not involve breaking up two families to create a new one. When we get to the other side of this mess, I would like to be your friend.

"For I know the plans I have for you, declares the Lord, plans to prosper you and not to harm you, plans to give you hope and a future."

JEREMIAH 29:11

Anne

Helen's home looked considerably more expensive than ours. It was on a street full of other immaculate-looking homes in a high-end but character-free subdivision.

I pulled into her driveway feeling nervous. *God, I can't do this without you,* I prayed. *I ask you to come with me, and that this morning Helen could have a meeting with you not with me. Amen.*

With that, I grabbed the ornamental gift bag full of my supplies, got out of the car, and rang the doorbell.

A short brunette opened the door.

"Hi, Helen?"

"Yes. And you must be Anne."

I had to look down in order to see her eyes. She didn't look much taller than 5'6". *Why had she boasted about how tall she was?*

She looked at me questioningly, as if she were comparing herself to me. I studied her face too. She had dark hair and dark eyes like mine.

"I just got my hair cut," she said. "It used to be cut just like yours."

So we had even worn the same hairstyle? Disgusting, I thought to myself.

She led me through an immaculate hallway with light-colored hardwood floors towards her kitchen. Both of us now in stocking feet, so not a sound could be heard.

Her home looked like a show home. Every decoration was perfectly suited. Nothing was out of place, yet the whole thing appeared cold and sterile as if no one really lived there. There were no signs that a child also occupied this home. I felt sorry for her daughter. *Was she accustomed to being brushed aside so her mother could engage in sexual encounters of her passing fancy?* I wondered.

Helen offered me coffee, but I declined and brought out an herbal tea bag from my purse.

"I hope you don't mind. A lot of people don't have herb tea, so I just brought some along."

"Do you normally drink coffee?" she questioned.

"Yes, normally I love coffee," I said. "But lately I can't actually stomach it."

She cringed a bit. We both knew perfectly well what "lately" meant.

She leaned down and opened a cupboard, drawing out a kettle. She was dressed in a suit, with a short sleeved blazer and capri pants in an off white color. Underneath the blazer, I could see that she was wearing only a bra, which she apparently didn't need. She had a completely flat chest. And here I had been imagining a big bosomed sex goddess! She was so thin I wondered if she had an eating disorder. I doubted she weighed more than a hundred pounds. Her figure resembled that of a ten year old. *Had her daughter been adopted?* She stared at my cleavage. *Did Brian prefer women with no curves?* I wondered.

When our beverages were ready, Helen offered me a cookie from a delicate china plate with a beautiful floral design.

"I haven't been able to eat since Brian told me about the affair," I said. "But thank you for offering."

She winced a little. I wasn't going to play politeness games with her. She might as well know the extent of the pain she was causing me, as much as it was possible to reveal.

She motioned for me to join her in the living room. I took my seat on the sofa, carefully placing my bag of teaching supplies on the end table beside me. Helen didn't ask any questions about the gift bag I was toting along like a purse.

"Brian is a very special man," she began, sitting in a rocking chair, facing me head-on. She said this as if she was delivering some enlightening information I had never been aware of before. She must have assumed I was like many wives who seemed to have disdain for their husbands rather than respect.

She was wrong. I smiled at her, feeling totally relaxed and in complete control. The reason for this was unexplainable.

"Yes, he certainly is," I replied. "I love him very much. So tell me a little bit about yourself. I would like to get to know you a bit."

"Well Richard is my second husband," Helen said.

She looked extremely nervous, and I felt I was intimidating her. I knew that I often did this unwittingly, therefore I usually made an extra effort to be friendly when meeting people.

But today I made no effort to soften the impression I was making. When a moment of silence came in the conversation, I used it to my advantage. I was comfortable with the silence. Helen quickly filled in the pauses, revealing more of herself.

"I married my first husband young. He was a lot older than me. I really wasn't ready for marriage but my father kind of pushed me into it. Richard is quite a bit older than me too. How old are you?" she asked.

"I'm thirty-eight. How old are you?"

"Thirty-seven," she replied apparently disappointed. "I thought you were a lot older than that."

I wondered why she thought that, or maybe she was just trying to insult me, indirectly saying that I looked old. I knew I didn't.

"What was your first husband like?" I questioned as if I were just making small talk.

"He was a bad man, very violent," she said. "But I didn't realize that before we were married. It's funny how people seem to change after you marry them. I saw my first husband recently, while I was with Brian, shopping on Robson Street." Robson is a famous shopping area in downtown Vancouver. I was glad Brian had already told me about this shopping day. It would have been rough to hear it for the first time in this situation.

"Yes, Brian told me all about your shopping adventure. So tell me about seeing your ex husband. What happened? Did you and Brian talk with him?"

"No, we were walking down the street, and we saw him about a block away. I quickly grabbed Brian and told him we had to go the other way. The moment I saw him, I remembered the violence. He used to beat me sometimes. I had a flashback. Brian didn't really know what to say. We went the other way for quite some time, before I was ready to head back to Robson. I was so afraid," she told me.

Normally, I would have felt sorry for a person relaying such a story, but I wasn't really feeling sorry for Helen.

"What attracted you to your first husband?" I asked once again as if I were just making conversation, really I had an ulterior motive. I was trying to get to know Helen and she was doing an amazing job of revealing her life to the woman whose husband she planned on making her third husband.

"Well my first husband was the strong silent type. I didn't know how important it would be to have a husband who could share his feelings, someone soft and gentle. My first husband wasn't very good in bed either. He was really fast. He had no idea how to please a woman. Brian is a very talented lover."

I honestly thought she was going a bit far here and purposefully being insensitive or trying to provoke me.

"Yes, I am the one who taught Brian how to make love so well. I am fully satisfied every time we make love. It wasn't always this way in the beginning. When Brian and I first met, he got so turned on by me that we were married for well over a year before I ever saw him without a full blown erection. The moment he saw me, he had a rise." I said. I could see this had not been her experience and it made her feel a little inadequate. If she wanted to play games of subtle intimidation, I could certainly go there. She backed off from the topic of sex.

Throughout the conversation, she was fidgeting nervously and unable to look me in the eyes. Whenever she looked towards me I looked straight at her. I wanted to make eye contact, but it didn't happen. I thought it was good for her to sit face to face with the woman she had hurt.

"Also my first husband refused to have children," she continued as if explaining these things would suddenly make me understand that she needed to marry Brian.

"Why didn't you leave him sooner, if he was violent?" I questioned.

"I was just trying to make it work. I didn't think divorce was right. I really am a loving, caring person." I wondered why she felt a need to keep making this statement. The only reason I could think of was that deep down, she didn't believe it. She was trying to convince herself.

"How soon did you meet Richard after your divorce?"

"Actually, I met Richard before my divorce. He works for the company my dad founded, you know. At the time, I was working there too and my father introduced us. We shared a common interest in sports. I love sports." I hardly needed enlightenment about this fact.

It intimidated me. Nonetheless I listened patiently, careful not to lose sight of my motive.

"Were you attracted to Richard, because he was good at sports?"

"Well that was part of it. He talked about wanting to have children. He was very caring and sensitive and he really listened to me. I was so hurt from my first marriage, I found him irresistible."

"Did you end up making love to Richard, while you were still married to your first husband?"

"Yes," she confessed. "I couldn't resist." I saw her pain, and I actually felt compassion for her.

"If I had lived your life perhaps I would have done the same," I heard myself say. This statement implied *I don't condemn you, nor do I condone what you have done, but I identify with you and do not think of myself as better than you.* I saw that she liked me and knew she sensed the Love inside of me and longed for it, but she didn't know this Love did not come from me.

We talked like this for about half an hour. I stayed relaxed and controlled, surprising myself with the kindness and compassion I felt for this very real woman who sat in front of me under these painful and strained circumstances.

I wished Brian had included me in his initial desire to help Helen with her marriage to Richard. Brian had said if the circumstances were different he was sure I would have liked her. I felt he was right.

I was surprised by how easy it was to get Helen to open up and reveal her story, but then she didn't know what I was up to.

The time had come for me to illustrate to Helen how the pain in her life was not about to be magically resolved, like she thought it would be, by marrying Brian.

"Helen, before I go, I do have something I would like to say to you," I said, kindly. "Just one thought, if you don't mind."

She nodded for me to go ahead.

"I want to share an illustration with you that someone shared once with me," I said, carefully pulling my prepared sheets of construction paper and glue out of the bag. She looked a little surprised, but as if she was going to tolerate me.

I held up the first sheet, the bright solid yellow one.

"This sheet," I said, "represents you as a young woman. You are a loving and kind person. You are bright and full of energy like the sun. You are athletic, competitive and beautiful. You get good grades in school.

"You also have some aches and pains. You don't have a very good relationship with your father. He is too busy making money. And your mother is more concerned with appearances at the country club than she is about you.

"But you have dreams: you want to have a family, a husband to love you and a nice home with a white picket fence in a lovely neighborhood. You dream of being loved and adored by your husband, and of making him happy. You visualize family picnics in the park."

I was only repeating the things she had told me, filling in a few gaps. I had her attention. I was describing her dreams, longings and heartaches accurately.

Carefully I pulled out the blue sheet of construction paper.

"This is your first husband, Steve. Steve is strong, confident and older which you find very attractive. You see in him the potential to meet the void in your heart, which is there because your father didn't meet your emotional needs. Steve has established himself financially. He wines you and dines you in fine restaurants. He buys you flowers and gifts. He doesn't talk much, but you interpret his lack of communication skills as confidence. If only you could marry Steve, you would have a wonderful life.

"So you do whatever you can to win his affections. Eventually he asks you to marry him and you accept. Then you go about the happy work of making wedding plans. The future seems as bright as the stars. After all look at him. Mr. Blue, perfect, flawless."

I turned the undamaged blue construction paper about admiringly.

"Finally the big day arrives and you exchange your wedding vows promising to love, honor and cherish each other. Pastor Elmer is there to perform the ceremony," I explained squeezing glue in circles on the yellow sheet, representing Helen and attaching it to the blue one representing her first husband.

"And so here you are after the ceremony joined as one." I showed her the two sheets of construction paper, now glued together.

"You love each other very much," I said, pressing the two sheets firmly together at every inch.

"It's you," I showed the yellow side, "and him," I showed the blue side, "attached together married, Mr. and Mrs. One-unit-together and you both plan to spend the rest of your lives with each other in happy marital bliss.

"You know there will be bumps along the way, but right now you are sure you will be able to work everything out. You meant it when you said, 'for better or worse, for richer or poorer, in sickness and in health, until death do us part.'"

"Yes, I did mean it," Helen said, apparently completely drawn into the illustration. "You're exactly right."

"Yes," I smiled, "And how can anyone know just how difficult living with one person can be? And why is it that people seem to change after you marry them? At this point you are sure you will be married for a lifetime. After all you have enough money. You are attractive. He is attractive. You share friends in common. He takes care of you, buys you the finer things in life. It's going to be a great life," I said.

I kept talking about the confidence we often have when we are young, making sure that I allowed adequate time for the glue to dry.

"But then," I said, "there was that day, when Steve promised to take you out for dinner, but he stayed at the office until about nine o'clock and didn't even bother to phone home. You waited and waited, hurt and disappointed. It was completely thoughtless and insensitive of him. You had a big fight about it later."

I tore off a small chunk of blue, separating it from the yellow paper.

"After you had been married for a year, you realized he no longer bought you flowers like when you were courting."

I tore off another small chunk of blue as I told her story.

"Then he forgot your birthday, and when you challenged him he became angry. You had never seen this before. In his rage he slapped you across the face with an open palm, and it hurt."

I tore off another piece. Helen watched.

"You were committed to the marriage, so you forgave him, but the issue never got resolved. After two years of marriage you wanted to have children. Of course you would have children, you thought, but he refused."

I tore off another chunk of blue paper.

"And when you brought up having children again, he beat you, leaving you bruised."

I tore off a big chunk of blue.

"You didn't know who to turn to or what to do. You were scared."

I snuck a peak at Helen's eyes, they were red and misty. I could see that she was working hard to hold back tears. I was describing her story accurately.

"You longed for someone to love you, like every woman longs to be loved, like I long to be loved. Then he started to hoard his money, questioning you even on your grocery purchases."

I tore off more blue.

"And the beatings started to happen more often. Then you met Richard. Richard was a different color, let's say Richard is purple. By the time your relationship with Richard has developed to the point that you make love to him, your relationship with Steve is beyond hope."

I ripped the blue from the yellow as much as possible, but torn patches of blue remained attached to the yellow sheet. Once the glue has dried, you cannot totally separate them.

"So here you are, divorced. Free from Mr. Blue at last or are you? Pieces of him are still attached to you. You have hurts. You aren't as innocent as when you were younger. You decide you don't like blue anymore. The problem was you married the wrong man, the wrong color, you think. So you meet Mr. Purple, Richard. Surely purple is better than blue. After all Mr. Purple is kind and gentle. Mr. Purple talks! Most importantly Mr. Purple wants to have children. He even makes love better than Mr. Blue. So you marry Mr. Purple and the whole thing repeats itself.

"It turns out Mr. Purple is horrible. [I was using her phrase.] Mr. Purple is not a good father. You have arguments over how to discipline your child. You get in a car accident, and Mr. Purple drops your daughter off with your parents and doesn't even come to the hospital to visit you. You feel abandoned, unloved and alone. How could he be so insensitive?

"Helen, I can really understand why you are hurt. I would be hurt too. You know, I haven't experienced this kind of neglect from Brian. Richard doesn't buy you cards and gifts. You try to talk to him about it, but he justifies himself and says it's a frivolous waste of money. Still you don't have the affection you long for, the affection every woman longs for. So you are married but alone, and very empty. You care for your daughter, you excel in your career, but still you feel empty, unfulfilled and alone.

"Then you meet Mr. Red." I got this piece out extra carefully, showing only one side to Helen.

"This is Brian. Brian is different from any man you've ever met before. He doesn't have any blue tones at all! He doesn't swear. He is a gentleman. He opens the door for you. He speaks highly of his wife. He is charming and witty. He talks about the ingredients for a successful marriage. He talks about open and honest communication. You've never heard a man speak of things that matter like this before. You are attracted to him right away. You notice that he is good with children. He makes kids laugh. He is their hero. You wish your daughter had a father like this.

"So you went after him, and it appears you have won him over, but if you marry him there will be problems," I said, as I carefully glued the untainted yellow side representing Helen to the red paper representing Brian. This exposed the damaged side of the yellow paper with the torn pieces of blue still stuck to it.

"One of the problems is you. You are still hurt from your first marriage. This is why when you went shopping on Robson Street and saw your ex husband you were no longer able to enjoy yourself. And you also have pieces of Mr. Purple attached to you, hurts from Richard. But Brian can fix all that, right? Brian is the man of integrity who reads books on marriage. Brian puts effort into relationships. Surely if you are married to a man like Brian you will have a happy life, but there is another problem."

I flipped the newly glued yellow and red construction papers around to reveal a damaged red side with pieces of green attached to it which I had carefully prepared in advance.

"Brian has pieces of me, the green, attached to him. You see, Brian is not a free man. He is not free to marry you. Brian tells me that even though all this has happened with you, he still loves me. Perhaps he loves us both, I don't know. If you pursue a life with Brian, if in fact he does follow through with this and marry you, you will not have what you are longing for. You will not have that one man who will love, honor and cherish you and only you. You will compete with me every single day of your married life with Brian. And he will be a damaged man, a man who is disillusioned and doesn't believe in himself anymore. He will no longer be the same

Brian you met six months ago.

"I have one more thing to say. This will be difficult for you to understand because you do not share our faith in God."

Helen was still listening fully attentive. She looked as if she wanted to hear more, but was afraid. The words were coming to me with ease, so I kept going.

"God is real, and once you have had a personal relationship with Him as Brian has, you cannot just walk away from your faith and be happy.

"I know of a woman by the name of Arthelene Rippy. She and her husband knew God in this way. They were pastors and even founded a Christian school. They were very much in love and impacting their community and their world in a positive way. One day after many years in this solid marriage, Arthelene's husband suddenly and unexpectedly left her for another woman. One year later he committed suicide, and a couple of years after that, the other woman arrived on Arthelene's doorstep begging for her forgiveness.

"If Brian pursues a life with you, I am convinced that this is what will happen to him. He will not be able to live with himself. And I believe one day you will come home to find Brian dead on your floor, and that day won't be so far away. Then you will find yourself on my doorstep. There will be no more Brian, and you will be asking me for forgiveness.

"I know you want a man to love, honor and cherish you, and I want you to know you can have that. You deserve it. God wants you to have it too. But you will not have it with my husband. I don't know whether God will give you the desire of your heart through healing your relationship with Richard, or through a new man, who isn't married to someone else. But I do know if you seek God in your life, He will give you the desires of your heart."

Helen was speechless. I could see she had a lump in her throat and she needed me to leave quickly. I pulled out the card I had written for her.

"This is for you," I said. "I want you to know I really do care about you as a person, and I'm sure that had we met under different circumstances, we could have been friends."

I walked to the door, gave her a hug, and left, feeling an overwhelming sensation of love and compassion for the woman I had wanted to kill two weeks ago. I felt strong and powerful, filled with peace.

It didn't matter anymore what Helen thought. What mattered was that I had faced the thing I was afraid of, and I wasn't afraid anymore.

CHAPTER 14

unseen forces *pulling* Brian Home

DAY SIXTEEN – WEDNESDAY, MAY 31, 2000

The Light

As I drive through the darkness
The light comes to me.
It entices me and inspires me.
It makes me think I can press on.
It is not wavering – it is constant and strong.
As the light comes to me
I know I can go on.
As I drive through the darkness
The light bids me come.
It reassures me and comforts me.
It makes me think I can press on.
It is not unfaithful – it is loving and kind.
As the light bids me come

I know I can go on.
As I drive through the darkness
I am no longer alone.
The light is all encompassing.
It makes me think I can press on.
No more empty promises — instead a purposeful path.
I am no longer alone and
I know I can go on.

MARGIE THALER, A PERSONAL FRIEND
FIRST TIME PUBLISHED

Motivated by love, perhaps motivated by insanity, still behaving like a desperate and neurotic mad woman, I once again decided to do something proactive to get Brian back. I attempted once more to have lunch with Brian.

This time I heeded his warning from last week and phoned in advance. He agreed to this lunch. I concluded that was a good sign.

I started to get ready. It was an obsessive routine of perfecting to the best of my ability every detail of my physical appearance, as if looking like a sex goddess was the secret to winning back the affections of a straying husband.

I bathed, shaved my legs, styled my hair, manicured my nails, and then searched for the most flattering outfit in my closet. I came up with a short, sleeveless denim dress that hadn't fit me for a while, but was now perfect. It was also one of Brian's favorites. It buttoned all the way up the front, but I left the lowest button undone to expose a little extra leg.

During my hour-long drive to Brian's workplace, I felt anxious and afraid. Worried that I would say the wrong things.

In spite of my fear, I willed myself on, asking God for strength and for a miracle. I was still functioning in a state of shock, thinking that all I needed was for my husband to return home, as if we could then just carry on as if nothing had happened.

Although Brian did not smile at me when I arrived, he was less grumpy than the time I had arrived unannounced.

"Are you still fasting?" he asked.

"Yes," I replied.

"Well, what's the point of going out for lunch then?" he said.

"The point is being together," I answered. "Plus, I am allowing myself to eat some liquids. I'll order a bowl of soup." Brian drove us to a family restaurant, and I felt the pressures that come on a first date. I was out to be fun and exciting. I wanted to impress. Yet I was in a state of severe emotional shock and pain.

Brian asked me about me about my meeting with Helen on Monday and that made me smile. It was something I felt good about.

"Helen said you had your boobs hanging out," Brian said. That humored me.

"I didn't have my boobs hanging out," I replied playfully. "I was wearing my blue fitted tank top, you know the one. It just shows a little bit of cleavage."

"Yeah, I figured that's probably what you wore." He seemed somewhat amused that Helen was intimidated by me. "I thought it was funny that she kept talking about it. That's really pretty much all she had to say about the meeting. I think she's pretty self-conscious about her flat chest."

"Okay, Brian. I wasn't going to say anything about it, but now that you brought it up, I must say, I can't believe you are leaving me for a woman without breasts! What is wrong with you? I thought you liked breasts."

He looked a little embarrassed.

"Anne, it's not about the sex," he said. "It's about the friendship. Helen is just fun to be with. You're not."

Wow, that hurt! I tried to be mature and not respond to it. I wanted to cry, but I sucked it up. Fortunately the waitress arrived to take our order.

After some silence, I asked him why he thought I was no fun. He explained that he thought I was too serious, that he preferred Helen's sports-chat to my deep conversations. I restrained myself from criticizing Helen, as it would only put him on the defensive, drive him further away. I held my tongue.

When the waitress brought our food, I found it ironic that we said our customary mealtime prayer together before eating. Brian ate his meat sandwich enthusiastically, while I simply stirred my clam chowder around in its bowl. I didn't care about eating, only about being attractive to Brian.

"The problem with you Anne is that you never listen to me," Brian started in. "You are so self-centered. You only think about yourself. You don't even care about me."

"Well, after all these years, if that's how you feel, can you not give me a second chance?" I asked.

"No. You have not been listening to me. You don't even care about me," Brian said.

He continued, but I did not understand.

"But Brian, it's not true. I do listen to you. I do care about you."

"See, you're not even listening to me now," he said. "You're still just thinking about yourself."

As we left the restaurant, tears forced their way out of my eyes. I had been completely unsuccessful in being fun. I was humiliated and embarrassed.

As I said good-bye to Brian, his face looked strained and sad. I wished he would kiss me good-bye, but he remained distant. My best friend, who I had previously gone to for comfort, was now the one hurting me and there was no comfort to be had.

I am a big loser, I thought to myself driving home. *I am a big loser, and Helen is fun and exciting.*

Later in the afternoon, Brian phoned me.

"I'm thinking about coming by tonight," he said.

"Would you like to come home for dinner?"

"Yes. I was wondering, would that be alright?"

"Yes. Of course," I replied happily, as if he were a friend from out of town dropping in unexpectedly. After hanging up the phone, I excitedly told the kids. All three helped me prepare the house. Dustin and Tamara did the cleaning. Danielle made sure all the laundry was done. I prepared steaks for the barbecue and baked carrot cake, Brian's favorite desert.

We had a great meal together as a family that evening. The presence of the children made it easier for Brian and I to keep the conversation light. We talked about their lives, and Brian joked around with them, which made him feel more comfortable.

When Brian left after dinner, he told me he was on his way to meet Darrell Barnes. He hugged the kids good-bye, except for Danielle, who refused his embrace.

"Good-bye," he said to me warmly.

Perhaps there was hope for this marriage. We were two broken people who still loved each other and did not understand the mess we found ourselves in.

Once again it was Wednesday. That meant Bible study and a house full of guests.

During the evening, I checked my watch at regular intervals, so restless that I had little tolerance for people's questions and their lingering small talk. The whole study seemed to be moving along in slow motion.

"Look," I said finally, when I thought the evening would never end. "This study is supposed to be over by nine o'clock. It's nearly nine, and we haven't even closed in prayer. I'm still expected to serve coffee and refreshments."

My rude behavior got things moving. We rushed through the

closing prayer, I served cake and every last guest was gone by 9:05 PM.

Having regained the privacy of my living room, I sat alone on my sofa. This left me feeling unhappy as well. It seemed that I couldn't stand to be with people, yet I couldn't stand to be alone either.

I sat thinking, thinking about what I should do with my life, thinking about what had gone wrong, wondering how others survived betrayal, and wondering if my new companion, Sadness, would ever depart from me. After some time, the phone rang.

"Hello," I said.

"Hi. It's me." It was the voice of the man that I loved.

"Hi," I said.

"I just finished with Darrell here," he said. "It's a long drive back to North Vancouver. Would it be okay with you if I spent the night at home tonight?"

"Yes, of course, Brian," I said. "You are welcome in your own home."

"Okay, I'll see you in a few minutes then."

I greeted him at the door wearing a long, off-white, silk nightgown with spaghetti straps and nothing underneath. The silhouette of my nakedness was identifiable, but subtle.

In the bedroom, I stretched out on the bed and watched him wash up in the master bathroom.

I still felt attracted to him. He was only wearing his boxers, and I could see the clearly defined muscles in his arms, shoulders and back as he brushed his teeth. I wondered if he felt at all attracted to me.

"Did you have a good time with Darrell?" I asked.

"Yeah. Darrell's a good guy."

Of course, I wanted to know every detail of this conversation, but I knew better than to start fishing for information.

He lay down on the bed beside me. With the soft glow of our bed-side lamp shining on our faces, we simply stared into each other's eyes.

I wanted him. I wanted to touch him. I felt close to him.

I put my hand out to touch him gently on the shoulder. He was reluctant at first

"I shouldn't," he said.

"Why not?" I questioned. "After all, I am your wife."

He touched me gently on my shoulder in a reassuring manner. He hesitated. Suddenly, he leaned in and kissed me passionately. I allowed my body, my mind and my soul to flow gracefully with the moment.

We started to touch each other gently. He pulled me in closer, as if he longed for my comfort as much as I longed for his. The next moves became magically out of control. We were once again engulfed in the familiar harmony of playing the beautiful music of love together, only it seemed as if we had moved from the calming spirit of Mozart to the passion of "Beethoven's Fifth". We were entwined in a rhapsody of sensual pleasure, which went on as if time did not exist. Once again, we were one with each other.

When it was all finished, I knew I had pleased Brian in ways that Helen never could. I had also received the comfort I had longed for. Another battle was won in my personal war to save my marriage.

Eventually exhausted, we fell asleep in each others arms. When I awoke in the morning, Brian was already off to work. I was encour-aged by our night together, but still very unsure of my future.

DAY SEVENTEEN – THURSDAY, JUNE 1, 2000

Brian: "Hey, how you doing?" asked my good friend Darrell, in his distinct South African accent. "I'm wondering if you would like to have coffee again. I really enjoyed talking last night. I'm free again this evening if that works with you."

"Yeah, I'd like that," he said. "How about the same restaurant as last time? Around half past six?"

"See you then."

I knew Helen would not be pleased that I was meeting with Darrell once again. After my first meeting with him, I began to regain my senses and equilibrium concerning my affair with Helen. This was the first time that I was able to talk to someone who did not pass judgment on me, and who actually listened to how I was feeling.

This was a threat to Helen as she sensed a loss of control in our situation. Helen wanted me to talk with her friends, who would encourage me to leave my wife, and try to convince me that I was doing the "right" thing.

Most of her friends were less than positive when it came to long term relationships. Many complained about their marriages, and others were already involved in second marriages.

Helen's insistence that I talk with her friends was my first recognizable sign that she lacked concern for my happiness and well-being.

During my first visit with Darrell the magical grip of the affair was shaken, but not yet fully exposed for what it really was.

Darrell was the perfect person to talk to because he showed concern for me, he was neutral in the situation, and he had the experience of being divorced because of an affair.

In the end Darrell never married his affair partner. His actions, however, had cost him his marriage and his relationship with his kids, and that wasn't worth it.

I felt that as he listened he was allowing me to make my own decision about my future instead of trying to tell me what to do, and that he would support me no matter what decision I made.

Darrell was also a good person to talk to because he was there to listen. He only dispensed a bit of advice. "Brian," he started, "if you are planning to leave your wife and kids for another woman, you'd better make damn sure that she is way better looking, smarter and nicer. She has to be richer and respect you more. And she needs to be way better in bed than what you have now, because, if not, she isn't worth it!"

Of course Helen didn't meet any of these criteria. I told Darrell that I'd found Helen to be controlling and in a hurry to split up our marriages. I still had feelings for Helen, but the fairytale was starting to unravel.

"You're a smart man Brian," Darrell said. "Though right now you are thinking with your little head instead of your big head. I know that you are going to make the right decision."

———•———

On Day Seventeen, Brian came home again in the evening. He came home late and I was already sleeping when he arrived. I awoke slightly when I felt him crawl in the bed beside me.

I reached out for him, but he pulled away. I was half asleep, so I just accepted it and allowed myself to drift back into my dreams. I was still feeling a lot of pain, but knowing that he was there beside me again, after so many nights alone, made me feel better.

DAY EIGHTEEN – FRIDAY, JUNE 2, 2000

Brian: "For just the two of you?" asked the hostess, as we entered the usual restaurant that was close to my jobsite. This was about the fourth or fifth time that we had lunch together. My dining partner was Adrian Lee, a young Asian man who was one of the sub-trades working on the project I was running. Somehow we both seemed to hit it off as lunch partners and were slowly becoming friends, too. Adrian was a successful businessman whose warm personality, above average people skills and social graces made him stand out from the crowd of typical construction workers.

During our previous lunch conversations we had discussed work related issues, business, making money, and our mutual interest in hunting. He was highly educated which was not the norm. I found him refreshing. I respected Adrian for his integrity, honesty and quality workmanship.

I was happy for two things during our lunch talks. One, was that he was quite interesting. All his traveling, adventures and success made conversation easy and pleasant. Two, was the fact that we had not discussed family, specifically marriage. I was in no way feeling like talking about how screwed up my life was becoming, or that I had a wife, kids and now another woman in my life.

After we ordered our food, Adrian made this statement, "I'm thinking about getting married later this year. I proposed to my fiancée last night. I'm pretty nervous about it though, with so many marriages ending in divorce. What do you think?" All that was going through my mind at that moment was *Pal you are asking the wrong guy*, and before I could even comment I heard him ask me, "What about you? Are you married?"

"Yes."

"For how long?"

"Eighteen years."

"To the same woman?"

"Yes."

"Do you still love her?"

"Yes," I responded truthfully, having to really think about Anne and what she meant to me, still unaware of actually why I was doing what I was with Helen.

"That's great! I'm glad for the both of you. I would really like to meet your wife one day and also to see your kids, as that would confirm all that I believe about marriage and what it stands for. Do you think that would be possible?"

"I'm sure that can happen someday." I answered, not really certain that it ever would. I respected Adrian for what he had accomplished in his life and for the values he embraced. Somehow, I knew deep inside that I also embraced those same values, and I did not want to disappoint my new friend.

A couple of days and a few lunches later, we were once again discussing the topic of marriage. "Brian," Adrian said, "You have a good reputation with everyone I've talked with at the jobsite. Almost all the guys respect you for your honesty and the helpfulness that you show at work. I know from dealing with multitudes of men that you display a very high level of integrity and better than that, you have said nothing negative about your wife, marriage or kids.

"I want you to know that I hope that I too can be a husband and father like you. You have given me hope for my marriage. I can tell that you care very much for your wife and kids, and that encourages me tremendously."

I just sat there, feeling sickened due to my hidden hypocrisy. The very things that I stood for, the things that I believed in, the things that were of great importance to me, the very things that had value and meaning were conveyed to this younger man, yet there was now this distraction that was luring me away from those values. "Oh, what a wretched man am I," the old sage penned, "the good I want to do, this I do not do."

This encounter with Adrian replayed over many times in my mind that day.

"Have you ever regretted giving up your freedom?" Adrian asked at the end of our last lunch together.

"No, not at all, I have a beautiful wife and we have had a good life together."

———————

Day Eighteen was much the same as the others since heart and life were shattered. I ate no food, spent an hour in meditation, and took a walk with Lori in the park. This was the best I could do for exercise since I was weak from my fast.

I also had a tanning session, did some housework and prepared a nice dinner in case Brian decided to come home.

Returning home from a spa appointment at the end of the day, I saw Brian's van in our driveway.

I was pleased but apprehensive, wondering what this night would bring.

Entering the door, I saw that Brian was talking intensely with someone on his cell phone. He saw me and headed straight for our bedroom, closing the door behind him. I wondered if he was talking to Helen. I tried to listen for a moment from the outside and then decided to enter. After all this was my home and my bedroom. I slowly opened the door.

Brian was red in the face and looked like he had been crying. Seeing me, he jumped up off the bed and motioned angrily for me to get out. He didn't say a word to me, clearly not wanting the other person to hear.

I decided to respect Brian's wishes and leave the room. I knew things had gone well, all things considered, over the past two days. Maybe I had won. Maybe he was ending his relationship with Helen, and if I didn't grant him his privacy, he might change his mind.

I felt I had a right to hear what was being said, but knew I wasn't going to get everything I wanted right now.

"Who was that?" I asked Brian when he finally emerged from the room half an hour later.

"None of your business," he retorted, as if he had a right to secrets in our home.

Nonetheless, I ignored his rudeness and accepted the fact that he was not going to reveal the truth to me, at least not yet.

CHAPTER 15

success~*and*
an ultimatum

DAY NINETEEN – SATURDAY, JUNE 3, 2000

*Our God is a God of healing. He is a mender, a fixer of
broken things. And we need such a God, because we
tend to break and spoil much of what we touch. When
we allow Him to come into our fretful hearts, He works
quietly and gently; and with the skill of a tender craftsman,
He begins the work of restoring what is lost.*

FROM *HUGS FOR THE HURTING*
JOHN SMITH

Again Brian came home in the evening. It was the fourth evening in a row. We shared a nice meal together as a family and then watched the hockey game. Brian certainly seemed pleased with the newly installed cable.

In spite of the progress we were making, Brian still seemed distant and aloof, and I was very unsure of where I stood. Yet I sensed that perhaps we had had a breakthrough, perhaps Brian was home because he was making a decision to stay home with me.

But then maybe he was just saving the money he would otherwise be spending on a hotel. After all, I didn't doubt that our home was more pleasant than a hotel room, especially considering the special treatment he was receiving.

I hung around Brian whenever he was home, catering, as best I could, to his every whim.

After several hours of watching television together we went to bed.

Brian was fully clothed, and I wore a modest nightgown.

I really didn't know how to behave or what to do. I wondered, of course, what was happening with us, yet I dared not ask. We lay there quietly, staring at the canopy above us.

Finally Brian broke the silence and announced in a sad tone, "Well, I guess I'm home."

"I'm really glad Brian," I said.

Then we continued to lie in our silence. There was no big hug, no feeling of reconciliation. It all felt dry and cold. *So I had gotten what I had fought for or not? My husband was back. Shouldn't my pain be going away? Shouldn't I feel loved once again? I felt anything but loved right now. Where were the flowers? Where was the begging for my forgiveness?*

"I'm sorry for everything," he said next. But it sounded like he said it more out of duty than out of love for me. I didn't sense he felt genuine remorse for what he'd done.

"So that means you've decided to stay with me and work out our relationship?" I asked.

"Yeah." he said, looking anything but happy.

I needed to know one more thing. "Brian, last night on the phone, were you breaking up with Helen?"

"Yes," he replied sounding as if he hadn't really wanted to.

I felt happy to have won this victory, but the reality of the fact that

I was just beginning a journey to healing rather than ending it was starting to sink in. I was still engulfed in pain and questions: *Does he still love me? How could this have happened?*

DAY TWENTY – SUNDAY, JUNE 4, 2000

When we awoke in the morning, Brian was withdrawn. He didn't talk, look at me or smile. He was unaffectionate and kept his distance.

This was not the homecoming I had envisioned. No great apologies or red roses.

What have I done? I wondered. *Do I even want him back, when he's all depressed and gloomy? How will we ever get better? Now what of my future? Can anyone help me? Does anyone understand how I feel?*

Brian was not willing to come to church with us that morning. In a way, I didn't blame him. I could understand how difficult it would be to go there and face the people in our congregation who did know what was going on.

Yet, I felt that he should own up to his mistake. I wondered where he stood with his faith, this common ground that had meant so much to us throughout our marriage.

As far as I was concerned, we were currently not married. The vows were not only broken, but they had been declared null and void. I wondered if Brian would reinstate them. Now that he had chosen to come home, would he renew his sacred promise to me?

I had become a more independent person over the past nineteen days. I would no longer be making decisions based on what I thought Brian wanted. It was my desire to go to church so I would go with or without him. I would face whatever humiliation I might, going alone and making excuses for his absence.

———•———

We had experienced a lot of rain over the past month, but driving home from church, I was pleased to see the sun had broken through the clouds. Weather-wise, it was a glorious day.

Yet when I arrived home, I found Brian watching sports in our basement rec room with the curtains drawn.

I wanted to be with him. I tried to sit with him for a while, but I struggled with it immensely. I still did not understand most sports well enough to be drawn into the entertainment. Besides I was consumed with thoughts about where our relationship was at, why this had happened and what our future held.

I wanted to talk, but the timing seemed wrong. I longed for the bright sunshine outside, so I left the basement. Eventually, Brian did come to join me outside to do some yard work. To anyone driving by, we might have appeared to be a normal family, enjoying a sunny Sunday afternoon in June. Yet things were anything but normal. Yes, our family was back together, but we had a long way to go. Would we make it?

That evening, our friends Vincent and Alexandra invited us over for a barbecue. While we were there, Brian and I did not discuss our situation with them at all. We were there to have fun and be together as a couple.

However, Brian did not display any of his usual kindness towards me. He was cool and distant. It was obvious to our friends that Brian was still not treating me well, in spite of my efforts to forgive him and accept him back into my life.

Alexandra knew all about my fast and was concerned about my health, worried that I was headed for an ongoing eating disorder. She pointed out that my "fasting and praying" efforts had already netted the desired results: Brian was back in my life.

So that evening, at her insistence, I had my first small meal in weeks. I was afraid of the food and afraid of getting fat. I had lost sixteen pounds in twenty days and worried that even one pound gained would drive Brian away.

One might have thought that on the next morning, I would start to eat again having broken the fast the night before. I did not. I had become afraid to eat. I continued my partial fast with my fruit and meal replacement drinks.

DAY TWENTY—FOUR – THURSDAY, JUNE 8, 2000

Helen phoned Brian to tell him that she didn't think they should speak to each other anymore. Funny that she felt a need to announce it suddenly, when in fact they had not spoken since their split six days prior. The fact that Brian told me about his conversation with Helen was en exciting step forward. With this new openness, he was slowly gaining my trust again.

DAY TWENTY—FIVE – FRIDAY, JUNE 9, 2000

When Brian came home from work, I joined him in the bedroom to talk to him about his day.

"Helen phoned me twice today," he said.

"Wow, I thought she just called you yesterday and said that she didn't think you two should talk to each other again," I said.

"I know," said Brian, "I think she might have just been saying that yesterday because she was mad that I hadn't called her.

"What did she say to you today?"

"She's really mad at me for coming home to you." I was fuming back at her, but working hard to keep my anger hidden from Brian. *How ironic is that?* I thought. *She thinks it's okay to steal my husband of eighteen years, but it's wrong for him to return home to his wife and family!*

"You know what she actually said to me?" Brian continued.

"What?"

"She said, 'How dare you have sex with your wife!?!?'"

I was astonished, incredulous, amazed.

"Wow, that's amazing," I said. "She thinks it's wrong for you to sleep with your wife whom you've made a sacred and legal lifetime vow to, but okay for you to sleep with her?"

"Yeah, well she kept trying to get me to go along with this agreement that we wouldn't have sex with our spouses anymore."

"Did you agree to that?"

"Well sort of," said Brian. "I didn't really want to, but she kept pressuring me. It was ridiculous."

The nerve! I thought, *Here this woman is trying to break up my marriage and manipulate my husband into promising not to have sex with me. She is some piece of work!*

"What else did she have to say?" I asked.

"She's putting a lot of pressure on me to leave you," Brian said. "She keeps telling me I need to get my own apartment and think about things for awhile, but I don't want my own apartment. I'm sick and tired of other people trying to tell me what I should do."

Then Brian told me that Richard had beaten Helen, and she had wanted Brian to come and rescue her, but he told her to call the police instead. Richard ended up spending a day in jail, with a restraining order against him, and Helen was referred to victim services for support. It was a complete mess.

So this is how the glamour and fantasy of an affair ends, I thought. *From ecstasy to disaster, like a mouse eating the cheese just before the trap snaps shut with disastrous results.*

Helen seemed to be living in a world different than the one Brian and I lived in. A world where no marriages last, commitment is a short-term thing, and you eventually toss your spouse aside for another. She had bargained that once she had slept with my husband, I would be so angry that I would toss him out and make her takeover easy.

She had not bargained for either my forgiveness or my fight. Simply put, she tried to take over the wrong man. Yet, my war was far from over. Brian did care for her, and I would have to be very careful and very wise in how I conducted myself.

Somehow Brian's relationship with Helen had to be completely severed.

DAY TWENTY—SIX – SATURDAY, JUNE 10, 2000

On this day I began to eat again. I did so very slowly, eating only very healthy foods and only very small quantities. The total length of my fast had been twenty-five days. I had lost sixteen pounds and reached my ideal weight. In my pain, I had drawn the false conclusion that my weight was crucial to the success of my marriage. I feared that if I gained even one pound back, Brian might divorce me.

As we sat talking in our living room in the evening, the phone rang. It was Helen's husband Richard, yelling at Brian.

"If you would like to talk to me, I would be happy to," Brian said. "But you're going to have to get a grip on yourself. Look, if you're just going to scream profanities at me, I don't think this is going anywhere."

Finally he hung up without saying good-bye.

I looked across at my husband, the man that I loved, and admired his restraint. He looked pensive, remorseful and pained.

DAY TWENTY—SEVEN – SUNDAY, JUNE 11, 2000

After having a full and intense work day, Brian came home in the evening and said he wanted to take me out. I reacted excitedly. I was a changed person.

In the past, I might have questioned him, asking if we could really afford it. But I would never pose such a question again. Money matters were up to him. I knew that if I questioned him spending his hard earned profits on me, he may well spend them on another who wouldn't complain.

I also dared to dress sexier than ever before. I chose a tight-fitting short denim skirt and a snug and slightly low-cut red top to go with it. I took the time to do all that I could to look like a "babe." In the past, my look would have been more conservative. Pretty yes, but not so sexy.

Brian looked impeccable as always.

We drove to a small sea-side city not far from Brian's current work site. He took me to a romantic seafood restaurant that specialized in oysters.

He talked about some of the people and projects that made up his work day, and I felt like I was becoming a part of his life again. I resolved that I would never let the cares of my daily existence pull me away from Brian again. I would never get so caught up in details that I stopped having fun with my husband.

We enjoyed the wine and the oysters together and managed to just have fun. After dinner we took a walk along the beautiful seaside. We talked and enjoyed the warm summer air.

"You know," Brian said. "I now see the one really big difference between you and Helen."

"What's that?" I asked.

"Helen is being totally selfish, thinking only of what's best for her. You are selfless," he said. "All the time I have been married to you, you have been thinking only of what's best for everyone else."

These honestly shared insights brought us even closer together and led to another evening of unprecedented intimacy, tenderness and passion between us. Our love reunited again, we just couldn't seem to get enough of each other.

DAY TWENTY—EIGHT – MONDAY, JUNE 12, 2000

In the evening, I took my daughters out to see a movie. I wanted to connect with them and see how they were coping. I could see that Tamara was at peace and happy, satisfied to know that her father had decided not to leave her after all. Danielle, on the other hand, was not doing so well. It was clearly going to take some time with her, and I wasn't going to rush it. Pain like this doesn't go away overnight. Only time, coupled with understanding and acceptance, can eventually work the miracle of healing.

After my evening with the girls, I lay down to sleep once again with the man that I loved. "Anne, you know I was thinking of another major difference between you and Helen," he said.

"What's that, Handsome?" I called him Handsome often. It was my special expression of affection for him, and it felt good to say it again.

"Helen is a very shallow person," he said. "You have great depth."

Apparently he had phoned Helen because he was concerned about how she was coping with Richard's assault.

"Anne, all she could talk about was the physical things. She wouldn't talk about what really matters, the emotional things," he said. "The emotional wounds are far deeper. They can take a lifetime to heal. I know that if you would have been in her shoes you would barely have mentioned the physical soreness. You would have been busy talking about your feelings on the inside. It's becoming evident to me how you have so much depth in your character, which stands in stark contrast to Helen's shallowness."

These words brought healing salve deep into my heart, and my trust for him grew.

Brian also acknowledged what I'd been through by saying that there was a lot of work ahead of us. While I was still numb, emotionally, and hadn't even begun to experience the inevitable anger over the affair, he had a sense of what lay ahead.

"You won't be able to just get over it, Anne," he told me. He was aware that the upcoming months would not be easy for him or for me. He was fully aware of the cost, yet he was man enough to face the consequences and pay the price.

I was soothed by his insight and his fine words of praise for me, comforted that I was outshining Helen now in his eyes. I was also comforted that he was telling me about all these conversations with Helen. But there was a problem. A very big problem indeed: he was still talking to Helen.

In essence, he still had a friendship with her. I knew I could not live with this, but wondered how I could effectively tell him to break off his relationship with her.

"Brian?"

"Yes."

"I'm not really sure it's such a good idea for you to remain friends with Helen under the circumstances," I said, afraid that I'd push him away with my words. "I can understand your genuine concern for her, but I am not comfortable with you continuing your friendship with her. I think somebody else needs to be her friend right now, not you. I think you need to break off your relationship with her completely, and not speak with her anymore."

"Stop telling me what to do," he snapped. "Helen's my friend and I care about her. I'm not about to stop being her friend. I'll be her friend if I want to be and you can't tell me what to do!"

"Okay," I responded lamely. But it was not okay, not okay at all. I knew I could not stay married to him while he maintained a friendship with a woman he had cheated on me with, a woman who was bound and determined to break up my marriage so she could marry him.

———•———

As the early days of our healing continued, I inwardly blamed myself for Brian's affair. I became obsessed with being a flawless spouse.

Unfortunately I had the false idea that affairs happen because the third party is in some way better than the original spouse, probably sexier. So if the original spouse had just been a good spouse (and a sexy enough spouse), this wouldn't have happened.

I believed it was up to me to perform to keep my marriage together. Subconsciously, I thought it all depended on me. Without realizing it, I gave up my freedom to just be myself. This was not healthy, attractive or necessary. If I had understood more about affairs and why they happen, I would not have suffered as much as I did.

During my long days when Brian was at work, I took some time to connect with my children and talk to them about their feelings about the affair.

This openness helped the younger two children to continue on with their normal lives and to heal quite quickly. I was honest with them and didn't give them false hope for the future, but I did not discuss my insecurities with them. When they saw my confidence, they felt confident too, so that's what I tried to show them. I told them that their father was a good man and that we were both working on our marriage.

Danielle was another story. She became infuriated whenever her father was brought up in a conversation, and she put a lot of effort into avoiding him. She disrespected him and refused to listen to him.

In spite of my brave face for the children, I had no confidence that Brian or I could heal our marriage without outside help. After all, I had been completely clueless that anything was wrong in my marriage, while the affair was going on. Who was I to think I could heal the future?

I recalled a quote from Albert Einstein: *Insanity is doing the same thing over and over and expecting different results.*

Obviously something needed to change in our marriage, but what? What had gone wrong? My present belief system was a paradox. On the one hand I blamed myself for Brian's affair; on the other hand I viewed myself as the *good* person who had not had an affair.

I concluded that Brian and I needed the help of a counselor if our marriage was going to be repaired.

Brian was outraged when I suggested it. "I'm not going," he told me.

I was incredulous. *I forgave him his unfaithfulness and he isn't even willing to cooperate with my plans to save the marriage.*

"What do you mean you're not going?" I questioned.

"I'm not going. I don't need it," he said. "All our marriage you've been telling me what to do. You've been bossing me around. Well, I'm not going to be bossed around by you anymore."

I didn't think I was controlling at all. On the contrary. All these years, I viewed myself as the one who supported his dreams.

Clearly we needed help. I had to learn to identify problems in our marriage, I had to learn to forgive Brian, and I also needed to be able to trust him again. For these reasons I wanted to see a counselor, but in the end I respected Brian's wishes.

He didn't think counseling was the answer for our marriage, and I decided that he was entitled to choose his own way. However, I knew that if healing was not achieved, I would be forced to leave. I had no intentions of remaining in an unhappy marriage.

In order for our marriage to work, I knew I would have to be able to truly forgive. I knew I wasn't good at forgiving. I wasn't sure if I would be able to do it. I knew I would have to be able to come to a place where I didn't bring up the affair anymore, at least not in an argument or in a hurtful way, where I was holding it over him like a never-ending debt he could never repay. If I could not reach this forgiveness, it would be unloving of me to continue in this relationship with him.

———•———

On a Saturday afternoon, I had to take Tamara to her volleyball team's end-of-season party in a sprawling home of a posh suburb. Parents were encouraged to stay and visit and enjoy the breathtaking views.

This should have been a simple task, but I struggled with too many dark thoughts to keep on a happy face.

On this day, I was a devastated and broken woman. I felt humiliated and shamed. I felt not good enough for this world and not good enough for these people. I was convinced that I was going through the worst experience a person could, and that my situation was worse than anyone else's. I thought affairs happened to people with problems in their marriages, but I had had a good marriage. I was confused and upset. Brian was still stubborn about continuing his friendship with Helen and that wasn't going to work for me. I was having a very bad day, wrestling with unceasing negative thoughts.

When Tamara and I arrived at the party, I was imagining my life as a single parent, feeling bitter after all of my work to be a good wife. *If only I can make it through these cordial greetings without crying. If only I can look and act normal for just a few minutes,* I thought to myself.

I managed my way through polite greetings and got away with my lie that I had another commitment. My real commitment involved a secluded place and a stream of tears. I could barely hold them back.

My steps continued to gain momentum as I walked down the driveway. I walked faster and faster. It was over. I had done it. I had made it out of there without bursting into tears. I walked on, my mind racing, and the tears began to stream.

My heart was beating faster and faster as I continued, as if I was pumping adrenaline from an emergency situation.

My mind raced with my heart. I thought of the good things in my marriage. I thought of the bad things in my marriage. I thought of my Christian values, what I had been taught in my eighteen years in the church. I questioned those things. I was mad at the church. I continued to walk.

Then suddenly I stopped and wondered, *Where am I?* I couldn't remember. Some fancy residential neighborhood, which was unfamiliar. *Why was I here?* I couldn't remember that either. *Why am I walking around in this neighborhood? Where am I going? Where am I supposed to be? What am I doing?* I was lost, blanked out.

It took a lot of concentration to remember. Yes. I was supposed to be in a car, not walking! I was so excited to make it through the drop-off that I had forgotten my car. Now, I was blocks away.

I laughed at myself between my tears. *How can you forget your car?* I thought. *It's such a large item!* I turned around and made my way back, hoping no one would see me. I got into my car and found my way home safely.

No, I was definitely not in good shape, but there was no escape from the road which lay ahead of me. Whether my marriage stayed together or I ended up single, the journey was going to be difficult.

———•———

With the help of a book I had been reading[3], I decided it was time for me to grow up and face reality. It helped me see that up until this point I had been fighting with everything within me to save my marriage.

Now it was beginning to sink in that it was not *all* up to me. I could not control my husband's choices, only my own.

Maybe Brian would not be willing to give up his relationship with Helen, and it was my choice not to share my husband with another woman. I realized now Brian would have to choose: Helen or me. Period. No other way. If he wouldn't break ties with her, I would file for divorce.

I decided to deliver this ultimatum in the form of a letter. I brought it to him on a Sunday afternoon after enjoying a nice lunch together in our backyard.

June 25, 2000

Dear Brian,

I've been through some very tough moments since you told me of your affair with Helen and, to my horror, that you actually weren't sure who you wanted to spend the rest of your life with. Now you say that you have decided to stay with me, however I feel that there are some things that I need to say to you, and have decided that the best way for me to say them is through this letter.

My love for you is so profound, that my initial reaction was not only to forgive, but to do whatever I could to win back your affection. I couldn't believe how willing you were not only to hurt yourself, but to hurt me and your dear children as well. I could barely face the possibility of it all. To a person like me, who expected to marry only once and to remain committed for the rest of my life, it was a severe shock to see our relationship almost come to an end just like that.

Now it seems that you choose to stay with me, however, I have done some very deep thinking and soul searching and I realize that there are some things in our present relationship that I am not prepared to live with. Brian, you are putting our relationship under a severe strain.

You say that you will remain a friend to Helen and that you think of her only as a sister now. However, you also say that your whole affair with Helen is not based on sex, but rather on friendship. That tells me if the friendship continues the affair is also continuing. Whether it leads to sex or not is not the issue. The friendship is.

As a woman I also know that whatever you may think of her, Helen will not be able to think of you as just a brother. Every time you talk to her you are nurturing your friendship and thus the affair, and increasing the hurt she will feel if you one day break off your relationship completely.

So if you want to stay with me you will have to put an end to this "friendship" completely. If you don't want to, that's fine. It's your choice.

We dedicated ourselves to one another exclusively when we got married, and if our relationship is to continue it must continue to be that way. If you can't be faithful to me for life, then I'd rather separate now. I will not share the affections of the man I love with another woman. For me it must be all or nothing. If you choose to leave me I will be severely hurt, because my love for you is very deep.

I have reflected on how we met and were married in such a special way. I'm reminded of the fact that you married me of your own free choice. I did not blackmail you, twist your arm or offer you a bribe. It was your own decision. Suddenly it seems you have questioned that decision.

I only want you to stay with me if you are choosing to do so because you love me above all others, not because you feel like you have to out of duty or obligation. You married me of your own free will, and I want you to know that you are free to leave if you like. I will not make it difficult for you.

And if your friendship with Helen is so important to you, perhaps it is best that you do leave. It seems peculiar to me that you find it so difficult to hurt Helen by breaking off your relationship with her and yet it was okay to hurt your faithful wife of eighteen years and your own children.

I do not find this inspiring. I wonder if I can ever trust you completely and if I will ever feel the same as before about you. I have not been a perfect wife, but no other man has touched me since I pledged myself to you.

But you have violated my trust. You pledged eternal love and commitment to me on our wedding day, but now I see that that could be gone at any time, unexpectedly, without notice, and really without cause.

If you choose to stay with me, there are a couple more things that you need to know. You need to know how seriously I take all of this. I will not live with a man who has coffee or meals one-on-one with other women or who drives in a vehicle alone with another woman. So if those are things which are important to you, you might as well leave now. In the past you always seemed to understand how important it was not to be found in these compromising situations. Now you don't seem to think it should matter and are calling it maturity.

Finally, I think that you need to know that if you ever have an affair with another woman again, our relationship will be over. I'm extending this grace only one time. I will not be hurt in this way again.

I am not sure how you are going to react to this letter and I do not know what you are going to choose. Ultimately what you choose is between you and God. We will both have to answer to him one day in our own way, and my conscience is clear.

I admit that this entire experience has been painful, but I will make it regardless of what you choose to do with your future. The Lord has been with me thus far, and He'll go with me in the future. You and I have had some wonderful times together, Brian. You have been my only real love up until this point, and I'll never forget the memories that we have shared. If you choose to leave me, I will pray for you and trust that God will guide you in the years ahead.

I want to be sure you really understand exactly how I feel. I want you as my husband more than anything in the whole world. And if you can pledge yourself to me for the rest of our lives together, I'll do everything I can not only to forgive and forget, but to be the most awesome, beautiful, exciting, wonderful wife a man could ever have. But if not, then there's no better time than right now for you to leave.

With Love,

Anne

I watched him as he read the letter in front of me. He was not pleased. He threw it down on the floor in disgust as soon as he finished reading it.

I was surprised. I thought it was a very kind letter, all things considered, and that it clearly expressed my love for him.

---

3. *"Love Must Be Tough"* by Dr. James Dobson

(Above) Our wedding, October 31, 1981, Houston, Texas. (Opposite top) Leaving our wedding on Brian's motorcycle in the pouring rain. (Opposite left) Brian on our honeymoon.(Opposite right) Anne on our honeymoon – somewhere in New Mexico or Arizona???

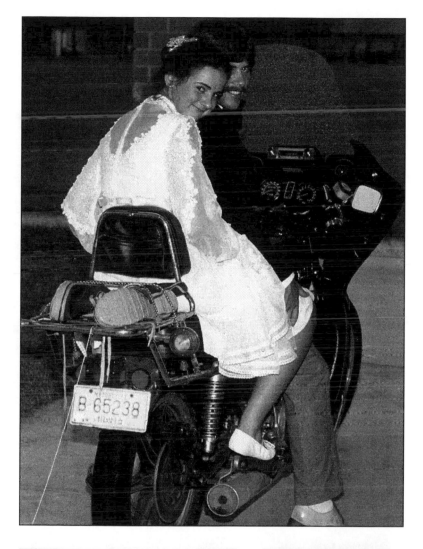

*(Opposite top left) Anne on our honeymoon wearing that inconvenient helmet.
(Opposite top right) Brian and Anne taken at our wedding reception, held by
Brian's family in Vancouver, November 1981. (Below) Brian and Anne
with Danielle as a newborn baby, October 1983. (Above) Brian and Anne
with children, from left to right, Danielle (6), Dustin (4) and Tamara (2),
November 1989. (Photo by Dave O'Kamura)*

(Above) Brian and Anne on the way to a Christmas party in 1999. This photo was taken just a couple of months before the affair began. (Right) Danielle ready to accompany her boyfriend, Jason, to his graduation ceremony on May 27, 2000. (This was the day she got upset about her hair style and called herself Curly Sue.) (Opposite top) From left to right are Tamara, Brian, Anne, Dustin. Celebrating my 39th birthday in August 2000. We were putting on a front, trying hard to be happy and get along, during the darkest period of our lives. (Photo by Danielle) (Opposite right) – I had this picture taken in November 2000, because I was afraid I was going to lose my family forever. I wanted a keepsake of my precious family together. I marveled that the photo could turn out so well, during such a dark time in our lives. (Photo by www.imagemakers.bc.ca)

(Above) A casual snapshot of Brian, Danielle and I enjoying being together in January 2004, just as this book was entering into the final stages of editing.
(Right) A recent photo of Danielle, April 2004.

CHAPTER 16

Trouble *with* the Law

JULY, 2000

Friends share a special something that is rich, rare, powerful, and persuasive. They offer it without cost to each other, and yet it holds extreme value. If it were a commodity, it would be considered priceless. If it were a precious stone, its value would be immeasurable. If it were a painting, it would be the most coveted of all works of art. What is it? Forgiveness. One simple word, phrase, or touch that transforms heartbreak into healing, sadness into celebration, and tragedy into triumph.

FROM *HUGS FROM HEAVEN*
CELEBRATING FRIENDSHIP
G.A. MEYERS AND LEANN WEISS

Brian never spoke with Helen again. She had gotten the message that their relationship was over when Brian referred her to the police rather than coming to her aid after her husband's assault.

Nonetheless, I did not trust Helen even slightly and I wanted every trace of her removed from my life and Brian's life.

Two days after giving Brian my ultimatum, I began to challenge him to decide.

"What is your decision? Her or me?" I demanded.

"Okay," he snapped. "I'll have nothing to do with Helen any-more." This was the answer I was looking for, but not the tone. "Do you promise that if she ever calls you again you'll say, 'Helen, our relationship is completely over. Don't ever call this number again. I love my wife and I never want to speak to you again'?" I demanded.

"Yes," he replied, matching my loud volume.

"Do you promise to tell me about it if it happens?"

"Yes."

"Do you promise never to try to contact her again yourself?" I asked.

"Yes," came Brian's now exasperated reply.

I was comforted to hear the words I longed for, yet I was far from feeling secure.

Next I asked him if they'd ever exchanged gifts. He told me that Helen once gave him a card with a photo.

"Where is it?" I demanded. Brian retrieved the card and threw it at me.

"There, it doesn't mean anything to me," he shouted.

I opened the envelope that had been thrown towards me.

To Brian, my soul mate ... Looking forward to our future together, I'll love you always, Helen.

I looked at Helen's photo.

"I want you to destroy this picture yourself," I said handing it back to Brian. Brian immediately ripped the photo in half and threw it in the garbage.

"No, that's not good enough." I shouted, grabbing the two halves of the picture back out of the trash and handing them back to

Brian. "Rip it into a million pieces," I continued to shout, giving way to some honest anger.

He looked at me and tore it into as many small pieces as was possible. It seemed that he wanted to get rid of every trace of Helen and this nightmare as much as I did.

"Is there anything else?" I asked. "Are there any other traces of that woman in our home?"

"No," he said, reaching out gently and embracing me tenderly. The intensity of my anger gave way to sobbing.

"Thank you. Thank you for doing that," I said, soothed by his willingness to give me what I needed. He hugged me for a long time and let me cry in his arms as long as I needed to. It was just Brian and I now. No more third party wreaking havoc in our marriage.

The next day after dinner, Brian asked me if I would like to go out for coffee. It made me feel special that he was initiating yet another date.

After ordering our coffees, we found an empty table outside. It was a cool summer evening, but heat lamps kept us warm. We enjoyed the fresh air and the bustling city life at the same time.

"Ask me anything you want about the affair," Brian offered.

He knew I needed to be free to talk about my feelings and to understand. Many months later, I learned that he was a rare spouse to be willing to share the details with me. Many adulterers are unwilling to talk about their affair, and think their betrayed spouses should be able to just suck it up and get over it. They desire to bury it when what is needed is many hours of honest dialogue. The pain of an affair doesn't go away by pretending it doesn't exist.

This coffee date was an important part of our healing journey. Over the next two years, Brian took me out for many more dates where we discussed the affair and why it happened. Brian willingly answered all of my questions, holding nothing back. For me the healing came gradually through learning the details. The pain is in the details, but so is the healing.

I have heard the importance of open discussion between spouses regarding affairs explained through an analogy involving a window and a wall. When affairs take place, the third party is given a window into the relationship, because the unfaithful spouse generally talks about his or her marriage with the person they are having an affair with.

However, the unknowing faithful partner sees only a wall. They are not allowed to see beyond the marriage into the affair, which is always hidden with lies and deception. If healing is to take place, the window and wall must be reversed. The faithful partner must be given a window into the affair, and the third party must be given the wall instead. Their window into the marriage must be boarded shut permanently.

I have seen no better explanation of the importance of full disclosure than in the following letter by a man whose wife had an affair. He later posted the letter on a website so others could benefit from it.

Joseph's Letter[4]:

To Whomever,

I know you are feeling the pain of guilt and confusion. I understand that you wish all this never happened and that you wish it would just go away. I can even believe that you truly love me and that your indiscretion hurts you emotionally much the same way it hurts me. I understand your apprehension to me discovering little by little, everything that led up to your indiscretion, everything that happened that night, and everything that happened afterwards. I understand. No one wants to have a mistake or misjudgment thrown in his or her face repeatedly. No one wants to be forced to "look" at the thing that caused all their pain over and over again. I can actually see, that through your eyes, you are viewing this whole thing as something that just needs to go away, something that is over, that he/she doesn't mean anything to you, so why is it such a big issue? I can understand you wondering why I torture myself with this continuously, and thinking, doesn't he/she know by now that I love him/her? I can see how you can feel this way and how frustrating it must be. But for the remainder of this letter I'm going to ask you to view my reality through my eyes.

You were there. There is no detail left out from your point of view. Like a puzzle, you have all the pieces and you are able to reconstruct them so you understand the whole picture, the whole message, or the whole meaning. You know exactly what that picture is and what it means to you and if it can effect your life and whether or not it continues to stir your feelings. You have the pieces, the tools, and the knowledge. You can move through your life with 100% of the picture you compiled. If you have any doubts, then at least you're carrying all the information in your mind and you can use it to derive conclusions or answers to your doubts or questions. You carry all the "STUFF" to figure out OUR reality. There isn't really any information, or pieces to the puzzle that you don't have.

Now let's enter my reality. Let's both agree that this affects our lives equally. The outcome no matter what it is will affect us both. Our future and our present circumstances are every bit as important to me as they are to you. So, why then is it okay for me to be left in the dark? Do I not deserve to know as much about the night that nearly destroyed our relationship as you do? Just like you, I am also able to discern the meaning of certain particulars and innuendoes of that night and just like you, I deserve to be given the opportunity to understand what nearly brought our relationship down. To assume that I can move forward and accept everything at face value is unrealistic and unless we stop thinking unrealistically I doubt our lives will ever "feel" complete. You have given me a puzzle. It is a 1000 piece puzzle and 400 random pieces are missing. You expect me to assemble the puzzle without the benefit of looking at the picture on the box. You expect me to be able to discern what I am looking at and to appreciate it in the same context as you. You want me to be as comfortable with what I see in the picture as you are. When I ask if there is a tree in such and such area of the picture you tell me don't worry about it, it's not important. When I ask whether there were any animals in my puzzle you say don't worry about it, it's not important. When I ask if there was a lake in that big empty spot in my puzzle you say, what's the difference, it's not important. Then later when I'm expected to "understand" the picture in my puzzle you fail to understand my disorientation and confusion. You expect me to feel the same way about the picture as you do but deny me the same view as you. When I express this problem you feel compelled to admonish me for not understanding it, for not seeing it the way you see it. You wonder why I can't just accept whatever you choose to describe to me about the picture and then be able to feel the same way you feel about it.

So, you want me to be okay with everything. You think you deserve to know and I deserve to wonder. You may honestly feel that the whole picture, everything that happened is insignificant because in your heart you know it was a mistake and wish it never happened. But how can I know that? Faith? Because you told me so? Would you have faith if the tables were turned? Don't you understand that I want to believe you completely? But how can I? I can never know what is truly in your mind and heart. I can only observe your actions, and what information I have acquired and slowly, over time rebuild my faith in your feelings. I truly wish it were easier.

So, there it is, as best as I can put it. That is why I ask questions. That is where my need to know is derived from. And that is why it is unfair for you to think that we can effectively move forward and unfair for you to accuse me of dwelling on the past. My need to know stems from my desire to hold our world together. It doesn't come from jealousy, it doesn't come from spitefulness, and it doesn't come from a desire to make you suffer. It comes from the fact that I love you. Why else would I put myself through this? Wouldn't it be easier for me to walk away? Wouldn't it be easier to consider our relationship a bad mistake in my life and to move on to better horizons? Of course it would, but I can't and the reason I can't is because I love you and that reason in itself makes all the difference in the world.

Brian was willingly handing over the puzzle pieces, allowing me to view the entire picture in my own way and at my own pace. He patiently explained to me what went wrong and what his experience had been, as I asked the questions.

Mid-July arrived, and the kids were well into their summer vacation. Because Brian's construction business was in full-swing, we were able to get away as a family for a short time only. We planned a camping trip at a beautiful, warm lake, four hours north of the city.

To take full advantage of the little time we had, I left a day early with the kids to set up our site. Danielle didn't join us for this trip. At age sixteen, she decided she'd rather stay in town and pick up some shifts at her work.

It was a gorgeous hot sunny day as my two younger kids and I drove along the winding curves of the beautiful Fraser Canyon. Driving along, I marveled at the remarkable engineering feat this whole road represented, carving its way between cliffs and the roaring Fraser River.

The kids and I listened to soft rock music as we swerved through the canyon. They indulged in soft drinks and chips, while I enjoyed a refreshing cold apple juice. We chatted as we headed north, reminiscing about things we'd seen and done on previous trips.

Then when they dozed off, I thought about my marriage and all the good times Brian and I had enjoyed on past family vacations. *How had this awful thing happened in our marriage? Would I ever be able to get over it?* I was thankful to get away from home, away to enjoy the therapeutic effects of nature and all of her beauty.

Dustin, Tamara and I had no trouble setting up camp. We were the three easy-going, quiet ones in the family. We assembled our tent for the kids to sleep in and removed the seats from our mini-van, so Brian and I could make our bed in the back. We accomplished everything at a relaxed pace, without stress. Around the campfire that night, I read them stories as I had done so often in the past.

The next day I woke up to perfect weather: warm sunshine with a gentle breeze. I started my morning off with a refreshing swim in the lake, and then spent hours reading a good book while the kids entertained themselves. The two of them had always been buddies and never fought.

At around dinnertime I used the campsite's pay phone to give Brian a ring. I was pleased to catch him already an hour into his journey. I looked forward to seeing him in a few hours.

The kids were also anxious for Brian to arrive. They always enjoyed his adventurous spirit and knowledge of the outdoors.

When the hours passed and it was clear that Brian was delayed, I started to worry. *What if he was in a car accident?* The thought of losing him made it clear to me that I loved him deeply in spite of everything that had happened. I didn't understand how he could have had an affair on me. Much less did I understand how he could have contemplated leaving our marriage altogether or how he could have been so cruel towards me, but I understood human nature.

I understood how we often fall short of our own ideals. We all do things we are not proud of, things we would like to hide from the world. I also understood that we have a tendency to judge ourselves by our intentions, but judge others by their actions.

I believed that I could forgive Brian. I wanted to forgive Brian. I believed that in spite of all that had happened he was a good man. He was fun and witty, charming and caring. He was an excellent provider and an excellent father. He was strong and handsome, yet gentle and caring. He was highly intelligent. Well, it didn't matter all that he was. The truth was that in spite of all that had happened I still loved this man.

It was now nine o'clock. Still no Brian. I tried not to worry, but where could he be?

I called again from the phone booth but there was no answer. I called home to see if he had left a message with Danielle. No message.

When it was dark I sent the kids to bed, assuring them that their Dad would be okay. Then I sat staring at the campfire and I worried. Again I tried calling his cell and our home. Nothing. I returned to my lawn chair in front of the fire and stared at the flames again. What else could I do? I tried to read but couldn't concentrate.

At 10:30 PM the park warden's wife drove her truck through the quiet campsite and stopped in front of me.

"Mrs. Bercht?" she asked.

"Yes."

"The police have contacted me," she said. "A Constable Wilkinson wants you to call him."

"What's wrong?" I questioned.

"I don't know. He wouldn't say. He only said that he thought you would be here and that you should call. There's a pay phone at the camp entrance."

"Thanks," I said taking the constable's name and number. In the pitch black, I managed to dial the right number. I was scared. The constable's voice broke through the silence of the night.

"Mrs. Bercht, I have your husband here in Clinton," he said. "I need you to come and get him, and then I'll release him to you."

"Is he okay?" I asked. "What happened?"

"Just come. I'll explain everything when you get here," he said.

With the help of my car headlights, I wrote out the constable's directions to Clinton, a forty-five minute drive from the campsite. He cautioned me to drive carefully as it was not unusual to strike a deer while driving in that area at night and at this time of year.

Before I left, I returned to our campsite and woke the kids slightly letting them know I'd be gone for a couple of hours, so they wouldn't be afraid if they woke up while I was away. I told them that something had happened and I had to pick up Dad. I was comfortable leaving the kids there sleeping, since it was a safe campground with other families close by if help were needed. Then I followed Constable Wilkinson's directions, my mind racing.

Release, I thought to myself. *That's a strange term. Why did the police officer say that he would "release" Brian to me? Is Brian okay? He mustn't be in that bad of shape if they'll "release" him to me? You would think he was in prison or something. Release?*

Tears made their way down my face once again. I felt emotionally weak. *I can't take anymore of this,* I thought to myself. *No more bad things, God. No more, please.*

At the police station in Clinton, Constable Davis, the on-duty constable, brought me to Brian, who stood behind bars! I couldn't believe it. I had never seen anyone in jail before, except for on TV, and this tiny town with its tiny little jail had a Western feel. I felt as though I had just traveled backwards in time. The whole situation was surreal. *What was happening to our nice family?*

The constable unlocked the cell. Brian's eyes were red. I was trying to be strong. I wanted answers.

"Brian, are you alright?" I exclaimed.

He looked at me, face full of sorrow and shame, yet he wasn't fully focused on me. He didn't seem to be fully coherent.

"Your husband was in a motor vehicle accident." Constable Davis said. He seemed pleased, as if this was the first police work this town had had in months. I wanted to go and grab my husband and get him out of that awful cell.

"Your husband has been drinking," Constable Davis continued. "There were no other vehicles in the accident. He drove off the road near a farmer's field." *A farmer's field!* I thought to myself. I considered the winding road full of canyons and cliffs and marveled. *Had Brian managed to drive off the road at the only flat place on that long journey?* His vehicle had sustained extensive damage but he was completely uninjured. It was a miracle.

For the first ten years of our marriage Brian and I had practiced total abstinence from alcohol. In the past eight years we had enjoyed the very occasional drink. *How could my husband be drunk?*

"What do you want me to do?" I asked the constable.

"We want you to take your husband with you. We usually keep impaired drivers here overnight unless we can release them to a family member," he explained. "He is not allowed to drive for three days. Then he can drive for thirty days during which time he has the right to appeal the conviction, after that he can't drive again until his court date which is set for the end of September."

As more details emerged, my heart sank. Brian could lose his license for a year. There would likely be a stiff fine. The car, undrivable, had been towed to Clinton.

I imagined that the Constable was judging us as bad people. *This man has no idea,* I thought, *no idea how even some of the highest quality of people, even the highly educated and model citizens sometimes have problems too. Life is not easy for anyone, and we can all fall sometimes.* I didn't understand how my husband had gotten from the happy man that answered his cell phone on his way to go camping with his family a few hours earlier to the man that was now inebriated and being "released" from jail, but I still knew that Brian was a good person.

I signed some papers and Brian and I drove back to the campsite. Brian kept apologizing.

"It's okay," I answered him. "Thank God you're okay." And I was truly grateful for that. I was also truly grateful that no other people or vehicles had been involved in the accident. I didn't think I could handle it if his negligent behavior had claimed an innocent life. *What was wrong with him,* I wondered as I drove down the dark road? *What was he thinking? How could he do such a thing? Take such a risk?*

As we continued to drive, I heard a strange sound beside me: a cry and a gasp for air. It sounded like crying, but it couldn't be. I turned on the light to see what it was.

To my astonishment my husband *was* crying. I didn't know what to think, but under the circumstances, crying seemed to me like a good idea. I thought about Helen and wondered if she would have been supportive of Brian in this situation. I was pretty sure the answer was no.

When we got back safely to our campsite, I helped Brian to our makeshift bed, and embraced him tightly as we fell asleep in each other's arms. I awoke in the morning to the sounds and vibrations of Brian crying in my arms.

"My life is over," he said. "I've really blown it."

"No, Brian. You're life isn't over. It ain't over 'til it's over. When we face our problems we can always get through them. You have a lot going for you. You have a wife who is willing to stand by you, who loves you and does not want to give up on you. You are a good man, going through a bad time. You are in the middle of your story, not as you think, at the end. Sure the past few months have been bad. Yes, you have made some bad choices and yes there will be consequences, but it ain't over 'til it's over. You have three kids to live for. Two of them are outside waiting for you to get up. We are here in this beautiful place today. You were in an accident last night, but you weren't even injured. No one was injured. We are together with the ones that we love and we have enough food to eat. Get up. Spend some time with your kids and we'll talk more later."

It felt good to hold my husband. He was devastated. Like children playing games who call for a "do-over," Brian needed a "do-over" in his life. He also needed what we all need sometimes: forgiveness.

After having our classic camping breakfast of bacon and eggs, Brian played with the kids in the water.

Then Brian and I headed off for a walk together.

"I've really screwed up this time, Anne," he said. I wondered how he could think the events of last night could be worse than the betrayal he had put me through.

"What happened?" I questioned him. "Why couldn't you just drive up here uneventfully? What the heck did you do?"

"I just wanted to relax," he explained. "There's been so much pressure for so long. I wanted to make the pain go away, so I stopped at the beer store and picked up a six pack. After one beer, I just wanted one more."

"How many beers did you drink?" I asked.

"I don't know. A six pack I think."

"You drank the whole thing!" I naïvely thought that that was a lot.

"I just needed a break from the pain," he said. "I just wanted to relax. I didn't realize how many I had drunk."

I could hardly believe he had made such a poor decision.

"Anne, my life is over. I'm going to lose my driver's license," he said. "I won't be able to get to work. I'm so sorry. I'm such a loser."

"You have really screwed up big time, but it's not over," I said. "We'll see what happens. We'll figure something out."

We put our arms around each other as we walked. We were two broken people. *How could things be going so wrong in our lives?* We had both tried so hard to do what was right. We pulled each other close. The pain was great, but so was the love between us.

We told the kids there was an accident, but didn't mention the alcohol. When we headed home and I did all the driving, we just told the kids we were in the mood for a change.

Back at home, Brian still refused to go for counseling. However, he did agree to attend a marriage course for couples starting in September. The leaders of the church promised us that this was just what we needed, the answer to all of our problems, so we sat tight and waited.

The week after the accident, we phoned the Clinton auto repair shop and learned that the repairs on the van would cost more than it was worth. With no collision insurance, it was not worth keeping.

I drove to Clinton to retrieve our belongings from the van, but first stopped at the police station to pick up some paperwork.

At the station, I talked to the on-duty officer, saying that Brian was not a drinker, and that only one six pack had led to these unfortunate circumstances.

"Ma'am," he said shaking his head compassionately. "Your husband's blood alcohol level was very high. He drank a lot more than a six pack."

"How much did he drink?" I asked, desperate for a straight answer. I was sick and bloody tired of being lied to. *How many times would I be deceived*, I wondered? All I wanted from anyone was truth right now, the whole truth. No more lies.

"I'd say your husband would have had to have drunk at least a twelve pack in a couple of hours to get his blood alcohol reading that high."

Again I was shocked, embarrassed and humiliated.

When I went to the van to get our belongings, the officer's comments were confirmed: The van was full of empty beer cans, scattered around from the impact of the accident. I counted more than six.

As I made the long drive home, I was so angry that I had been lied to again. I considered never trusting him again, getting out of the marriage and cutting my losses.

"How dare you lie to me again?" I asked Brian that evening when I picked him up from work.

"Well I don't remember how much I drank," Brian defended.

"Brian you made me look like a fool. You should have seen the way that policeman looked at me as though I were some sort of a hopeless basket case, believing that a man could get that drunk on six beer," I said. "Don't you realize that if we are going to rebuild this marriage I need the truth? I never want to appear that foolish again."

"Really, Anne, I didn't know how much I drank," Brian said. "I lost track. It was hot and I was so thirsty. I didn't mean to make you look bad."

"Brian, you should know better than to drink and drive," I said. "Drinking even impairs your judgment as to whether or not you should have another beer. You should have just waited until you got there to relax."

Again, I thought that a person could be forgiven once, but they had better make sure that they learn from their mistakes!

---

4. This letter was originally posted on Peggy Vaughan,s website, www.dearpeggy.com, by a member of the Beyond Affairs Network. It is reprinted here, as it was posted, with permission.

CHAPTER 17

.

fire

AUGUST, 2000

"In our sleep, pain which cannot forget falls drop by drop upon
the heart until, in our own despair, against our will, comes
wisdom through the awful grace of God."

EDWARD M. KENNEDY
(FROM HIS EULOGY FOR SEN. ROBERT F. KENNEDY, JUNE 8 1968)[5]

August arrived and found us far from healed, far from secure in
our marriage. We were on an emotional roller coaster, and the consequences of Brian's affair were hurling themselves upon us like the
mighty winds of a great storm.

Danielle was not coping very well with the crisis that had come
upon her family. She no longer regarded her father with respect,
and she still avoided him as much as she possibly could.

Neither was she emotionally stable. She often slept all day and
went out all night, disregarding our requests, as we were trying to
protect her from harm. If we gave her ultimatums to behave or get
out of the house, she would usually just get out. We were two loving
parents and both wanted the best for our girl, but differed in our
perception of the best approach to helping her. Neither one of us
understood what was happening with her.

We found out later that Danielle was being treated by doctors for depression, but had requested that we, her parents, were not told. Had we known that she was dealing with a chemical imbalance in the brain, we would have been able to deal with her behavior appropriately.

For Brian and I at this time, broken and devastated as we were, trying to cope with these problems on top of our crumbling marriage was too much to bear. It seems that when things get bad, they get worse.

———•———

A ringing noise. A ringing of some sort. We were asleep, sound asleep. It was four o'clock in the morning. Perhaps it was a dream. Ring, ring, ring, the sound persisted unceasingly. Slowly, gaining a mild sense of consciousness, I realized it was the doorbell. I rolled over in the bed.

Oh no, I thought. *Not another problem with Danielle. What's she done now? Uggghhh, I just can't take any more.*

I pulled the blankets over my head, trying to hide from the noise and the possibility of yet another disaster. Whatever it was was Danielle's problem. I wasn't getting up.

Ring, ring, ring, ring, ring. Brian jumped up, grabbed his robe and headed for the front door. I rolled over and tried to fall back into my escape of sleeping bliss. Soon I heard the sound of water running through the household plumbing system. Someone had turned on the garden hose. *It must be Brian,* I reasoned in my state of semi-consciousness. *What a good idea. If you're awake at four o'clock in the morning you may as well water the grass.* Shortly after that, I heard the blaring sirens of a fire truck screaming down the road, getting louder and louder until they reached a crescendo and suddenly stopped.

I jumped into my robe and ran to find a fire truck parked directly in front of our home.

One scene at a time, I took in the unbelievable sights. The blaze was already out, but dense smoke was still rising from the driveway, revealing a melted version of what had been our minivan. Part of the garage door and siding around it had also started to burn.

Firemen worked in a rhythmic fashion cleaning up the mess. Brian stood holding our garden hose while talking with a woman I'd never seen before.

"What happened!" I shouted, my heart pounding as I watched a police car pull up behind the fire truck.

I approached Brian and the woman he spoke with. She explained that she was the person who had been frantically and unceasingly ringing our doorbell. She was a neighbor and a police officer who spotted the flames while getting ready to leave for work.

She had called the fire trucks and done all she could to wake our sleeping family. Then Brian, thinking quickly, had doused the flames with the garden house before the fire truck had arrived. If the fire had burned unnoticed for a few more minutes, our entire home could have burned to the ground. Who knows if our family would have escaped in time?

It was an unquestionable case of arson. Rags soaked in gasoline had been placed on our vehicle and a large outdoor candle had been lit and placed underneath to ensure the van would burn. And it had.

After talking with the firemen, the police told Brian they were sure this was not a random act. They were confident that someone intentionally wanted to hurt us. They questioned Brian, asking who might be angry enough to start this fire.

"I had an affair on my wife," said Brian. "I'm pretty sure the other woman's husband is mad at me."

The police officer shoved his notepad back in his pocket without writing anything more down. I was certain I saw him roll his eyes with an exasperated expression. I wondered if he now thought Brian deserved this devastation, if he would be unwilling to solve the case.

His partner, a female officer, overheard and gave me a mixed look of compassion and disdain. *Did she see me as dysfunctional because I was willing to stay with a man who had cheated on me? She doesn't understand,* I thought. *Doesn't understand at all. She doesn't understand that we once had a good marriage, a long-term marriage. And she doesn't understand that I still love my husband.*

The police also questioned the curious neighbors who were slowly emerging from their homes, and they found further evidence, the gas can, stashed in some bushes down the street. Eventually the police and the firemen finished their work and left, leaving us facing our neighbors in housecoats. We talked with them briefly, everyone discussing how awful this was. We did not, however, tell our neighbors about the affair. We could see that they felt fearful. *Would their vehicle and home be next?* We told them that they were probably safe because it likely wasn't a random act.

Finishing our polite verbal exchange with our neighbors, Brian gently took my hand. We walked back into our house and sat in our darkened living room, shocked. It was not yet daylight, but we had no desire to go back to sleep. We both felt knots in the pit of our stomachs as we began to talk about what had happened. Our two younger children were still asleep in their bedrooms. They had not even been awakened by the potential danger that threatened our home and our lives that night.

We argued a bit over who might have started the fire.

"Well, I'm sure it was Helen," I told Brian.

"No, I'm sure it was Richard," Brian replied. "Helen wouldn't do something like that. I'm sure it's not possible that it's her."

"I doubt it. I think she's perfectly capable Brian. She wanted you really bad, and she was not going to stop at anything to try and get you."

The police never did find the person who committed the crime, and they told us little about the investigation. We got the impression that this was a small crime in comparison with other things that were going on in our city. They would not disclose whether Richard and

Helen were ever questioned about it, and no one was ever charged.

Ten days after the fire, having received the insurance settlement, I drove a brand spanking new minivan off the dealership lot. I had always dreamed of having a new vehicle.

It was a practical, yet sporty van with a shiny bright red coat of paint. It rode smoothly and had that wonderful new car smell. I felt happy and grateful for the van, but deep inside I wanted to cry.

The new vehicle was lovely, but it couldn't take away my intense pain. How gladly I would have traded it for an old beater and a marriage unscarred by adultery.

---

5. He was quoting his favorite poet Aeschylus

CHAPTER 18

suicide Attempt

AUGUST, 2000

Mom and Dad, can't you hear me? I want your attention.
My home is now filled with brokenness and dissension.
I know you are hurting. I know you are struggling.
I know your world is shattered, filled with fighting and tension.
But what about my world? Don't you care about me?
Aren't you listening? Don't you understand what you're doing to me?
Don't you see my burden's too heavy to carry?
Too much for a young soul who just wants to be free?
You think that I'm bad. You don't see my heart.
You don't understand that I want to do my part.
You misunderstand and punish, but don't stop to ask me,
Honey, are you okay? Has your world also come apart?
I'm hurting. I'm dying. I'm lost in a sea.
My burden's too heavy. It's choking, squeezing me.
Mom and Dad, can't you hear me? I want your attention.
Do you love me? Do you want me? Do you still care about me?

AFTER A LONG AND HEALING MOTHER-DAUGHTER CHAT,
I WROTE THIS POEM TO CAPTURE DANIELLE'S FEELINGS.

Originally this entire chapter was written in my voice alone. When Danielle read it, she told me it was inaccurate. So I asked her if she would write the story from her own point of view. I was astonished when she gave me her version. Comparing them, there was no discrepancy in facts, but a major discrepancy in the way we each experienced the same event. The story is therefore told by both of us, so you, the reader have both perspectives. I never knew the whole story until after I had written the first version.

Danielle: A few days after Mom got her new van, I went to bed at a decent hour, no later than 10:30 PM, trying to get some much needed rest. I didn't sleep well anymore. I often had nightmares. But tonight I was determined to have a good night's rest.

Before heading to bed, I called Jason to say goodnight. He told me he was going to a buddy's house for a guys' night out, which I thought was a good idea, because I knew that being with me over the last couple of months had been stressful. He needed to have some fun.

I tossed and turned for a bit, then drifted off to sleep. At around 1:30 AM, I woke up to the sound of my cell phone ringing.

"Hello," I said, wondering who was so desperate to get a hold of me.

"Danielle, what are you doing?" the caller asked. It was Luke, Jason's older brother. *Weird.* He had never called me before.

"I am trying to get some sleep, why?" I asked, confused.

"Danielle, get up. I am coming to pick you up right now."

"Luke, what is going on?" I said, panicked. "Just be ready in ten minutes outside your house. I will explain it in the car," he said, then hung up.

I got ready in the dark, careful not to wake my parents because they would not allow me to leave in the middle of the night. Sneaking out of my bedroom window, I escaped. When Luke's car pulled up, I jumped in.

His face looked like someone had died.

"What's going on? Where are we going?"

"Jason's been in a car accident. He's in the hospital."

My heart dropped. Thoughts raced through my mind. *What? Why? How? Is he going to live? How could this happen to the only sane person who cares about me?*

"Danielle, try to calm down," he said. "He's hurt pretty bad and he's pretty drugged up, but when he manages to speak, he asks for you."

I started to cry. *Not him, anyone but him.*

I located Jason's room and found his parents standing by his bed. Jason looked awful. He had so many tubes, cords and needles attached to him. Blood, cuts and bruises covered him.

Tears ran down my face. I told Jason I loved him, but the hospital staff pulled me away.

They told me that he had hit his head pretty bad. They were still unsure of his condition and needed to run tests. Their talking continued, but I zoned out. Someone sat me down in a waiting area. I cried. *I have no one,* I thought. Jason's parents came to console me, but I was dead to the world.

When Jason awoke, he asked for me again. For the next few hours, I sat by his side. I talked to him and prayed for him. Eventually, the doctors told me I had to leave. Jason got mad, *really* mad. I looked to his parents for guidance. They told me to reassure him I was not going anywhere, that the doctors would do what they had to and I would be right there waiting for him. I did what they said, kissed him and promised not to leave the hospital.

After an hour, the doctors told us they had stabilized his condition. They told us all to go home, get some rest and come back in four hours. I was panicked. I told the doctor that I could not leave the hospital in case he awoke and found that I wasn't there, but the doctor promised me he would not be awake for at least four hours. I was to go home, get some rest and then come back.

I told Luke that I would get my mom to drive me to the hospital in exactly four hours, at 10:30 AM. I was sure my mom wouldn't mind giving me a ride on a Saturday morning.

Arriving home at 6:30 AM, I snuck back in through my bedroom window and changed back into my pajamas so that no one would suspect I'd been out.

Not much later, I pretended to get up to the sound of my alarm. I showered and tried to occupy myself until it was time to go back to the hospital. I tried to figure out how to tell my parents that Jason had been in an accident without telling the truth about sneaking out. I was sure I would get in trouble if they knew.

I don't know exactly how I told them about the accident, but I do remember being specific about the need to be there by 10:30 AM. They didn't seem too concerned.

I was panicked, overwhelmed with emotion and exhausted. To pass the time until it was time to go, I occupied myself by making chocolate pudding, Jason's favorite. I figured if he was hungry, even though his face was swollen, he could at least eat chocolate pudding.

On Saturday morning Danielle was extremely eager to get to the hospital to see Jason, who had apparently been in an accident the night before. While waiting for me to drive her to the hospital, she made some chocolate pudding to bring to Jason as a gift. The pudding had been placed in Styrofoam cups and was now to be carefully transported open and without lids. It was a sweet gesture.

Danielle: It was 10:00 AM, time to leave. I told Mom, who seemed unconcerned.

"In a minute honey," she responded. Like hello? Did she not understand? I was in a hurry. *Jason is in critical condition and all she is concerned about is drinking her stupid coffee and reading a book.*

"Mom, I really need to get to the hospital, could we please go now?" I said, trying to be nice when really I wanted to scream.

"Sure honey, just let me finish this page." *Grrrrr!!! Okay, fine.* I sat waiting by the door, holding the pudding, which I'd carefully spooned into two small containers. Minutes passed. It was now 10:12 AM. I wanted to be there already. *What if Jason wakes up and realizes I'm not there? Okay, calm down, you are stressed and tired. Mom is standing up, she is coming.*

"Okay honey, I am just going to brush my teeth and change, then we can go," she said, as if she was being sweet about it.

"Uh Mom, I really need to be there now. Can we just go now?" I asked. "Do that when you get home. You aren't going to see anyone."

It was now 10:17. She didn't seem to understand the seriousness of the situation.

"If I am doing you a favor by driving you, then you can just wait a couple more minutes for me to get ready."

Okay, seriously, I gave her plenty of notice, an hour and a half. She is normally on time for everything else. Nothing I do is very important. Just a couple of minutes ... she had a couple minutes to finish reading her book, now a couple more. Well, I don't have a couple of minutes. My boyfriend is in the hospital. They don't know what is wrong with him. If I did this to her when someone she cared about was in the hospital she would freak.

Finally she was ready at 10:33 AM.

We climbed into our new red minivan with its immaculate factory interior. Danielle placed the chocolate puddings into the cup holders so they wouldn't spill over. We did up our seatbelts and headed down the hill towards the hospital. She seemed to be in a hurry, but then Danielle did everything in a hurry and whenever anything needed to be done, she seemed to expect it to be done yesterday. Boom, boom, hurry, hurry, fast, fast. That was always her style.

Danielle: *Oh boy, I could not have picked a slower person to drive with. The speed limit is 30 MPH and she is only driving 20 MPH! No traffic anywhere, no pedestrians, nothing, a straight road, yet she is only doing 20 MPH I am thirty-five minutes later than I planned, and she cannot even be kind enough to drive the speed limit. I wish she would get a ticket for going too slow!* Okay stay calm, I coached myself.

We arrived at a T-intersection, where turning left would be about ten minutes faster. Normally it is hard to turn left at this intersection because of traffic, but today there were no cars to be seen. Mom stopped at the stop sign.

Do you need to stop for thirty seconds to check both ways, I wondered? Is she trying to make me mad? Well, I won't say anything. We'll be there soon enough. I sure hope Jason hasn't woken up yet.

Mom signaled right.

"Mom, we are going to the hospital," I reminded her. She sometimes forgets where she is going.

"Yes I know," she said.

Doesn't she know how to get there? Turning right is a huge detour. We are in a hurry. Still looking both ways, I guess, sitting at the intersection.

"Just turn left mom, it's way faster," I said, frustrated. Then I decided to take control of the situation by pushing the steering wheel left.

My mom freaked out, saying it was illegal to turn left at that intersection. She cranked the steering wheel as hard as she could in the opposite direction. Thank God there was no traffic. For a moment we were all over the road. Then it was too late. We were taking her way: the long way. I was furious. I swore and screamed at her.

I cannot imagine a more insensitive person. Both of us were yelling.

I am holding back. Everything inside me just wants to smack her. I continued to yell at her and she continued to yell back at me. Then she missed the next turn. I looked at the clock inside the van, 10:47 AM.

Why, why, why does my mom have to be so mean?

I drove straight through the next intersection, where I would have turned left if I was still going to the hospital. I was not going to do Danielle any favors while she was addressing me with undeserved disrespect.

"What are you doing?" she yelled, reaching and grabbing the steering wheel again, this time with ten times the force. I held on for dear life and slammed on our horn to alert other vehicles that everything was not okay in our car.

"Get your hands off the wheel!" I shouted, while trying to steer us over to the side of the road where we wouldn't endanger others.

I was frightened, humiliated, incredulous. *What was wrong with my once sweet daughter?*

Danielle: *She's pulling onto a side street. I can't breathe. I can't think! What should I do? I have to get to the hospital. Why is this so difficult? She doesn't care about me or what I need at all.*

Finally I managed to park safely on a side street. I sat, adrenaline pumping, completely unsure of what to do, wishing someone had seen what happened and would offer me help.

Danielle: *My mom yelled at me. I think she was freaked out because I tried to turn the steering wheel while she was driving. But there were no cars around and we were barely moving. It wasn't dangerous.*

"I need to get to that hospital now!" Danielle shouted.

"I'm not taking you anywhere behaving like that," I shouted back, trying to remain in control of myself. "And you will never address me with those terms again. I will not drive you anywhere ever speaking to me like that. I'm doing a nice thing for you. I don't have to drive you to the hospital to see Jason. If you want me to do things for you, you have to treat me with respect."

There was silence. I thought about just jumping out with my car keys and walking home.

"If I start this car up and drive home, will you keep your hands off this steering wheel?" I asked.

"Take me to the hospital! Take me to the hospital to see Jason, now!" she shouted back.

"It's not an option. I'm not taking you anywhere after that episode," I said. "If you want to get there you'll have to get out of this car and get there yourself."

I knew my boundaries and we had definitely reached them. She would have to apologize before I would drive her anywhere again.

I sat with my heart pumping. We were silent, for a few minutes, wondering what to do. Realizing I was serious about not driving her to the hospital, she said we could drive home and she wouldn't touch the steering wheel while we did.

I looked seriously into her eyes to see if I could trust her to make it home safely. Deciding to take the chance, I carefully restarted the car, turned back onto the busy road and headed towards home. Danielle was crying.

Danielle: The whole way home my mom freaked out, yelling at me. I felt lonely and hopeless. I was incredibly upset and worried about Jason.

Mom doesn't care about me. I could feel my adrenaline pumping. *Mom thinks I'm crazy. She says I'm being disrespectful and irresponsible. Fine, I will show her. I can't take this anymore.*

It seemed there was nothing I could do. But as we pulled into the driveway, I spotted the pudding, which obviously was no longer needed. *Oh I'll show her,* I thought. *She cares more about the freaking van than me.*

Danielle grabbed the chocolate pudding. Swiping giant handfuls of the gooey desert with her bare hands, she began to smear the chocolate pudding all over my lovely new vehicle. I tried to grab it back from her, but it was useless.

"There, take that, and that, and that," she shouted with each new chocolate swipe. Within a few out-of-control moments, my windshield, upholstery, dashboard, steering wheel and face were covered in pudding.

My new vehicle was one gigantic chocolate-covered mess. I might as well have put a bunch of kindergartners armed with chocolate pudding into that vehicle and told them to have a food fight. Few spots remained untouched.

I was devastated and at a complete loss of knowing what to do. I got out and walked into the house, wishing for a moment to regain my composure and to make some sense out of this disaster.

Danielle: *Well, if she didn't hate me before she sure must now.* I was crying and shaking. I didn't feel like myself anymore. I felt like I was watching someone else in my body. The emotional pain was very real. I paused for a moment. *She does hate me. She does. My own mom hates me. Fine, if you hate me, then I will just go kill myself.*

Danielle came running up behind me shouting, "You hate me. It's all over. I have no reason to live. Everyone hates me. I'm going to kill myself."

And with those last words I was overwhelmed with sadness, disappointment, disillusionment and fear. I was devastated. I didn't know what to do or say. I felt so alone, so helpless, so confused.

What was going on for this child?

Danielle: I was so hurt, so tired and so enraged, that I ran to our medicine cabinet and grabbed a bottle of painkillers. I opened the bottle and just as Mom came in the door, I began pouring them down my throat. She grabbed me and tried to stop me. I pushed her off and locked the door behind me. I swallowed two hundred extra strength Tylenols. As soon as I realized what I had done, panic and fear set in.

"Open up, open up," I shouted desperately. "Danielle, don't do this. I love you. Please honey. Let me in. Don't do this. I love you."

I didn't care about anything except saving my kid.

Realizing that she had taken a whole bottle of pills and was now locked in the bathroom, I ran for the phone and dialed 9-1-1.

"Ambulance," I shouted when the operator answered. "My daughter's trying to kill herself."

Danielle: *Oh no! Mom is calling the cops. I can't let anyone know I took the pills. They might think I'm crazy.*

Taking the pills was a mistake, but I decided to get to the hospital and fix it myself. I didn't want people to think it was a suicide attempt. It was dumb, not suicide. I could feel my body temperature rising. I began to feel sick, yet was determined to get to the hospital on my own.

Danielle then came running out of the bathroom, grabbed the receiver from my hand and slammed it down before I had a chance to say another word.

She ran out of the house fast. I chased her, but I didn't know what I should be doing.

I needed help. I didn't see the point of running after her. She wasn't going to allow me to help her. She was too big for me to manhandle. I couldn't force her to come to the hospital.

I ran back into the house and phoned Brian's cell phone. He was playing golf with Dave. He said they would come right home and help. I waited, overwhelmed.

Danielle: Fearful that the police or ambulance might show up at the house, I ran as fast as I could to hide in the ravine behind our house. Feeling dizzy, I tripped and fell into some blackberry bushes, where I scraped my arms and legs.

I was hurt and afraid.

I wanted my mom to come and help me get back home, but I wanted to find a way to get to the hospital by myself. I was nervous about how I could pull that off.

Crying, I called my mom on my cell phone.

"Mom, I'm afraid." It was Danielle, sobbing.

"Danielle, where are you?"

"I'm in the ravine. I'm in the bushes. I've hurt myself."

"Do you want me to come and get you?"

"Yes."

I ran down our street and then down the path leading through the ravine with its thick vegetation. There I found Danielle crying in some bushes. I supported her, putting her arm over my shoulders and walked with her back towards our home, being gentle and compassionate, yet moving as quickly as possible. We made it back to the house and the phone rang again.

"This is 9-1-1. Someone from there just phoned here."

"Yes," I said. "My daughter just tried to kill herself. I don't know what to do."

"Is she there?"

"Yes."

"How did she try to kill herself?"

"She swallowed an entire bottle of Tylenol."

"We have an ambulance waiting close by, but they are waiting for the police to arrive at your home first to secure the situation."

"Okay," I said.

Moments later the police arrived. One of them questioned me and the other questioned Danielle. The ambulance drivers arrived and began to monitor Danielle's vital signs. In the midst of all this commotion Dave and Brian pulled up. They were horrified, in addition to the situation at hand, by the chocolate-covered interior of our new vehicle, which they passed on their way into the house.

Danielle: I have great respect for police and others in authority, so lying to them scared me. It was weird, everything was so blurry. I thought I might pass out. It took forever to explain to the police, paramedics, Dad and Pastor Dave that I had not taken the Tylenol, but only pretended to do so. The ambulance attendants checked my vital signs and somehow I was fine. *They believed me! Wow! I hadn't really thought I could pull this off.*

Eventually, two police officers and two ambulance attendants were persuaded that Danielle was okay. So were her father and Pastor Dave.

Dave talked with Danielle for a while and eventually convinced her to come and stay with his family for a few days. Danielle told Dave that she was really tired and needed to rest for a while. She said that after resting she would pack a few things and come to his home.

We believed her.

In the meantime, 200 Tylenol tablets were on the way to the liver of one beautiful sixteen year old.

Pastor Dave left. Danielle lay down on her bed, and two shaken parents with a marriage hanging on by a mere thread sat down in the living room and tried to make some sense of the drama that had just transpired.

Danielle: I was finally able to be alone. As soon as they weren't paying attention, I snuck out of my bedroom window. I knew I didn't have much time to get to the hospital. I called a cab and arrived there in a matter of minutes.

When I went to check on Danielle shortly after she went to lay down, I found an empty bed, an empty room and a wide open window with curtains blowing in the breeze. Once again I was seized with fear.

Where had she gone? Why did she do this? Was she okay?

"Brian, she's gone!" I yelled.

He ran to the bedroom and stared with me in disbelief at the empty bed and room.

"You stay home," he suggested, "in case she comes back. I'll go look for her."

It seemed the most logical plan, although I was scared that it would once again mean I was left alone to deal with this wild teenager, whom I loved but had no idea how to handle.

I sat waiting, disillusioned. *Why had the police and ambulance attendants left us so soon?* I was unconvinced that Danielle hadn't taken those pills. I had seen them in her mouth and it looked to me like she had swallowed them. *Why had Pastor Dave believed that she would come to his house after a rest? Weren't professionals supposed to know the answers?* I felt helpless and alone.

How much pain could one person be required to bear? Could I die of an emotional overload?

Within an hour the phone rang.

"I found her, honey," said Brian. "She's going to be okay, I think. She's at the hospital. They're pumping her stomach right now. She got here just in time. After they stabilize her physical condition, a psychiatrist will be giving her a complete psychological examination."

Why did my daughter want to take her own life? I'm not just losing my husband, I thought. *I'm losing my whole family.* I'm losing everything. Tears once again filled my eyes as the emergency of the situation subsided and numbness gave way to grief.

How had I failed so severely as a mother? I wondered. Throughout Danielle's childhood I had done everything I knew to be a great mom. I was dedicated to my children, taught them values and gave up many things to ensure they had a great life. It seemed that my best was not good enough for this world. There seemed to be no reward for years of doing all the right things. I understood that there were no perfect families and that everyone had problems, but

I didn't think something as severe as suicide would ever be a factor in our lives.

I cried alone on my sofa.

When Brian came home, we didn't talk much. We were devastated, both handling our grief differently and certainly not strong enough to comfort each other.

The hospital, Brian said, had everything under control. She was going to be having a full gamut of medical tests and an extensive psychiatric evaluation. Danielle had requested confidentiality from her parents, so we were not allowed to be present for these tests. After the tests, Danielle fell asleep and slept through until the next morning.

The next day, we went to visit Danielle in the hospital, checking in first with the nurse on duty who informed us that she was about to be released. We were shocked! The doctor said she was now fine and could go home.

"You might want to rethink that," Brian said, "because we're not actually going to take her home."

The nurse stared back in disbelief.

"Our daughter nearly died yesterday yet we know nothing of her medical condition," said Brian. "She has had a complete medical evaluation and we know nothing. Perhaps she is in need of some special care, yet we know nothing and have been informed that because she has requested it and the law says so, we have no right to know anything about her medical condition. Yet now you want to send her home into our care and give us complete responsibility for her medical well being!

"We can't take her home," Brian continued. "We feel inadequate. We want to take care of her, but we are completely in the dark as to what her needs might be."

The nurse continued to stare, obviously pierced by the sharp truth in Brian's words.

"Furthermore, she has had a complete psychological examination of which I have been informed I have no right to know anything about. We don't know if she has special needs emotionally or how to go about meeting them, while trying to maintain sanity in our home. No, we are not taking her home. We are completely uninformed and therefore incapable of assuming full responsibility for her well being."

"I see your point," said the nurse.

Now it was my turn to make a point.

"And don't you dare go in there and tell our daughter that we wouldn't take her home, because she'll think we don't love her and that isn't true," I said. "We just need information in order to care for her properly."

"Okay, we'll keep her here and I will talk to the doctor, and I won't tell her you wouldn't take her," promised the nurse.

Brian and I sat on the hard waiting room chairs and talked, questioning the sanity of our country's laws. *How does a sixteen year old who has just attempted suicide have the mental capacity to decide for herself what is best for her future and whether or not her parents should know?*

We then went in and visited with our daughter. She was putting on a strong front and saying that she didn't need to be there. (She didn't know the doctor had planned to release her so soon.)

Danielle: I felt hurt, misunderstood and unloved. I felt like a bad person, who would never live up to my parents' ideals. I wanted to do the right things, I wanted to be good and I wanted my parents to be proud of me. Seeing them there in the hospital made me think of all that I wasn't. I knew they were disappointed with my behavior, so I yelled at them.

"I'll never be a good teenager!"

Brian and I looked at each other. We had no idea what to do. Brian left. I tried to calm Danielle down.

"We're sorry you feel that way Danielle," I said. "We love you just the way you are."

Within a few minutes we were interrupted by some of her friends coming to visit. It was awkward. Danielle was angry with me, and it showed, which embarrassed me in front of her friends. She didn't seem to want me there, and everything I said seemed to make matters worse, so I left her room and Brian and I went home.

Within two hours we received a phone call from the office of Dr. Johnson, the psychiatrist who had examined Danielle. The doctor had agreed to meet with us. In doing so, he was breaking the law. There wasn't much doubt about it. Brian and I would be there.

When we arrived, a tall well-built man with blonde hair greeted us warmly with appropriate handshakes. He appeared to be strong, physically, mentally and in his character. His eyes told me he was someone who could be trusted. Before we had a chance to say a word, as soon as he had closed the door to his office behind him, he started to speak.

"Mr. and Mrs. Bercht, first of all, I want to apologize to you on behalf of the Medical Association because you have been totally wronged as parents. Your daughter does not have a remote hope of survival without your love, support and help. Her condition is serious. I don't know how many teenagers this town, this province and this country have to lose to suicide before we get our inappropriate laws changed."

There had been an epidemic of teen suicides in our community that year. Some of the teenagers had attended the same high school as our kids. Some of the tragedies had been covered in the media. It was a common topic of debate and discussion around town. People in our community were grieving. Why was this happening in our nice city? People wanted to know, and they wanted solutions.

After Dr. Johnson made this statement he told Brian and I that Danielle had been prescribed antidepressant medications five months prior. We were also told that this was not her first, but her second suicide attempt.

We were shocked and felt violated as parents.

Can you imagine that a teenager can be so emotionally upset that he/she attempts suicide and then once the immediate danger has subsided is sent home into the care of parents who don't even know! How fair is that to either parent or child! Brian and I wondered.

We loved our daughter, but how could we help her when we didn't even know? If only the medical community and Canadian laws had given us a chance. We would have handled Danielle's behavior very differently had we known she was dealing with adverse reactions to various antidepressant medications her doctor was prescribing.

Some ask, *When do you give the right to a child for privacy regarding their medical situation?* It really isn't any question at all. The answer is simple. Freedom and responsibility belong together, not separated. You give children the right to complete privacy at exactly the same time as you give them complete personal responsibility for their own medical condition. At whatever age you set it, you put it together, but to give complete privacy and freedom to the child, while the parents remain legally responsible for the outcome is insanity.

We asked Dr. Johnson questions about how to care for Danielle and were told that Danielle was not able to handle any conflict right now.

"Whatever you do, do not fight with her, unless you are willing to lose her," he said.

We asked him if we could receive some help, explaining that we felt uncertain about how to handle the day-to-day situations that would come up during this difficult time. We were told that there was no budget within our medical plan for help for the parents.

The doctor said things were probably going to get worse before they got better. But he encouraged us by saying he saw that we were kind, loving and reasonable parents and that there was a lot of hope for the future healing of our family. We will always be grateful to Dr. Johnson for this meeting. I don't know if our family would have made it had he not shared this critical information with us that day.

We are happy to say that Jason made a speedy one hundred percent recovery from his accident, and was released within a couple of weeks.

We spent another thirteen months on this mood altering medication roller coaster, before Danielle recognized that the medications were causing her more trouble than help. She made her own decision to go off the medications expressly against the doctor's orders. As soon as she was off them, we had our sweet daughter back, but not before. Afterwards she told me, "Mom, I never had any problems until after my doctor put me on the medications."

A poem dedicated to every teenager who has hurt so deeply that they have contemplated suicide.

A Stranger

I was sitting in the park one day
Trying to find an easy way,
To ease the pain I felt inside
That's when I thought of suicide.
I knew I couldn't live another day
If I had to live my life this way,
Then suddenly a man appeared
He said, "Do you mind if I sit here?"
I nodded yes, my head hung low
Wondering, should I stay or go?
The stranger turned to me and stared
He said, "I know you're really scared."
What kind of man must you be
That can see the pain inside of me?
He said, "I know this look you have today,
I once looked the very same way."
He said, "Your train's come off the track,
Let me help you put it back.
Reach way down inside yourself
Find the strength to get some help."
And when he turned and walked away,
I knew he saved my life that day!

THERESA KLAVER, A PERSONAL FRIEND
FIRST TIME PUBLISHED

CHAPTER   19

Let the fights Begin

SEPTEMBER, 2000

God grant me the serenity
to accept the things I cannot change,
The courage to change the things I can,
And the wisdom to know the difference.

REINHOLD NIEBUHR

With all the terrible events that transpired in our lives that summer, life went on. We made it through the months, numb, living in fear, not really working on our relationship. Brian and I took time to go on some dates, and we had some good times as a family. We needed opportunities to escape from all the seriousness and pain. We needed to experience that life could still be fun together. But there were still problems we had to resolve.

Finally September came and the thirteen-week marriage growth group began. I went into the group with a positive attitude and high hopes that this would be the answer for our marriage. After all, it was the only outside help Brian was willing to seek.

The first session already presented challenges. It was about the wedding vows. One of the first activities involved looking deeply into your partner's eyes, while a love song was played on the leading couple's stereo.

While all the other couples looked so happy, I was thinking *Brian's not committed to me. We're not really married anymore, because he nullified our wedding vows.* I wanted to cry. Although we were studying the vows, re-saying the words to each other was not part of the agenda. I wish it had been. I needed this reaffirmation from Brian. Since it was a group, the study dealt with common issues, not specific needs. Brian refused to reaffirm the vows to me, since, as he explained, he didn't mean it when he nullified them.

The wedding vows just aren't the type of thing you can go around saying and retracting and reinstating at your leisure. I was still very stuck on this issue. Throughout the summer, I had done everything I could to win back Brian's affections, but now, the pain of what Brian had done was starting to sink in. I began to question whether or not I still wanted to be married to him after all.

We came home from our first group meeting with homework. Our assignment was about our wedding vows, and so we fought.

Instead of answering the questions, Brian wrote in giant letters across the page *I STILL MEAN THE WEDDING VOWS.* He yelled the words at me while he wrote them out. Somehow this did not meet the need I had for reassurance. I cried and hoped the next week would be better.

In mid-September, Brian finally had a much needed holiday from his work. Because our kids were in school, we couldn't get away. Instead, we hoped to spend time golfing, relaxing and pursuing other recreational activities together.

However, we were now fighting all the time, because we were

beginning to deal with the issues in our relationship. Brian told me that all throughout our marriage he had listened to me talk about my feelings, but that I hadn't listened to him.

So now it was my turn to listen, apparently. I was to listen without becoming defensive or trying to explain myself. Rather, when Brian spoke, he wanted me to understand him, to see things from his perspective and to comprehend his feelings. He felt that if I really cared, I would ask him "why" questions to understand him further, rather than answer right away with my side of the story. This I was not doing very well. My emotional pain was very intense, my heart was broken, and now I was to hear about all the things I did wrong in this marriage! Why really, according to him, the affair was my fault!

"The reason why I had an affair and you never have," he said, "is because I have been a very good husband. Therefore you didn't need to have an affair, but because you haven't been a very good wife, I had an affair." Those unfair words pierced my already broken heart. I was speechless, out of breath. I felt as if I had been stabbed again.

What fault in a person could justify their partner's unfaithfulness? I wondered. *Unfaithfulness is never the fault of the faithful partner. How can I be responsible for something, if I didn't get to participate in the choice of whether or not to do it? All spouses have faults, but those faults do not force the other spouse to have an affair. There are healthy and constructive ways to deal with unhappiness in a marriage. Bad things happen to all of us. How we react to the negative circumstances in our lives is our choice.*

So Brian was determined to tell me all about my faults. He said again that I never listened to him. He said I had been a controlling wife. He said I didn't admire and respect him.

When I tried to tell him that I did admire and respect him, he said that I wasn't listening again. He told me that Helen listened to him. And again, he told me I was too serious and no fun.

In an effort to be a fun mate, I planned an outing to a football game with Brian. I was determined to be fun like Helen.

I dressed sexily for our outing: tight-fitting black pants and a snug top made from a beautiful leopard skin print. Brian took me to a very nice Italian restaurant in Vancouver before the game, and I tried to be funny (like Helen apparently was). Only there was a big problem with this: I am not usually naturally funny. I tried desperately to be someone that I'm not – never a recipe for success. My attempts at humor and "fun-ness" fell flat. Apparently I was downright irritating.

"You're not fun like Helen was," Brian informed me.

"What made Helen so funny?" I asked reeling from the sting of his words. "What did you two laugh about when you were together?"

He thought for a moment and then told me they laughed about how funny it would be if certain people found out they were together.

I envisioned Brian and Helen meeting secretly in a restaurant, laughing and joking around, having so much fun saying, *Wouldn't that be hilarious if your wife found out?*

This vision was depressing. We went from dinner to the football game, but I failed to have a good time, thinking about Brian and Helen laughing at me. (I was not one of the "certain people" they laughed about, but when Brian told me this, I made this false assumption.)

The next day I phoned Brian's friend, Darrell Barnes, for advice. He was stunned by Brian's words.

"Anne, that's ridiculous," he said. "That was cruel. Listen, Anne, you don't have to become a stand-up comedian in order for Brian to love you. Just be yourself."

What a relief to hear those words. Finally, I began to see that I was not the only one making mistakes.

As Brian and I continued on, both of us were, in our own way, putting one hundred percent effort into our relationship. One of the big things Brian was doing to heal our marriage was taking me out for dinner and coffee often, where he openly discussed the affair and our marriage, and answered all of my questions. He knew I needed to talk about things, and he facilitated these essential discussions even though it was very painful for him to face the pain and his failure. It would have been much easier for him to tell me I should just "get over it" like other unfaithful spouses often do, but then we would never have healed.

But in spite of the effort on both our parts, we faced many hurdles.

Brian's court date came and went, with a resulting fine and a suspension of his license for a year. This left Danielle and I taking turns getting up at 6:00 AM to drive a full hour to Brian's work and an hour back, only to turn around and repeat the process in the afternoon. We also found ourselves doing all of the errands for the family. We took the younger kids to their activities, got the milk from the store and rented the videos.

"Drive in this lane," Brian would direct. "Park in that spot, pass that car."

I tried to be patient with my "backseat" driver, but finally he sent me over the edge.

"You know, for years I have been driving and I have been perfectly capable of getting from point A to point B safely," I said. "Also, when you're not in the car, I never have any difficulty choosing a parking place."

All this driving was frustrating for me, and I could see that it was nearly killing him to be chauffeured around by his wife. But in some ways, we benefited from all the driving together: we each had a captive audience and were forced to work through some of our issues. Many times I found myself in tears. Still, we had to drive together again the next day.

In between all the fighting, Brian was treating me like a queen. Our lives were a paradox. He took me out on dates and to nice restaurants several times a week. Fortunately his business was prospering and finances were not a challenge for us.

He romanced me, opened the door for me and treated me with respect. On several occasions he took me out to a shopping mall. We went together into some of the ladies fashion stores, where he and I would pick out a large assortment of clothing for me. Then one by one I would try them on while he patiently waited.

"That looks great," he would often say. "You look amazing. You look beautiful. We're going to buy that one for sure. I'm lucky to have a wife like you."

Trying on all these beautiful clothes and being complimented again and again by Brian lifted me tremendously. He insisted that we buy most of the clothes I tried on, and he chose many items for me which I would have been too timid to try myself.

Over the course of several months, I acquired an entire new wardrobe. Being pampered like this was like applying healing medicine to a life threatening disease.

Buying me gifts was Brian's way of telling me he loved me. He wanted to make it up to me for what he had done. He wanted to comfort and encourage me, and make me feel special again. He also took me on special outings, to live theatre performances, the famous Abbotsford Airshow and on a family whitewater rafting adventure as well as including me in his recreation. We started weightlifting at the gym together.

Danielle: Mom and Dad had made a decision to work things out and stay together. This is what I thought I wanted. But now life at home was a nightmare for me. I no longer respected my dad and definitely had not forgiven him. After walking out and abandoning us, he now had the nerve to try and tell me what to do (hard enough to take when I loved and respected him).

My parents fought and fought. It was difficult to be home for any amount of time and not burst into tears. I never let them see me cry though. When I was crying and I felt like I needed to talk, I would scream at them instead. I was not going to let them know how much they had hurt me.

I was losing my mind. My Dad had hurt me so bad, I was never going to trust him again. I was never going to forgive him. He didn't even seem sorry. I think he would have liked it if I disappeared forever. Why, you ask? Because Mom seemed so dumb, so needy and she was so forgiving, wanting everything to work out. I was not about to forget about my Dad deciding he didn't love us anymore and deciding he wanted to leave. I wanted him to suffer.

Mom and Dad would fight and fight, yet then go out for fancy dinners and buy new clothes. They even bought a fancy new van. I was happy for my mom, but no one asked me how I felt. No one bought me anything. I spent so much time helping Mom, for what? Nothing. I probably wouldn't have told them the truth about how hurt I was if they did ask, but it would have made me feel like they cared.

My boyfriend Jason was the only person I talked to about what happened. I was too embarrassed to tell anyone else. Even though he was an amazing listener, he didn't know what to do. He bought my mom flowers to cheer her up when my dad left. I thought it was so sweet, but she didn't really notice. I felt like I had no one besides Jason to care about me. My parents definitely did not care one little bit. Otherwise, they would have talked to me. Jason told me that I should talk to someone, but who? There was no one, so I would cry and cry.

I would sneak out for walks late in the night and cry and scream and wander around hopelessly, as if I might bump into someone who would listen, care and give me advice. But that never happened.

One day I felt I could no longer deal with my life. Jason and I were talking seriously and I was bawling as usual. I told him that I wanted to fall asleep for a month or more. Maybe when I woke up Mom and Dad would no longer be fighting. Maybe if I slept long enough, someone would notice that I wasn't around. Maybe after a month of not talking to me, someone would care. I knew Jason loved me. I tried to think about him as much as possible, because I felt that he was the only person in the world who cared about me. I just couldn't get rid of my overwhelming pain and crazy emotions.

I thought that I was strong and tough, physically and emotionally. That is why I didn't have to tell anyone anything. I could handle things alone, I thought. That's why my mom could tell me her problems and I could help her, because I thought I was stronger than she was. She didn't seem able to handle things since my dad's affair.

I tried to protect Dustin and Tamara from the fights. I had to be strong, since Mom and Dad weren't doing a very good job of keeping them safe. Everything seemed too hard now. I had no adults to talk to, no one who cared and no one who I gave enough credibility to, to receive advice from.

What a pressure to be sixteen and to feel as if you have no one in the world, yet to have problems dumped on you every day. I felt like I was choking. I didn't want anyone to know how much I cried, wishing I had never been born. It probably would have been better. I cost my parents a fortune. I got in trouble for everything. I had no clue what to do. What I did know was that I was no longer capable of dealing with all this stuff.

The thought of sleeping for a whole month sounded so nice, but how? It was impossible, or was it? What about sleeping pills? One pill puts you to sleep for twelve hours, so could sixty pills put me to sleep for a month? They didn't have a maximum per day warning on the bottle, so I figured it might work. I bought sixty pills. I was aware that there was some danger in trying this, but I thought if I could just fall asleep and never wake up it would be better.

That night I got ready for bed and put on nice warm comfy pajamas, as I planned to be sleeping for a while. *Ha*, I thought, *I hope they miss me* (thinking about my family). Soon I was ready for bed and I called Jason to say goodnight and that I loved him. Then I took the pills with a glass of milk. I felt really, really hot. Dismissing it, I got into bed so that I would be lying down when the pills took effect.

As I was getting into bed, I took a look around. I had cleaned my room that day and I thought briefly what a great idea this was. I would be like Sleeping Beauty in my comfy pajamas and clean room, surrounded by fluffy blankets. As I shut my eyes I drifted off peacefully.

On the first night of Brian's much-needed two-week holiday, in the middle of the night as we were sleeping, I was awakened unexpectedly by some strange rattling noises that seemed to be coming from our main bathroom. I got up, put on my bathrobe and went to investigate. To my horror, I found our sixteen year old daughter, shivering and convulsing.

"Danielle, Danielle," I tried to talk to her, but she was not coherent. I could feel the adrenaline shoot instantly through my body as I ran to get Brian for help. He was just as devastated as I was to see our lovely daughter like this. Neither one of us knew exactly what to do.

We worked together as a team to help her, to get her to the hospital, yet we were not getting along with each other. We had another unresolved fight that night before we went to bed. Since Danielle was convulsing, she felt heavy. It was difficult to lift her and it was frightening to see her this way. As we carried Danielle to the van, her eyes opened, yet looking into them, it was as if she couldn't see us, like looking into blankness.

Arriving at the hospital emergency entrance, some staff assisted us in bringing her in with a wheelchair, while she continued to shake. I was scared. I wondered how many catastrophes I was going to go through. I felt like I couldn't handle another one, yet they kept coming with unrelenting persistence. I looked at the nurse with humble desperation. *How had this happened to us? What had we done wrong?* Tears were streaming down my face.

"She's probably taken an overdose of a drug called ecstasy," the nurse said. "She'll probably be okay. Don't feel bad," she tried to comfort. "This is not the first time we've seen this." The hospital staff took Danielle away and encouraged us to sit and wait. It would probably be best if we didn't watch, we were told. We took their advice.

Brian and I sat for an hour, numb, just staring. We didn't talk, but we held hands. After about an hour the nurse came out and told us Danielle's condition had been stabilized and that she was going to be okay. The doctors had run several tests but had been unable to determine which substances may have been in her system to cause this. They suggested Brian and I go home and get some rest. We were exhausted and took their advice. What else could we do?

The next day neither of us was in any mood to enjoy a holiday. Brian's much-needed rest was ruined. We were supposed to be attending a wedding that morning. I decided to go anyway. I wanted to honor my friends and I reasoned that it might be good for me to distract myself from the pain for a few hours. Brian chose to stay home, which I understood.

I sat at the wedding glad to share in someone else's happiness. I myself felt stiff, as if I were moving in slow motion. I knew I was having tremendous difficulty producing a smile on my face. I wondered if I would ever know happiness again.

Danielle was released from the hospital two weeks later. Now at least the doctors were working with us rather than in secrecy against us as before. They had not been able to identify the substance in her body, but later Danielle told us that it had been sleeping pills. At this point, I blamed myself for her attempt to escape from life. I saw it as my responsibility to prevent her from putting herself in such danger.

The psychiatrist we'd met before, Dr. Johnson, was assigned to Danielle's case and she was scheduled to continue to see him on a regular basis. After a couple of sessions, Dr. Johnson felt we were ready for a family session together, Danielle, Brian and I. He explained it was not just Danielle that needed help, but the entire family dynamic needed to be changed. Brian and I were willing to do whatever it would take to heal our family, and save our hurting girl.

During our first and only family session, Danielle became very angry. Dr. Johnson was trying to get a commitment from her that if she ever felt like killing herself again, she would give him a call first. Danielle kept refusing and never did make the commitment he was asking for. Brian and I sat quietly and listened. Finally Dr. Johnson said to her, "You are right, Danielle. If you want to kill yourself, you can kill yourself. There is absolutely nothing we can do about it. We can put you in a straight jacket in the psych ward and you can swallow your own tongue. We won't be able to do a thing about it. Your life is your choice."

As painful as it was to hear him say these words, the truth in them set me free. I realized, for the first time, that I was trying to control something I didn't have any control over. The choice for her to live or die belonged to her and not to me. And if she made the choice to die, it would not be my fault. Her decision was not something I could control.

We are all given the freedom of choice, and that is something no one can take away from us. Realizing for the first time that Danielle's future was up to her, and not me, set me free from a painful bondage and obsession, and it freed me to just love her. It also freed me to be myself. Now I realized that if a child has problems, it does not mean their parents have been bad parents. Even people from the best of homes, with the best of parents can have major problems. And those with the worst of childhoods are also free to choose to heal, learn and have a great life in their adult years. What we do with our life is an individual choice.

CHAPTER 20

chicago?

OCTOBER, 2000

We do not understand:
Joy ... until we face sorrow
Faith ... until it is tested
Peace ... until faced with conflict
Trust ... until we are betrayed
Love ... until it is lost
Hope ... until confronted with doubts

AUTHOR UNKNOWN

Several weeks into our marriage course, I felt completely discouraged and disillusioned. It was supposed to be the answer to all our problems. Although it may have been a wonderful course for those wishing to improve a reasonable marriage, it was hardly the place for a couple with a marriage in crisis.

It was as if I was having a heart attack, and after being rushed to the hospital they were busy giving me a liver transplant. It may well have been a life saving operation if it was the one that I needed, but hardly helpful when a different ailment was threatening my life. When dealing with the devastation of an affair and its phenomenal impact on the marriage, people who have never been there, well-meaning and kind as they are, are often far from helpful.

One night on the way to one of our meetings, Brian and I were having another fight, triggered by the weekly homework assignment. Again I was supposed to listen to him, without interrupting to share my side of the story. I was so tired of being told I didn't listen, and didn't admire and respect him, that I just exploded. I stopped the car and insisted that he get out. I went to the meeting alone. When they asked about Brian, I told the truth, we had a fight. Brian walked over six miles home in the cold, in the rain and in the dark. That was the last time we attended the course that was supposed to save our marriage.

Shortly after that evening, I decided to see a counselor on my own. I felt Brian needed counseling. I felt Danielle needed counseling. I felt sure I was the only sane individual among us. However both Brian and Danielle refused to see counselors, so I went alone, hoping to learn to live through the mess I found myself in.

At the first meeting with the counselor, I started to unload my horrendous story: the affair, the teenage battles, the drunk driving and the burning vehicle. After about ten minutes, he interrupted me. Unlike my friends, he was unimpressed by my noble efforts to try and save my family. Instead he questioned me.

"Exactly what motivates you to do so much good for your family?" he asked.

I was stunned. Instantly I knew the answer: I was motivated by an obsessive drive to fix my childhood in my adult life. Suddenly the pain of everything I suffered as a child flashed before me, especially the pain of growing up in a broken home. This made me subconsciously decide to do anything to stay married to my husband.

Now if I was going to have any hope of a happy home, "anything" was going to need redefining. All of a sudden it was clear that what had appeared to be noble was really just codependency. It was time for me to stop trying to save everybody else. I was astonished to see how much I was a part of my problems.

With the counselor's help I began to learn what a healthy relationship really looks like and I began to change drastically. I stopped trying to please everybody, stopped taking responsibility for other's mistakes and stopped apologizing all the time. I set clear relationship boundaries. I began to think and act more independently. It was all for the better, but the change was also difficult for both of us. At one point Brian remarked, "Anne, you are changing and growing incredibly as a person. I see that it is a good thing, but at the same time it scares me."

The next time I talked to my mother on the phone and updated her on the events of my life, she gave me some unexpected advice. She conceded that my father was not all bad, that he was sometimes wise, and that he might even be able to help me. She strongly recommended that I call my father and tell him of Brian's affair. She told me that it was not fair that my father had no chance to help me through such a trying time and that one day when he did find out, he would feel hurt that I never told him.

My mother's words carried a great impact. Besides, deep down I really did want to talk with my father. Deep down, I didn't agree with the advice others had given me to keep my troubles a secret, in order to "protect" Brian.

I wasted no time phoning my father in Chicago, and I told him everything. He listened compassionately and without passing judgment.

Two days later he called me back.

"I'm going to be arriving in Vancouver in two days," he said.

"But Dad," I said, shocked, "really, you don't need to come here. I'm working things out. I wasn't expecting you to do anything. I just thought that it was only fair that you knew what I was going through."

I was terrified at the thought of having my father arrive in the midst of what seemed more like a war zone than a family. It was not unusual for me to have difficulty getting along with my father at the best of times. But I saw that he viewed it as an opportunity to show his only daughter how much he loved her, and after several attempts to dissuade him from coming, I realized that he wasn't going to budge on this issue. I knew he wanted to help, and he said he wouldn't interfere. He also promised to pretend to know nothing of the problems in our lives.

"My father's coming to visit," I told Brian when I picked him up from work that evening.

Brian was surprised. "Does he know about our problems?"

"No," I lied. It was the first time in my life that I had ever told a lie to my husband. I knew Brian would feel embarrassed if he knew my father knew.

I don't know why I thought it was suddenly okay to start telling lies in my marriage. What I do know is because of what had happened I was now questioning the truth in every value I had ever held dear. Since I could no longer believe that my own relationship was secure, how could I trust anything else in my life? How could I know my friends, family and children would not betray me also? I was now questioning everything I had ever trusted or believed in.

On Friday afternoon I met my father at the airport. On the way home, we had a nice seafood lunch at a charming oceanside village. It felt good to discuss my mess openly with my father, and as my mother suggested, I found him to be quite reasonable.

"Dad," I reminded my father, "I have told Brian that you don't know about our problems, so it is imperative that you not say anything to him."

"No problem," he assured me. "I am not coming here to cause any trouble, only to help out in whatever way I can. When my daughter calls me with a problem, I come to help."

On Saturday morning I made bacon and eggs for breakfast and we gathered the family around the dining room table, attempting once again to act like normal people in the midst of our turmoil. No sooner had a simple prayer been uttered and people started to eat then my father said, "So Brian, I guess we're having some problems here. This is quite serious that you have lost your driver's license."

Every fork stopped. I felt blood rushing to my face and my heartbeat quickened. I gulped. Brian stared at me in disbelief.

"I think we should continue this conversation after breakfast," I suggested, wanting to avoid the discussion in front of the children.

I couldn't believe that the first time I had ever lied to my husband, I had been caught red-handed almost immediately. Oh, how I wanted to get out of this one!

We made it through breakfast cordially discussing the weather, the kids' schooling and the current position of the solar system (one of my father's favorite topics).

Afterwards, Brian and my father tried to find excuses to get away from the inevitable discussion. Determined to face this issue head-on, I brought them back to the table.

"You two are the two men in this world that I happen to love more than any other men on the planet," I began. "You have also both hurt me more than any other men ever have or probably ever could." I hoped this would level the playing field. No sense my father thinking he was a better man than Brian. He wasn't. He had certainly done as much, if not worse, than Brian in his day, and I knew it.

"Dad, for the first time in my eighteen years of marriage, I have lied to my husband," I said. "Brian, I want to apologize to you for that. I out and out lied to you and I am truly sorry. I shouldn't have done it. It was foolish of me. Dad, I'm already feeling betrayed and as though I can't trust anyone in this world and here you promised me that you wouldn't say anything. Once again you have hurt me."

"Well, I thought I just wasn't supposed to talk about the affair," my father tried to justify himself.

"Don't start with me Dad. You know perfectly well you weren't supposed to say ANYTHING." I was uninterested in any more game-playing.

"Both of you have let me down. I'm sick and tired of it and I'm not taking any more garbage from either one of you. I expect both of you to face this and to be nice to each other. I don't know if Brian and I are going to make it, but I love you Brian, and I am fully committed to rebuilding our marriage. Dad, I appreciate your wanting to help, however, I think you need to let us work this out ourselves. I don't know where we go from here, but I think I have said what I need to."

Both men sat silent and startled. "Well Brian, obviously I cannot claim to be a better man than you," my father said. "We all make mistakes sometimes. Why don't we go and have a beer and talk man to man, alone?"

Brian declined. And I guess I couldn't blame him. He had had enough of people pressuring him to do this, that and the other thing.

I spent most of my time with my father that weekend. He took me out and spoiled me a bit. He also talked with me about my problems and offered me helpful perspective, reminding me that most men are unfaithful to their wives at some point. He reminded me that I wasn't alone in my experience and that this was a problem in our society as a whole.[6]

The fact that my father had gone to a big effort and expense to visit me, showed me that he loved me in a way that I had never understood before. This was something I desperately needed. It was with a lot of emotion that I saw him off to his plane on Monday morning.

Journal entry, October 6, 2000:

    My dad came to visit on the weekend, and all-in-all it was a good visit. Brian withdrew all weekend.

    As I meditate on my talks with my dad, I feel he has offered some valuable advice. I have to get myself and my family out of this state of continual crisis. I have done nothing but sacrifice myself for my family and it is ending with them walking all over me and abusing me. If I keep on like this I'm going to lose my health and then I'll be no good to anyone.

Journal entry, October 11, 2000:
  I went to see the family doctor today and he inspired me greatly. He told me that he was a good judge of character and that he knows Brian, and that he knows that Brian is a good man. I know that's true too. He told me that we can make it through this. I believe it. He says that if our family unit breaks up we will each always live with a pain that will haunt us, but if we keep this family unit together and heal and restore the relationships, we can all go on to have happy lives. I believe that too.

Within a couple of days, my father called me up to offer me a free trip to Chicago to visit him and my half–brother, Charles, who I hadn't seen in fourteen years. Apparently it was my brother who was offering to pay for this trip.

Now that my family knew, they were doing everything they could to support me.

I was not going to pass up a free trip to my old home town. I hadn't been there since I was sixteen years old. In the past I might have stayed home for Brian, but now, I didn't hesitate. He had hurt me. I didn't know if I could trust him anymore.

My family was offering me help. I was taking it. Period. I was making my own decisions now. I was far more independent than I had ever been before. Danielle had agreed to drive her father back and forth to work while I was away, so there was nothing holding me back.

When Danielle drove me to the airport two weeks later, I was buzzing with excitement. This trip was a big deal to me. It was a time to reflect on all that had happened and decide where I wanted to go from here? What did I really want out of my life? I was at a new beginning. My marriage and my life as I had known it were over.

I was Linus, from the Charlie Brown cartoon, without my blanket.

I was like an acrobat who had just let go of the trapeze, somersaulting through mid-air, wondering if I would catch the next. I could go wherever I wanted to go with my life from here. I could leave my marriage and start a new life if I wanted to. I had every right to do so. I was confident in my own ability to support myself and my children. I was a knowledgeable teacher and a confident business woman. What did I really want?

In the airport, while waiting for my flight, I wrote a letter to myself:

Dear Anne,

You have begun an incredible journey. For eighteen years you thought you had one of the greatest marriages ever. Now this year your life has totally fallen apart. Your husband left you for another woman and now has come back. Your daughter has tried to kill herself. You have walked around in devastation and in shock. The pain has been overwhelming. As Brian accurately puts it, the clock struck midnight, your husband turned out to be a toad and your Cinderella fantasy has ended. Now you realize that what you really had was a codependent relationship and you are equally to blame for these problems. Brian is a good man and he is working on his issues right now. As long as he is, you will keep working on this family. But you have no guarantees for the future, except that you can fix yourself. Now you are going to be healed, and you are no longer going to make decisions based on pain from your past.

Arriving in Chicago, I was excited to see Charles once again after so many years. He greeted me with a great big hug and told me that I looked just like Cher. Must have been the black hair and leopard print jacket Brian had bought for me.

My brother looked great too. He was wearing a slick suit and a confident walk. A professional wine-taster and business owner, life was treating him well. He encouraged me to check out the career opportunities in Chicago.

"Get out of the remote West and come to the East where you can really make some money," Charles advised.

"But I may still want to stay in my marriage," I said.

"Then bring the whole family," he said. "This is a much better place to live."

My four-day visit was fantastic. My brother and father treated me like royalty, taking me to Chicago's finest restaurants for great food and expensive wines. I took a nostalgic tour around my old stomping grounds and visited some of Chicago's tourist attractions with the only Chicago friend I had stayed in touch with over the years.

Charles took me to Evanston, Chicago's elite suburb, because he thought it would be the best place for me to live. And it was beautiful, right on Lake Michigan and only a short commute from the city. He showed me what a wonderful life I could have living there with my children. He even offered me a good job with his company, plus the financial support I would need to move and get set up. I could also see that he and his lovely wife would be a good support network while I got my bearings.

I now had an easy way out of my marriage. I was totally free. I was seriously tempted by his offer. I told them honestly that I was considering their offer and I would give them a definite answer within a month. We did a lot of important background work while I was there, investigating places to live and actual costs. The salary he offered me was very generous, and would provide a decent lifestyle for myself and my kids. I really wanted to move there. I wanted a new beginning, but I still loved Brian.

I felt sad to leave, sad to leave this wonderful treatment and return to my family problems, but my vacation had given me much-needed strength I needed to face the looming battle that waited for me at home.

I arrived to find Brian in a miserable state. As far as I could tell, he wasn't going to rest until I was just as unhappy as he was.

I tried in vain to do the "right" things. Everything I did seemed to be wrong. Then he confessed to me that he was jealous that I had been on such a wonderful trip and jealous that I had people in my life who were there to love me and help me through my troubles. He also confessed that he had spent the past four days imagining that my family had set me up with some man, who he imagined was much more worthy and wealthy than he was. He feared that I wouldn't come home and that he would never see me again. I now felt compassion for how he must have felt.

Danielle told me that Brian had been so worried about losing me that he had stayed in the bedroom and had become physically ill. She had heard him vomiting repeatedly throughout the night. Sad as this was, it comforted me. The man must really love me, if he became physically ill over the prospect of losing me, I reasoned to myself.

Journal entry, October 26, 2000:

The misery continues. I had to drive the kids to youth group at the church, drive Danielle to work, buy a saw blade for Brian and rent a movie. The kids were mixed up about where the youth meeting was being held and it took me nearly an hour to find the right place. On my way home alone in the car, I started screaming as loud as I could and ended up sobbing. I was afraid that Brian would be angry with me for taking so long.

Then I realized this was totally unhealthy and I felt like I wanted to separate. I also took some of my anger out on the kids. That's bad even though I did apologize. It's like right now I'm happiest when I'm not with Brian. As it worked out, I phoned Brian right away and explained my problem and he wasn't angry. I still had no opportunity to talk to him. But there is still hope for our relationship and I so much want things to work out. I don't know what to do. I need wisdom.

Journal entry, October 30, 2000:

Things are going really well between Brian and me. We had a great weekend. The hockey game didn't go so well. We had numerous difficult talks until finally I forgave Brian in writing, absolving him from his guilt, but even more so promising not to continually bring his faults before him anymore, except in the context of counseling for the purpose of healing. This seemed to make all the difference. Yesterday we had a great time together. We tried on rings in the mall just for fun.

The best thing about it was that last night Brian said yesterday had been the first day in a really long time that he had had a good time. I think all the quality time has also paid off. It has been so difficult I didn't feel like doing it and wished someone else could have spent the time with Brian and had all the difficult talks with him. But I think that it had to be this way. Ultimately I want to be with him, I believe he wants to be with me and we are the ones who in the end have to work out our relationship. No one else can do it for us. Others can provide a little help, but we have to do the work. Only we can pay the price.

---

6. Conservative estimates are that 60 percent of men and 40 percent of women will have an extramarital affair. If even half of the women having affairs (or 20 percent) are married to men not included in the 60 percent having affairs, then at least one partner will have an affair in approximately 80 percent of all marriages. *The Monogamy Myth*, Vaughan, Page 7.

CHAPTER 21

9-1-1

NOVEMBER, 2000

*Love is a double-edged sword. It brings the greatest joys
and the greatest pains people can know. It wants to hold
and nurture, to rescue and protect. This is its nature.
But the moments of growth and steps toward maturity will often
be taken against the pull of those we love. Don't let this fool you:
Love is not the enemy. Give thanks for those who care for you and
seek to guard your way. See them not as obstacles, but as opportunities to grow and love in a different way.*

FROM *HUGS FOR GRADS*
JEFF WALLING

The fighting and the emotional roller coaster continued. One day
it seemed as if there was hope. The next day all seemed lost, but I
continued to fight my personal war to recover from the affair,
unsure of whether my marriage would make it.

Journal entry, November 7, 2000:

*I'm really frightened. I don't know what to do. The past week has
been crappy. Brian seems to be losing it. I can't fix it for him. I'm
afraid that I'm doing the wrong thing by staying with Brian. It
seems that there are signs telling me to leave and at the same time
there are signs telling me to stay.*

I had tea with Danielle today, and we had a good talk. She told me about a recent visit she had with Brian's mother and that it seemed to Danielle history was repeating itself. The things that Brian is doing are just like the things his father did, and his father never got better. He only got worse and worse.

Danielle says that Brian and I sound like her grandmother and grandfather. It's so much the same that it is totally scary. I find myself falling into the same trap as Brian's mother, trying to please, working so hard to keep the house cleaner, cook better, be prettier, be totally available for Brian's needs every moment of every day. I find myself giving up things that are important to me in my effort to try and please him. I'm losing my own sense of self.

I don't know if I can change, stop being "nice" when I should be taking a stand. Danielle tells me I am losing some of my sweetness. That really scares me. I never want to be a bitter person. I wish I knew what to do. Maybe a separation is the only answer.

I was making personal progress with the aid of my counseling. I was beginning to understand myself and the unhealthy buried roots from my past that were wreaking havoc in my life. Even though I was living in a present-day reality full of ups and downs, I was growing as a person at a tremendous speed. Most importantly I was recognizing codependent behaviors in myself and I was consciously replacing them with healthy patterns.

My change forced Brian to also change. We were permanently rewriting patterns in the way we related to one another, and that wasn't easy. We were changing the dance in our relationship.

One evening, we sat having coffee and talking together privately in our bedroom. It started as a good time, with us communicating honestly and enjoying each other's company. Once again Brian was willingly answering questions about the affair, and I was struggling to understand what weaknesses in our marriage led to infidelity.

I told Brian that I did not feel I could be myself in our relationship, I didn't feel loved for the person I was. I felt he was expecting me to become something I wasn't. This hurt Brian. He said it wasn't fair, that I didn't realize how much he was doing to show me he loved me. He was agitated, but I didn't back off. Then he told me I never listen to him. I disagreed. Next he said I didn't respect him, because if I did I would be asking him "why" questions. *How dare he tell me whether I respected him or not?* I thought. He could tell me that he didn't *feel* respected, but he had no right to accuse me of not respecting him because it simply wasn't true.

"You don't understand what I'm saying," he said with rising volume.

"Don't you dare tell me what I do and don't understand," I yelled back.

Then he stood up and continued yelling. He refused to sit down.

"I'm not remaining seated. I'm sick and tired of you bossing me around," he said. "I can never talk with you because we always have to spend forever discussing how to talk instead of just getting right to the point."

"When you stand up and start raising your voice at me, I feel intimidated," I said. "I can't even hear what you're saying any longer. My mind just shuts off. This conversation is going nowhere right now, so I'm leaving."

I only meant I was leaving briefly, to regain my composure, but I was so worked up that I didn't even think to make my intentions clear to Brian.

I brushed past him heading towards the door. He grabbed me and restrained me, keeping me from leaving our bedroom. He had something to tell me and he was determined to tell me right then and there. To him it couldn't wait.

I was determined to prove that he could not force me against my will. I had learned that I didn't have to put up with behavior that I deemed inappropriate, that I always had a choice whether to stay and take it or not.

"Anne, I just need you to listen to me right now."

"No, I'm not listening. You can't make me listen," I yelled. And I wasn't listening at all. I was frightened by the intensity of the moment. I was determined to show that I could not be forced or manipulated. I deserved to be treated with respect.

He held my wrists as I struggled and squirmed to move past him. I began to kick him. I was now fighting with all my might. As we squirmed together, we spun around and I fell over on our bed.

He fell down on top of me and held me down by the wrists. I tried to bite him, now desperate for my freedom. Finally I got one arm free and rolled to my side, reached over to the telephone on our nightstand and dialed 9-1-1 before he had a chance to stop me. He quickly hung up the phone.

At this point, I realized that he was too strong for me and I would not be able to physically free myself.

"Anne, just listen to me," he said. "I just need you to listen to me."

We continued yelling at each other. The phone rang. He wouldn't let me go. The phone rang one more time and stopped. It had been answered elsewhere in the home.

I continued to fight for my freedom but I was still pinned, against my will, to our bed. Brian continued to fight to be heard. Eventually I submitted myself helplessly to his control. I stopped fighting.

"That's it," he said. "I never want to be treated with such disrespect again."

"I don't think our relationship is going to work out," I told him. "You better pack your bags and get out of here."

That drove him over the edge and he grabbed his duffel bag and once again began packing, almost like the night he had left now nearly six months prior. He threw in a few basics. Then he headed out the door. Having him gone I began to regain my composure. *Where would he go?* I worried. *What should I do? Maybe I overreacted.* I was so confused.

Grabbing the phone I dialed his cell phone number. When he answered, I told him that I may have overreacted, and if he wanted to come home and sleep on the couch that would be all right. I wasn't really sure how we had gone from a pleasant constructive evening to something so out of control in such a short time period. We hung up with barely a cordial good-bye. Within a few minutes, Brian was back home. I didn't want to talk to him.

Minutes after Brian returned, our doorbell rang. I didn't want to talk to anyone. I was disheveled and broken. My eyes were red with tears. I heard Brian answer the door.

"Hi. Someone from this address called 9-1-1 this evening," a man said in an authoritative tone. Obviously it was a police officer. "I'm here to see if everything is alright."

"Everything is fine," Brian said.

"Who dialed 9-1-1?" the officer questioned.

"My wife did," Brian answered honestly.

"Was there a domestic dispute?" the officer asked.

"Yes," Brian answered. "My wife and I were fighting, but everything is fine now."

The officer continued his line of questioning, and I realized that he wouldn't leave until he saw with his own eyes that I was physically okay. I couldn't hide any longer.

I came out to face the officer's questions. No, Brian didn't hurt me. Yes, he held me against my will. No, I don't know who answered the phone when the operator called back. It must have been Danielle.

My heart sank when I remembered the phone ringing. Danielle was trying to protect us, told them everything was fine.

"Did your husband hurt you?" the officer asked me again.

"No," I said. "After the fighting I told him to leave, but later I changed my mind and told him he could stay as long as he stayed away from me and spent the night on the couch."

"And you agree to spend the night on the couch, sir?" the officer asked.

"Yes," Brian replied, humiliated beyond description.

Finally the officer left. The evening had somehow become a disaster. I could hardly believe that once again the law had to intervene in our once happy home.

The next day, I avoided Brian before he left for work. I didn't know what to think of the night before, and I wasn't ready to face him yet.

Brian: How does one complete a marathon? One step at a time. I was on my own marathon of a different kind. One that would determine the future of our marriage, yet one I was not solely responsible for. No matter what the outcome was to be, I was determined to do whatever it took to win back Anne's love, trust and respect. To me she was worth it. I believed we could overcome this terrible deed I had committed.

From the very beginning, I knew this would take a lot of time and effort, and that Anne would not "just get over it."

I realized Anne had many questions, and I would have to answer each and every one of them, and answer them more than just once or twice or three times! I was taking her out for coffee as often as I could in order create an atmosphere for discussion. Much of the talking had to do with the "whys" and "How could yous?"

It was painful to look into the eyes of the woman I truly loved and see the pain I caused her. It was not easy to revisit the why and how come questions, yet discussion was the only way for her to get the answers she needed. My openness was helping her to slowly regain trust in me. Many times though it felt like we were not making any progress forward, and this painful night was one of them.

Instead of going to counseling with Anne, I was reading books that were helping me to understand myself and how I could have done something that I was morally and intellectually opposed to. This helped me to avoid defensiveness about my actions, when Anne asked questions that made me look bad or selfish. I needed to recognize my own weaknesses and overcome them to ensure I would never have another affair.

I was trying to treat Anne like a princess. I wanted to make it up to her for what I had done. I took her out shopping for new clothes, to fancy restaurants and on other special dates. I wanted to show Anne that in spite of what I had done or how she was feeling about me, I really, really loved her and was willing to prove it to her by my words and my actions.

Yet no matter how much we talked, how many times I answered her questions, how many coffees we shared, or how much money I spent on her, it felt like we were not moving ahead! Yet, I wasn't prepared to give up, because I loved her.

So I wrote this letter to her during my lunch hour at work, in hopes that she would understand me. I gave it to her when I got home.

Dear Anne,

These are the things that went wrong last night from my perspective.

It appears to me that you cannot understand what I am saying. I think you think I'm asking you to change the person you are and I am not. I love you just the way you are.

I could not communicate to you the idea that if I make every effort to control my anger so that we can communicate properly, and yet I still blow it, I do not want to be punished over and over again for that mistake by needing to talk about "Why did you get mad Brian?" We never seem to be able to discuss the issue that made me mad in the first place. We only discuss the fact that I got mad.

I have to give an account for my behavior. My aggressiveness was inappropriate. What seems to be missing is you taking responsibility for your behavior which triggered my aggressive response.

It seems to me, and I might be wrong, that certain things I do (like yelling) trigger a response in you (like shutting down and tuning out). I have to deal with my behavior properly (ask for forgiveness, change), but there is no indication that you feel you had any part to play in causing my behavior. You do not have to deal with what you did (over exaggerating), but I have to deal with what I did!

My response might be just as instinctive as yours (your way of protecting yourself). So we both might respond instinctively to a situation. The difference is that how I respond is viewed as extremely negative and unacceptable (which it is!) but how you respond is deemed noble.

My behavior that provokes your reaction is viewed as intolerable and destructive (which it is), but your behavior that provokes me is never questioned because we now focus on my reaction. I feel that I am stuck on a treadmill and can never get past a certain place because we only deal with my reaction and never with your provocation.

I feel that in order for our relationship to get beyond this point (wherever this is), I have to:

1. Never make you feel threatened – keep total control over my actions (this I want to do).

2. Always react properly to any provocation from you – train myself to react totally different from what might be instinctive.

3. If I blow it, I have to start all over again, go back to the beginning and once more try to never do 1 or 2.

For me it feels like this: I want to have a warm bath, so I plug in the stopper and start filling the tub. As I begin to step into the full tub I accidentally splash some water out. Because of this I am told to drain the tub completely and start again. Once again I repeat the procedure trying to be more careful as I enter the tub, but this time I bump the shampoo bottle into the water thus resulting in water splashing out again. I am then told that because I splashed water out I must start the procedure over. So I do.

I keep anticipating this nice warm bath to soak in so I persist. The third time something else happens. The wash cloth falls in first. Again I am told that I must repeat the procedure until everything is done right.

By this time I am getting cold standing there. I am frustrated. I am getting somewhat angry. But the thing that I feel the most is hurt and rejected, rejected because I didn't do things well enough, though I wanted to and tried to, to get to the thing I desire.

There seems to be a level of measuring up that I can never reach. It seems that no matter how much I desire to have that bath or how hard I try to do things just right, something prevents me from going in. There almost seems to be some weird ritual of leading right up to the Promised Land only to be turned away time after time. Maybe I have become so used to this journey that in order to prevent feeling devastated I don't let myself think about the Promised Land. I just keep walking up to the locked gate habitually?

Maybe I have been discouraged so many times that now I don't believe I will ever get in? Maybe I don't really want to get in? Maybe I am not really welcomed in the land? Maybe the inhabitants of the land won't share its goodness with me? Maybe I can't see myself there? Maybe, maybe, maybe.

Honey, I am trying to understand. I love you and I want to work out our relationship, but I don't know if I can take much more of feeling the way I am. I need you to listen to me.

Love Brian.

I was touched by this letter. I wanted to work things out with him too. I loved him also, but it all seemed so difficult.

We talked quite a bit that evening about the letter, and I listened to him explain his feelings. I promised to control my reactions in the future and to listen to him. He promised to work on communicating in a calm manner, so I wouldn't feel intimidated. We were on the right track again.

A few days later, we went to work out at the gym together, which had become part of our routine. We had a lot of fun there and it was exhilarating to be getting in such great physical shape. I had reached my ideal weight, and since I was finally eating properly, I was able to develop attractive muscle definition. Physically, I was feeling and looking wonderful. This provided a much-needed boost to my wavering self-esteem.

After our workouts we would enjoy a nice relaxing soak in the hot tub. This evening was no exception. Except for the security camera, viewed by the girls at the front desk, we were alone. This was a good opportunity to discuss our relationship. It was times like these that I asked questions I needed to, to recover from the affair. I struggled with many uncertainties: *Am I beautiful? Am I sexy? Does he really love me? Will he be faithful to me in the future? Do I understand him? Was Helen better than me? Is he maybe still seeing Helen and I just don't know about it? Am I meeting his needs? Is he happy?*

Before long, our discussion turned sour. Brian wanted to tell me something and thought I wasn't listening. He got aggressive in his tone of voice and was almost shouting right in my face, violating my personal space.

I began to shut down and stopped listening. Brian's frustration level began to rise. The next thing I knew, he got up out of the pool and gave me the finger, right in front of the security camera.

I felt I had been violated, pushed over the edge. I didn't see how anything any wife could do or say to a husband could warrant such behavior.

We left the gym, not speaking to each other. Passing the front desk I was embarrassed, wondering if the staff had watched Brian's behavior on camera.

Again Brian chose to communicate with a letter. He gave it to me the next day.

Dear Anne,

It appears to me that no matter how bluntly and honestly I tell you how important it is for me to feel respected by you, you don't seem to get it. No matter how bluntly and honestly I tell you that I need to feel I have a positive impact in your life, you don't get it. When I make suggestions or give you advice, I need you to stop ignoring my words, and start putting weight in them.

And no matter how many times and how many different ways I tell you how very much I love you, you still don't believe me. I have come to realize that you must not respect me, so I think that you should find someone who you will respect and let have impact into your life.

I tried to do what I thought was right. I tried to do what you wanted! But this has not worked. So you should park your boots under someone else's bed because I cannot bear the thought that the person I love cannot respect me.

You can let me know how soon you plan to do this because I do not plan on sleeping on the couch for more than tonight.

I am sorry that I react to the words you say. I am sorry I have not made it plain or clear enough. I ask you to forgive me for how I gestured you in the pool. That was completely wrong and it will never happen again.

Brian

I was frustrated. I did respect him and he did have an impact on my life. I didn't understand why I was falling hopelessly short of communicating that love and respect to him. I felt sad that I had hurt him so much.

So after I read the letter, we talked some more. I apologized for not listening, and explained that I was trying to understand him. We talked for an hour or two, and I felt a little more hopeful about our future, until Brian shared something a friend told him that day.

This friend suggested that, considering the way Brian was feeling, it was surprising he hadn't had an affair years earlier.

I was burning with fury on the inside. *How dare some person stand around and say more or less that I deserved for this to happen to me?*

How dare they say that it was almost inevitable that my husband hurt me so tremendously by betraying me with another woman? How dare someone insinuate that it was inevitable? What kind of stupid person could say such a thing, I wondered? *Did this person have no compassion at all in their entire body? Did this person not have a clue how painful affairs are to the one who is betrayed? Did this person actually think that anyone could be deserving of such cruelty?*

I demanded to know who it was, but Brian wouldn't tell me.

"Anne, it doesn't matter. It's just something someone said. The fact is that I have felt disrespected and not listened to by you for some time. And considering the way I really felt, this person thought it was surprising I hadn't had an affair sooner."

"Why didn't you tell me that you felt disrespected and that I didn't listen?" I questioned.

"I did try, but you would never listen to me. You became defensive, and told me I was wrong for feeling that way. Then you would get depressed for days, and start saying that I didn't love you, and I would have to spend what felt like forever re-proving my love to you. You never seem to believe that I love you."

I felt as though I had been living inside a bubble, in a fairytale world believing only what I had wanted to believe; only what I had been strong enough to believe. Now my bubble was being burst. I could no longer remain in the idealism I longed for. Reality was bursting in. I was doing everything within my psyche to keep that painful truth and reality out. I did not want to see my own fault in the relationship breakdown. It hurt too much.

I kept pressing Brian to tell me who had made this statement.

"Look, it's someone who cares about you and you don't need to know who it is," he said.

"Someone who cares about me would never say such a thing," I said.

I pushed and I pushed and I pushed. I was not going to rest until

I knew who it was. Finally, Brian told me. It was Pierre Desportes.

Two of our closest friends were Pierre and Jackie Desportes. Pierre was a man who spoke with kindness, confidence and wisdom. He had moved to our small town outside Calgary to start a church in 1985. We bonded with him and his wife almost as soon as we met. We became the first members of their new church, and in the years that followed we dedicated many hours to helping out in whatever way we could.

One year, 1988, Pierre and his wife Jackie dedicated themselves to meeting with us once a week, taking us through a study on the principles of healthy marriage relationships. They had done this because they loved us. Pierre and Jackie were open and honest with us about their own marriage, sharing their personal struggles and how they overcame them. This deepened our friendship, respect, and trust for them, a trust that was to last a lifetime.

And this was the person who had said he was surprised Brian hadn't had an affair sooner! A man, who had given so generously to us, brought so many positive things into our lives, our mentor and our friend. I *knew* Pierre cared about me. Was this the man who said such a hurtful thing?

I was stunned, also slightly calmed down. If it was Pierre who said this, there must be some explanation. There must be some truth. If anyone else had said this, I would only have been angry, but Pierre had earned the place in our lives to say such a thing and have me hear the words. I called him the next morning, to get an explanation.

"Pierre, this is Anne," I said.

"Anne, how are you?" he said. "How are things going?"

"They are not going very well at all. That's why I am calling," I said. "Something is really bothering me. Brian told me you said considering the way Brian was feeling it is surprising that he didn't have an affair sooner. What do you mean? Are you saying I deserved for this to happen to me?"

"No, I'm not saying that you deserved for this to happen to you," he explained kindly. I'm saying that considering the way Brian has been feeling on the inside, it's surprising he didn't have an affair sooner. The man has been so frustrated. You do not communicate your respect towards him."

Pierre explained to me how I was always expecting perfection from Brian, how I really wasn't overlooking his faults, and how I didn't listen because, unless Brian got his communication perfect, I spent all my time correcting him instead of giving him the respect of just hearing what he had to say.

I listened as Pierre, who knew and understood Brian, explained to me what Brian's needs were, what his perspective was and how I was not innocent in this relationship. I saw how I had caused pain in my husband's life, much the same as he had caused me pain.

For the first time I was able to see my part in the relationship breakdown. I opened up my heart to the truth and allowed the false security of my fairytale bubble to fade away, replacing it with reality. What was reality? The reality was I was not a perfect wife, Brian was not a perfect husband and we did not have a perfect marriage, but in the midst of all of our imperfections our love for one another was very real.

This was a major turning point in the healing of our relationship, and I don't believe we could ever have healed if I hadn't reached this point. The point where I stopped just looking at what Brian had done to me, and started to see what I also had done to Brian.

After talking with Pierre, having a big cry and really thinking about what he said, I wrote this letter to my husband:

Dear Brian,

I am writing to you first of all to apologize for disrespecting you, for not allowing the things you say to impact my life, for giving more respect to others than to my very own husband, for placing more weight on the things other people say than on the things you say, for completely exasperating you by getting stuck on what people say or on what you say

*and harping on them over and over and over again regardless of any-
thing you say to make it better.*

*I apologize for belittling and berating you and making you feel like a
bad person in my subtle and manipulative little ways. I apologize for
tearing you down and chipping away at and destroying your self-esteem,
the whole time convincing myself I was doing the opposite. I apologize
for making you look bad to other people and trying to make myself look
like such a great person in contrast.*

*I have not loved, honored and respected you as a wife ought to love
her husband. The truth is I don't even know how to do this. And the
thing that I now realize is that the wrongs that I have committed against
you are equally as bad as your sleeping with Helen.*

*I am not one bit better of a person than you. My mistakes are not
lesser mistakes than yours. I have crushed and just about destroyed you,
as much as you have done to me. Like me your pain is also so great that
you feel it is unbearable. My greatest pain is knowing how much I have
hurt you. Perhaps, today for the first time I catch a glimpse of what you
have been suffering for the past nine months. No wonder you have been
asking, "Doesn't anyone want to know how I feel?"*

For all of the above I ask your forgiveness.

*Now comes the hardest part of all. I have made a decision to change.
Awareness is the beginning of change. Today I have become aware of my
part. The reason I have treated you this way is because of my own emotional pain. I do not mention this as an excuse, but because although I
can change considerably on my own effort right away, I will not be able
to fully respect you as you deserve until I am fully healed myself.*

*However, I now see that we need to open up and fully share our pain
with each other. I have not been willing to really hear about your pain
yet. I am now willing to listen. Let the truth be told. Let the real healing
begin. I am committed and willing.*

*Brian, I know that when we get through this, you will truly be as
great a husband as any woman could ever have. There is not a man out
there anywhere who is better suited to me than you. I love you.*

Anne.

Brian: After receiving this letter, for the first time I felt relief, and hope for our future. Through everything, even the affair, I loved Anne deeply, but I had been unable to communicate my needs to her. Finally I knew that Anne had been able to really hear me, to hear the truth of my side, how I was feeling. For the first time I felt understood.

CHAPTER 22

from fighting to Healing

The Tree

The tree that never had to fight
For sun and sky and air and light
Never became a forest king
But lived and died a common thing.
The man who never had to toil,
Who never had to win his share
Of sun and sky and light and air,
Never became a manly man,
But lived and died as he began.
Good timber does not grow at ease
The stronger wind, the tougher trees.
The farther sky, the greater length
By sun and cold, by rain and snow
In tree or man good timber grows.

DOUGLAS WALLCOCK
"SELFLESS LOVE," BY JOYCE SIMMONS

Even though Brian and I had reached this major breakthrough and significant turning point in the healing of our marriage, things were still tough. Dealing with the real issues in our marriage and facing the truth was painful. It required courage and patience on both our parts. We continued to fight as we wrestled to understand each other's needs, while we were both hurting.

As the Christmas holiday approached, I was fearful that I may have to leave my husband permanently, and that Christmas for my kids would always represent "the time that Mom and Dad broke up."

I didn't dare tell Brian about my real fears for the relationship, but we both agreed that we'd had it with the fighting.

We agreed to put our problems on hold over the holiday and just have fun together. For the first time since our world had fallen apart, we began to relax. Surprisingly, we enjoyed a wonderful time together as a family and Brian and I emerged from the season feeling a renewed sense of love and appreciation for one another based on reality, not on fantasy or a Hollywood portrayal of what romance should look like.

Putting my problems on hold and just enjoying myself helped me to see how very much I loved Brian. And I didn't just love Brian. Love is something that speaks of self-sacrifice and commitment. I liked Brian too. I truly enjoyed his company and the wonderful human being he is on the inside, in his heart. All this fun was like spending a night in a luxury hotel after months of traveling through the wilderness, sleeping in a tent every night. At last hope was restored and I could see a light at the end of a very long, very dark tunnel.

I was still on leave from work, but one day it became necessary for me to stop by the office. I hadn't been for months, fearing that my coworkers might sense that there were serious problems in my life. If they found out, I feared, they might not view me with the same level of respect.

Finally, I felt strong enough to make the trip. I walked into the reception area and greeted the receptionist cordially, while requesting the necessary papers. I had no intention of speaking to anyone I didn't have to, nor had I any intention of staying any longer than absolutely necessary.

My boss heard me from his office and came out to greet me warmly. He seemed pleased to see me after my long absence.

"Anne, come on into my office," he said. "Tell me how you are doing."

Rats, I thought. *This is exactly what I didn't want to happen. If I am going to make it through this errand without anyone knowing anything is wrong I am going to have to sit through this polite visit.*

"So tell me, how are you really doing?" He asked. "You look great."

"I'm doing fine. Brian and I have had a few problems in the past months, but everything is working out fine," I said as nonchalantly as possible.

He looked at me discerningly for a moment and said, "Was it another woman?"

I was shocked. How could he have guessed? In the same moment, I became aware that lying about my situation was going to be useless. My facial expression had just given the truth away.

"Yes it was," I answered, trying to keep tears at bay. I had been totally unprepared for such a conversation.

"Do you want to talk about it?"

No, I didn't. But, then again, I did. My boss was a man of integrity. He was respected for understanding human nature, and for showing genuine concern for the well-being of others. In the past, he had been a minister and had counseled others through life's challenges.

"It's been a devastating experience," I said. "I'm not sure if we are going to make it or not, but I've decided to give working on my marriage an honest effort and to reevaluate the situation after a year. The darn problem with the whole thing is that Brian and I love each other so much."

"The fact that you still love your husband and he loves you, tells me you have something worth fighting for," he said. "As you know, I have counseled many couples in my lifetime. Do you know that many people never know what it is like to experience the love that you and your husband share?"

His words gave me a great encouragement. I left the office with greater confidence that I was doing the right thing, fighting for my marriage now under reconstruction despite the size of the boulder that had been dropped in our marriage path.

Armed with renewed hope and a realization that we still enjoyed each other's company tremendously despite all the things which had transpired in our relationship, Brian and I entered the New Year ready to resume the work of healing our marriage. I was also finally emotionally ready to return to my job. My leave of absence had been nine months long.

In January, we attended a weekend personal healing, development and growth seminar, which had been recommended to us by our family physician. During this seminar, we made a giant leap forward in our healing experience. The couple facilitating the seminar had also experienced the devastation of an affair in their marriage at one point.

Having been there herself, this woman truly understood my pain. Affairs, like many things in life, are something you just can't really understand unless you have actually been there yourself. Seeing that she had recovered gave me courage to believe that it just might be possible for me to move past the pain and recover as well.

The most valuable lesson I learned during the weekend was how being neglected as a child had resulted in believing, in my subconscious mind, that I was an unlovable person. This was why, no matter how much Brian showed me that he loved me, I could never really believe it. I had sealed shut the valve to my love tank.

In my lifetime many people, including my parents, had loved me and shown that love to me in various ways, but I never received it. As a child, I processed abandonment and neglect as proof that I was unlovable, so although I enjoyed people and my friendships very much, I never really let the love of any person into my heart, because after all would they not also one day abandon me? All of this had taken place for years on a subconscious level.

Brian was an outstanding man who surpassed most husbands in ability and effort to communicate love towards their wives. Yet continuously throughout our marriage I would ask him, "Do you love me?" My frequent asking of this question made Brian feel inadequate. *I must be a lousy husband*, Brian thought, because if I was a good husband my wife would know that I love her. She wouldn't need to keep asking this question.

Unbeknownst to me, my insecurity and constant asking of the same question chipped away at Brian's self-esteem. No matter how many times he told me he loved me, I never really believed it.

As a result of what I learned this weekend, I was able to go back and reprocess with truth the events that took place in my childhood. Abandonment and rejection I had suffered were due to the shortcomings of the individuals involved and not due to my being unlovable or not good enough. Once this incorrect childhood tape, "you're not loveable," had been reprogrammed, I was able to open the valve and at last receive the love that others showed me. I wish I had asked myself years earlier: What baggage from my past may affect my present, my future or my relationships in a negative way?

The next issue I had to deal with was trust. How could I ever trust my husband again, after such a devastating and unexpected betrayal?

The first step in rebuilding trust was Brian's willingness and cooperation in breaking all ties with Helen. If he had insisted on remaining friends with her, I would not have been able to trust him again. From time to time, I would ask him if he had heard from her or seen her and he would always answer honestly.

He told me about the time he saw Helen at work, only two weeks after the affair had ended. To his astonishment, Helen was walking around arm-in-arm with another man. She was already dating someone new.

Brian: Seeing Helen with this other man, only two weeks after I had allowed my relationship with her to nearly end forever my eighteen year marriage to the woman I really loved, significantly impacted me. All this time, I had been deluded into believing that I was really special to Helen. Seeing Helen dating another man so soon after our relationship ended, helped me to realize how wrong my thinking had been.

I saw that it was never really me Helen loved. Rather it was the reflection of herself which she saw through my eyes. She had been looking for an escape from her present unhappiness. Any man who could provide this would do. And here I had nearly ruined my entire life for the shallow relationship I had with her.

One may ask: How could I believe Brian was telling the truth about his contact with Helen? I contemplated playing the role of an obsessive detective by checking his cell phone bills, showing up unexpectedly at his work at lunch time and questioning guys he worked with. But I decided if my marriage was only based on my checking these things all the time, then really there was no trust in my relationship. And if there was no trust in my marriage, was it really a marriage of value at all? I decided to extend to Brian a measure of trust and forgiveness. I did believe him.

At the same time, I would no longer blindly or naïvely trust. I was now well aware of the possibility of affairs and how easily they could take place. Certainly I would act on any intuitions I might have in the future, to check up on him.

The second factor that enabled me to rebuild trust with Brian was his willingness to be totally open and honest with me. If he had been unwilling to answer my questions, I would have thought he was still hiding something from me.

There was no room for hiding and privacy in our relationship after the affair. Brian may have had a right to some privacy before hand, but there is a price to pay for betrayal, and part of that price is full disclosure to one's spouse so that trust can be rebuilt. Brian revealed everything to me.

Of course I had to do my part to create an atmosphere that encouraged his honesty. I did not react to things he shared with me, nor did I judge him or tell him he was wrong. I listened now, truly listened. When Brian shared things with me, I did not spend the time that he was talking formulating my next response, rather I tried to come into his world and really imagine what it might feel like to be him. *What was he saying really?*

At times after he shared, I remained quiet. It was often painful, but because there is something intensely sacred about real honesty, it brought us closer and closer together.

I have found that most couples are far from truly honest with one another. We enter our marriages with a pile of preconceived ideas about how our mate should act and think, and we tend to punish them without realizing it when their way of thinking is not in line with our expectations. It doesn't take long before we have thrown away true honesty from our relationships without realizing it.

The third factor that helped me to trust Brian again was his willingness to hang in there and work on our relationship through the months it took me to recover from the betrayal. He considered me worth the work of rebuilding.

In the initial days following Brian's disclosure of his affair, I just wanted him to come home. I was experiencing the normal human reaction for anyone experiencing major change. I wanted to get my life back to exactly what it was before.

"Just come home," I had told Brian. "I'll forgive you and everything will be fine."

"You won't be able to just get over it," Brian had said. And he was right.

For months, I asked questions, I became obsessive about things, I misunderstood things, I cried and I argued. It was not easy for Brian. Yet he hung in there. This proved his incredible love for me. This work he did, this price he paid for me, helped me to trust him again.

The levels of trust we have in people can be likened to a bank account, a trust bank account. There are separate accounts, how much I trust you and how much you trust me. Usually when we meet people we start with a zero balance. (People who have been hurt before may start you with a deficit account, because they have already learned not to trust.)

When people do nice things for us, are thoughtful, share their secrets, keep their word and are faithful – they make deposits into the account. When people break their promises, hurt us, tell lies or do other things which lack integrity, they make withdrawals.

For eighteen years, Brian had been making ongoing deposits into his trust bank account with me, and very few withdrawals. So before the affair he was a very rich man as far as his trust account with me was concerned. The night he told me of his affair, he instantly plummeted into a huge debt. And two nights later, when he told me our wedding vows didn't count anymore (that was then and this is now), he owed me thousands of trust dollars and teetered on bankruptcy. I almost closed the account permanently.

From that point forward every time he disclosed the truth, he made a deposit. Acts of kindness, quality time, explanations and answers to questions, holding my hand, and kept promises were all deposits. Dishonesty, unkindness and especially withholding information became withdrawals, something he could no longer afford.

Through *sincerity* (including breaking *all* ties with Helen) trust climbed perhaps thirty percent. Through *ability* (discussing the affair, answering questions and proven behavior) trust continued to climb.

At this point in our healing, I had probably gained about forty percent of my trust with Brian. His account with me was still not out of the red.

We had to be willing to face our problems rather than burying them, or pretending they would just go away with time. We faced our situation head on and we dealt with it, although it was far from easy.

The whole thing was so painful and uncomfortable for both of us. We would have welcomed an instant formula for recovery, but there is no such thing. There was no rushing it. It took time. We were both committed to honesty and to investing the time and energy necessary to deal with all of the ramifications of the affair. We actively worked on it together pursuing a better relationship.

Both of us decided we would not settle for a mediocre marriage. Either we were going to have a great marriage or no marriage at all. The worst relationships are not the ones where couples are fighting. At least then there is action, communication and emotion. The worst relationships are the lukewarm ones. You're okay, but you are not my favorite. There's nothing wrong with you, but there's nothing special about you either. You're just okay. Now that would be a true nightmare. We agreed we loved each other too much to settle for that level of mediocrity in our marriage.

We both viewed our crisis as an opportunity to "get it right" – something we hadn't done in the beginning when we had been functioning to some degree out of a blind trust and just assumed that we were going to be okay because we loved each other and were committed to continuing to love each other through thick and thin. These things alone were not enough to guarantee the monogamy of our marriage. What we didn't know did hurt us.

Another major hurdle we had to overcome was that of re-establishing trust with our children.

Dustin and Tamara were able to accept their father and forgive him quite quickly, through the quality time Brian spent with them, and our willingness to be open with them in answering their questions.

I could see that Dustin and Tamara were watching me. When I was insecure, they sensed it and were insecure as well. As I healed, they sensed my healing and I could tell this put them at ease. These teens were smart and perceptive. I could not pull the wool down over their eyes.

When I was having a bad day, I didn't lie about it or pretend otherwise. At the same time, I was careful not to fall into the trap of role reversal. I didn't allow my children to be my counselors.

Healing our relationship with our strong-willed oldest child was a different story. Perhaps Danielle had been affected more simply because she was older, and understood more thoroughly what was going on.

She had lost respect for her dad and still refused to listen to him. If he asked her to do anything or tried to place a restriction of any sort on her, she disobeyed it.

It was a high and painful price Brian paid for his actions. We came to a place where, if Brian wanted Danielle to do something, he asked me to talk to her. She complied with my requests, but not his. So in this respect, I was paying the price for the affair too. I needed Brian's help in this huge task of parenting teens. For months, I had to do the parenting alone. Danielle simply wouldn't listen to her dad.

I tried on several occasions to talk to Danielle about respecting her father and forgiving him. I explained that if I had forgiven him, she could do the same, that we all make mistakes sometimes and need to be forgiven, that her father had done everything he could to earn back our trust and respect and that we could not hold this against him forever, but it was all to no avail.

Then one day I finally had my chance. It was two years after the affair, and she herself had really screwed up (as we all sometimes do). She had taken our van out one evening, and had fallen asleep wherever she was. When Brian had gotten up to leave for work the next morning, she was not even home. We had tried to contact her, but were unable to and eventually Brian had to rent a vehicle to get to work. When she came home at eleven o'clock in the morning she was overcome with remorse. She wept bitterly.

"Mom, I'm such a screw up of a daughter. I'm screwing up my

whole life. I try to do the right things, but I keep doing the wrong things. I've done so many bad things, how can you even stand me? I'm not good enough to be your daughter. I'm not good enough to love." (Do you see the generational pattern?)

Instantly, I recognized my window of opportunity.

"Danielle, what you need in your life right now is a complete do-over. You need all of your past to be wiped clean, as if it had never happened. And I want you to know that you can have that. I see you are truly sorry. I see that it will be too difficult for you if I forever hold all your teenage mistakes against you. You can never go back and undo the things you've done. What you need right now is for your past mistakes to be erased, as though they had never happened. And I want you to know, I can do that for you. I'm willing to give you a completely clean slate and never mention your wrongs again."

"Oh Mom, it's impossible. How can you ever do that?"

"I can do it. All you have to do is ask." I explained to her some of the basic principles of forgiveness.

"Oh, Mom, will you? Can you?"

"Absolutely, I promise if you want you can start completely over with Dad and me from this moment forward. I promise never to bring up any of your past mistakes again. It will be just as though they never happened."

"Oh Mom, yes please, I want that," she said, a glimmer of hope returning to her eyes as the tears began to subside.

"Okay, I will give you a clean slate; I just ask one thing of you." She looked at me questioningly.

"You have to forgive your father. What is good for one is good for another. Your father also screwed up big time, but he is also sorry. He can never go back and undo what he has done. He, too, needs a clean slate. Sure it was painful what he did, but if I can forgive him, you can too. We can never have a happy family if we go around harboring unforgiveness in our hearts. You can be forgiven, but you must also be willing to forgive."

I could see that my words were penetrating. I could see that she understood. I held her close in my arms for a long time, and from that point forward her relationship with her father was restored. We gave her the clean slate we promised. From this point forward, we consciously thought only of the sweet beautiful girl that she was inside in her heart, and not of the unacceptable behavior we had witnessed in the past, her way of dealing with her pain. It was the miracle of healing a broken heart, the miracle of forgiveness.

CHAPTER 23

should
I stay *or*
should I go?

MY DECISION DETERMINES MY DESTINY

"I am convinced that life is 10% what happens to me, and 90% how I react to it."

CHUCK SWINDOLL

After one full year, Brian and I were well on our way to healing. Living through discovering Brian's affair had been the most painful experience of my life. Now that I personally understood the pain of infidelity, I would never be able to say to someone, "You should stay in your marriage after an affair." Each person must decide that for themselves.

At the suggestion of my counselor I set time landmarks for myself with the final one being two years. I promised myself that if I wasn't happy in my marriage at two years, or if I found myself unable to forgive Brian, I would leave. I felt it was the only right thing to do, not only for my sake, but also for Brian's. I felt that it would be cruel to expect someone else to stay with me if I could not sincerely forgive and get past it. I also decided that at each six month point along the way, I could leave the marriage, if I was unhappy, didn't feel any progress had been made, or if I just wanted to. In between, I promised myself, I would give it my very best effort.

Now at one year, Brian and I were no longer fighting. We got along very well. I felt like I understood Brian loved me and I understood the affair and how it had happened. I had moved far in my personal counseling and was still going. (I went for counseling for a year and a half.)

I knew I loved Brian, I wanted to stay, and I was fairly sure we were going to make it. However, I was not strong enough to put it all behind me yet, and I still felt very sad most of the time.

My trust in Brian had grown back to about fifty percent, and I think it would be safe to say we were finally out of the red. He had, I thought, done everything a man could possibly do at this stage to make it up to me. He was open and honest, he took me out for many fine dinners and coffee dates. He also finally gave me my first bouquet of roses since the affair. This meant so much to me that I dried them to keep on my mantle.

Taking so long to buy me these flowers had been a big mistake on Brian's part, and a dangerous withdrawal from the trust bank account we were trying to rebuild.

For me, floral arrangements were very special. Before the affair, Brian bought roses for me often, even without a special occasion. Somehow, I thought having an affair and then coming home warranted a bouquet of "I'm sorry" flowers, but I waited a full year. While I waited, I couldn't understand it. I even asked Brian to buy me flowers, but he didn't.

I waited another year and a half for the explanation.

You see, Brian had once bought Helen a bouquet of flowers, and knowing that gesture had always been something extra special in our relationship, he felt guilty about it. He thought if I knew about the flowers he gave Helen, I wouldn't want flowers from him anymore. He felt the fact that he had bought Helen flowers cheapened the meaning of this thoughtful act in our marriage. I disagreed.

Ironically, I was punished for something I didn't do. After all, I had believed Brian wanted to marry Helen. I knew he had slept with her. I almost expected that he had given her flowers and that detail could in no way hurt me more than all the other things already had. What did hurt me was the fact that I had to wait two and a half years to find out this truth. He had been keeping yet another secret, supposedly to avoid hurting me, but instead hurting me even worse. I did not want any secrets to remain between my husband and another woman. I needed to know *everything* about their relationship. Trust was rebuilt through *full* disclosure.

At the one year mark, we were having fewer heavy, painful talks, and more dates, fun and recreation. We spent time with good friends together and we went to the movies often. We were learning how to have an "affair" with each other, purposely creating the excitement of doing special things together.

Even so, at this point I was still unsure of the future. There were many difficult days, mostly just difficult inside myself, in my battle to overcome the painful emotions. I struggled with my self-esteem, and I was obsessive about my appearance.

Unfortunately, Lori's words to me after I told her about the affair were still impacting my life in a negative way. *We need to work on your appearance,* she had said.

I struggled to get my heart to line up with logic and truth. Brian and I had discussed infinite times that this affair had not been about my appearance, and that he did not find Helen to be more attractive than me. Yet I was still behaving as though, if even once I was not prettier than all other women, he would have an affair again. I was afraid to wear sweatpants, and afraid to be seen by him without makeup on. It was a terrible way to live.

In this state of mind, I couldn't even accept a donut from a box being passed around at my workplace. As far as I was concerned, that box full of donuts represented a box full of divorces. I equated the words "Would you like a donut?" with the words "Would you like a divorce?" I still had a long way to go.

In the summer of 2001 (just past the one-year mark), we headed back to Hinton, Alberta for a small holiday and visit with our good friends Pierre and Jackie Desportes. During this visit Jackie and I went for a long walk one day. I began to tell her of my fears regarding my appearance, how I feared that if at any point I were not able to keep up, Brian might leave me. I also shared with her the effort I was putting into "looking good" twenty-four hours a day, seven days a week.

I told her how many times I wished I wasn't even married to Brian. I would rather just date him, I told her. Then I could just go home after work, kick my feet up and not worry about putting my best foot forward all the time. Then I would be more than happy to get dressed up and go on a date with Brian.

As crazy as these feelings and behaviors might sound, I have found these obsessions to be quite common with affair survivors. It is, as one woman put it, crazy making.

It was Jackie who stopped me in my tracks that day and explained the futility of my thinking. "Anne, no one in the world can live the way you are trying to live. It's bondage. It's a horrible way to live. No one can be their best all the time. And it is totally unnecessary," she said. "I have known you and Brian now for sixteen years and I can honestly tell you that I have never seen a man who loves his wife as much as Brian loves you. You have nothing to worry about. If ever a woman has captured a man's heart it is you who has captured Brian's.

"Secondly, you are a beautiful woman. I don't think I have known another woman who has maintained her appearance and figure so well, even though you are now forty years old. Brian doesn't need, expect or want you to try to look perfect all the time. Besides if it were all about your appearance, don't you think your relationship would be too shallow? You have to get over this. This is no way to live."

I was grateful to have a friend who understood and told me the truth. Because she knew Brian and me so well, her words had a great impact.

From this point forward, I was able to let go of my appearance obsession and be myself again. I started to relax, still taking care of my appearance, but because I wanted to and not because I felt I had to. I even wear sweatpants and no makeup in the house sometimes. And of course, Brian still loves me all the same.

With all this progress and healing, was I now confident about the future? Or did I wonder if things would work out with my marriage? The answer is emphatically, YES to the latter. I wondered, regularly, throughout the first two years following disclosure. I oscillated back and forth. It was a "two steps forward, one step back" journey all the way. One day I was confident, the next day I was leaving.

I actually seemed to go through a little mental circle quite regularly.

Phase 1 – Things would not be going well or like I thought they should. The pain would be too great. So I would decide I didn't love my husband anymore and had more dignity than to keep him after cheating on me. I would decide to leave my marriage.

Phase 2 – I would begin to make plans to leave and figure out how to put myself and my children in the best possible situation. I was trying to be very smart and play my cards right, so I would not tell Brian while I was going through these mental gymnastics. I would be pretending all was well (probably acting nicer than usual, since I was acting). I would do the math and realize I could not afford to stay in our home, maintain our lifestyle, and all of the educational and other valuable opportunities our current lifestyle was providing our children. I would curse myself for allowing my husband to be the main provider for so many years. Even though I was doing well career-wise, it wasn't well enough and I wished I had pursued further education. *Look what reward being a dedicated homemaker got me,* I thought, *betrayal!*

I would also consider how I would care for my children both practically and emotionally. Brian (aside from having this affair) had always been an awesome father, and was continuing to make valuable contributions into their lives in spite of the problems we were having. I knew my kids were getting a lot from their relationship with their dad, which would not be the same if he lived elsewhere.

Phase 3 – I would decide I would just continue to "pretend" for a little while, use my husband's current support to springboard my career and get my degree, which I was working on, and enjoy his help with the children during this time. As soon as I was ready I would leave. I was faking it in our relationship for my own selfish benefit. In other words I was using him, but he deserved it. *Didn't he? Look what he had done to me.*

Phase 4 – While I was faking it, Brian would do a few wonderful things. We would end up having some awesome times together. I would find the man inside of him to be very beautiful. I would regain my feelings for him and decide I loved him and wanted to stay with him after all.

Phase 1 (again) – After a little while something would go wrong for me emotionally again, and I would start over at phase 1.

During these two years, Brian never knew about my mental gymnastics. He was quite hurt later to realize this had been happening, but he understood. So there it is, the not-so-pretty truth concerning my regular thoughts about leaving, as I struggled to heal.

At two years, I was very near complete healing from the affair.

One day, I went hiking in the mountainous terrain of North Vancouver by myself. I took with me a pad of paper and a pen. Reaching a secluded spot alone by a raging river, I took out my pen and paper and wrote down all of Brian's offenses against me, everything I felt angry and sad about, everything I could think of.

Then I confessed out loud, where no one but God could hear me, "I forgive you Brian for all of this and I am choosing to let it all go."

Then I crumpled the paper up and threw it into the river. I watched for as long as I could see the paper, and then it was gone.

I had forgiven Brian. I only had one more battle to overcome. My new friend, Sadness, was still hanging around all the time. I just couldn't seem to shake this unwelcome intruder from my life.

Then one day in November of 2002, I remember my friend, Sadness, left me, and he hasn't been back since. I don't miss him.

We had been attending another seminar, this one on money management principles. The seminar dealt with your inner unconscious thoughts and belief systems regarding money. Patterns of thinking we have developed from childhood, most of which warrant challenging. Amazingly enough, the biggest value I got from this seminar had nothing to do with money at all.

Both Brian and I grew leaps and bounds in our understanding of ourselves and each other. It's hard to explain, but I suddenly came to realize that I am a very loveable person and therefore I will always have lots of love in my life. It might not always be Brian. It might not even be a man. It could be countless friends, family or adopted family members. Whoever it is, there will always be lots of love. Embracing this thought made me happy.

Although I would like to be guaranteed my future with Brian, no one in life can receive such a guarantee. No one can be guaranteed what all of the future decisions of another individual will be. In fact, no one can be guaranteed how many days they or anyone else will have on this earth. Therefore we must all learn the simple art of living in the present, without forgetting to plan for the future.

Should I stay or should I go?

If I go, I carry on with my life alone. I go through divorce. I take on most of the responsibility of raising my teenagers alone. I make significant financial and lifestyle changes. I may meet someone else, although I don't think I even want to.

If I meet someone else that person also might have an affair one day.

Perhaps I can do what I want, when I want. I save a little pride perhaps, the "no one gets away with having an affair on me" mentality. But what do I really prove? The one thing I gain by going (if I stay single) is to give up the risk.

I will never be betrayed again, for sure. I will never be hurt like that again, because I have now closed myself off to love. But then I must live without love.

If I stay, perhaps we work it out. It seems we already have. If I stay I may get to live with the man I really love for the rest of my life, my best friend, the father of my children and the one I have shared my youth and countless memories with. My children get to live with their father and I have help to raise them.

I have someone to make me coffee on Saturday mornings and someone to change the light bulbs (not that I couldn't do it myself). He knows exactly what I mean when I mention the fight about a shirt in Phoenix, Arizona, the lightening storm in Atlanta, Georgia, or the Kahlua on a camping trip.

I have someone who comforts me when I'm sad and sets my thinking straight when my mind has formulated a problem which doesn't actually exist. And if I choose to stay, have I not won, rather than lost, a tremendous personal victory?

But whether I stay or whether I go, either way I can be happy or I can be sad. No one can make me happy. Only I can choose to be happy.

Happiness is not in the staying or in the going. Happiness is not in being married or in being single. Happiness is in me.

Brian has done all any man could ever do to make it up to me. And I still love him more than anyone else I have ever met.

I made the decision to stay. I fully recommitted myself to the relationship.

C H A P T E R 2 4

The Rewards

You're Still The One

Looks like we made it
Look how far we've come my baby
We mighta took the long way
We knew we'd get there someday
They said, "I'll bet they'll never make it"
But just look at us holding on
We're still together still going strong
You're still the one I run to
The one that I belong to
You're still the one I want for life
You're still the one that I love
The only one I dream of
You're still the one I kiss goodnight
Ain't nothin' better
We beat the odds together
I'm glad we didn't listen
Look at what we would be missing'
I'm so glad we made it
Look how far we've come my baby †

SHANIA TWAIN, *COME ON OVER*

In July of 2001, we had finally saved up the down payment for our own home. We found a tremendous deal on a slightly older home that needed considerable work. Inspired by my friend Jackie who has a natural flare for transforming neglected homes into palaces; it had been a long time dream of mine to buy a fixer upper, and work together with Brian to make it our dream, and work we did.

The project is still not finished (are they ever?), but every room in that house, including our garden, is for me a tranquil oasis from the bustle of life. And each painted wall, each piece of trim, each little representation of the work of Brian's hands reminds me that he loves me.

He renovated that house for me, because he wanted to make it up to me for the wrong he had committed. Symbolically, I suppose our marriage had also become a fixer upper, and now it was being transformed into a palace as well. Just like continuous improvements on our home, we will always be making improvements in our marriage. We are not finished with it either. The moment one thinks they have built the perfect relationship, and therefore stops working on it, one will find before long it has become nothing more than a neglected fixer upper.

In the months following our exciting move, we continued on like two people having an affair. Brian stunned me by giving me a diamond ring for my birthday. I didn't need Brian to buy me a ring in order to forgive him, but he did it anyway. It was his way of expressing his love for me.

A few months later, January 2002, we had an incredibly romantic trip to Canada's Europe: Montréal, Québec.

In the midst of the Montréal winter, we took a carriage ride through the city. Equipped with authentic furs for blankets, we snuggled up together behind our enthusiastic French guide and her horses, as we viewed all the special sights of the city. We ate dinner in a famous restaurant situated in Montréal's oldest building. The dinner we enjoyed that night was the most expensive dinner we had ever eaten, and I felt that it was worth every penny.

I had learned a lesson to allow Brian to spoil me whenever he felt so inclined. Never again would I be saying no to a date, in order to save money. Now I understood that he worked hard for his money and needed to be free to spend it in the way that he felt was best, and it seemed that often involved spending money on me. The Bible says "where your treasure (or wallet) is there your heart will be also." I guess his heart was with me, because he sure was eager to spend his money on me.

Flying home from the trip, he wrote me this letter:

February 17, 2002

My Dearest Anne,

Traveling home tonight I thought that I would jot down a few words. I have wanted to express to you how much I love and cherish you, yet I have not done so in a way that is truly meaningful for you. Roughly two years ago I made the biggest mistake of my life. This has been the hardest time that we have faced. And throughout this time you have had the courage, grace, love and commitment to stay by my side. I am so totally grateful for that.

I want to spend the rest of my life with you. I love almost everything about you. Even those things that I find annoying, I am beginning to appreciate. After all, I could never keep lists and details like you. I love all the thoughtful things that you do for not only me and our children, but for others as well.

You are an extremely smart person. One who's not afraid of challenges, and is willing to better herself. You have not ever held back from trying something new or different and I find that very exciting and rewarding. I truly appreciate how much you have given to improve yourself and better understand not only you, but also me.

I know that these last two years have been painful, whenever you think about what happened, and I haven't been very compassionate towards you, but I want you to know that I will be more sensitive in the future and try to put myself in your shoes more often.

Anne, you captured my heart twenty years ago and still have all my love and desire. Though I don't always show you in ways you need or understand, you are the true love of my life and there is no one I would rather spend my life with.

You make me want to be home and it is difficult to work out of town. I look forward to the times we spend together not only talking, but also in the bedroom. We are each quite fortunate to be married to someone that we love. I don't think we would be able to find solutions to our problems if it wasn't for the fact that we are truly committed to each other.

Well, I hope this letter will help you to know how much I love you and appreciate you. I don't take you for granted even though you might feel like I do at times. I want you to help me to love you more by teaching me how and by being patient when I screw up. I will be able to do it.

You are a great woman. I am proud to be your husband. After all who wouldn't be if they were married to someone who was smart, beautiful, thoughtful, loving, compassionate, a terrific mother, a learner, a teacher, a sex goddess and a very good friend.

I love you.

Brian

He gave me the letter when we returned home from the airport. I read the letter over and over again. I read it again in the morning. Over the coming months I kept the letter close by and pulled it out and read it whenever those painful feelings of hurt, self-doubt and inadequacy showed their ugly faces to torment me again.

In June of 2003, three years after disclosure of the affair, Brian came to pick me up from work one day. "I'm taking you to pick up your new car," he informed me. It was a complete surprise.

Setbacks from the affair had resulted in the fact that we had only one vehicle in the family for a three year period of time (with four drivers fighting for it)! I ended up taking the bus most of the time, but now there, on the dealership lot, was a brand new shiny white sports car for me.

"Here." Brian told me, "This is for all the crap I put you through, and thank you for never once complaining about having to ride the bus." I gave him a great big giant hug and kiss. Again, he didn't have to buy me a car. I had already forgiven him. But it was his eagerness to express his love for me in tangible ways that touched my heart so deeply.

I wish every person could know the joy of a passionate long-term marriage. Brian and I now live our lives together and face life's challenges together. Some days are good, some days are bad and some days the world is a very unfriendly place, but no matter what my day has been like, at night I lie in bed beside the man I love.

He takes me in his arms and holds his body close to mine. I feel him breathing and I feel his heart beating. And as he holds me, it's as if I feel something transferring from his body to mine, something spiritual and something comforting. It is therapy for my soul and it seems to be healing the wounds of the day. I wish for every married person, that they too can hold their best friend in their arms at night and feel this same special comfort, this healing from the big and small battles of each and every day.

Our children have all survived the affair, and this is a great reward. Following all our hard work to get our marriage back together, our children each came to us, individually, and said they really respected Brian and me for fighting for our marriage and not giving up. "Most of my friends' parents are having the same kind of problems that you and dad have had, only their parents just give up, quit, get mad and get divorced. You and dad worked out your problems. I really respect you for that." I was told, individually, in different words, from each of our children. Coming from the mouths of teenagers, I found this to be profound.

APRIL, 2004

Danielle: I thank God that our family pulled through that horrific time in our lives. People have asked me if I wish it never happened. Sure, if we could still be where we are today. But we wouldn't be the same family and people without it. Because we all faced the brutal reality, embraced the hurt, devastation and pain, we have earned the reward of renewed and greater honesty, forgiveness and trust.

Dealing with the pain has enabled me to move beyond bitterness, to true friendship and real love for my parents and family.

My parents are so much in love, so much happier, living and loving life like I have never seen them before. This makes me happy. It takes away the cold heart I was developing. I know true love is real and achievable, and I look forward to one day having with someone special of my own, the love my parents share for each other.

Currently I work full-time at a real estate law firm and have plans to continue my education, pursuing a degree in law, psychology or nursing. Challenges, to me, have become opportunities to learn, which I embrace, because part of everything I have today has been gained by facing past problems.

On weekends, I enjoy traveling, backpacking, and the outdoors, often with my boyfriend, who reminds me of my dad: fun, wild, crazy, adventurous and responsible like me. We go snowboarding, rock climbing, and research future travel possibilities together.

Things definitely go wrong sometimes, but what keeps me sane is my genius parents, especially my dad! I always sit down and talk with them. My parents really listen to me and give me awesome advice particularly about relationships. The older I get the smarter they seem! I love my parents and am grateful to them for all they've done for me.

I'm proud of my mother and father for sharing their story with the world. I hope it will help a lot of people. It's a subject most people don't want to talk about, but parents need to know that affairs hurt their children, too.

Dustin is eighteen and will be graduating from high school in a couple of months. During the past two years he has worked part-time with his father in construction. They have a great relationship, too. When we asked him how he felt about the affair crisis that came upon our family he said, "I'm sure glad it's over!"

He is an exceptional young man with a natural aptitude for physics and mathematics like his grandfather. He has played club football this past year, plays trombone for the school band and is a talented bass guitar player. He plans to join the Canadian military after graduation.

Tamara is an unusually highly-motivated, self-disciplined, goal-oriented young woman. Last year she received two outstanding student awards and scholarships from her high school, one for consistent high marks overall, and one for being the top student in her grade in science.

Two years after the affair, she was required to write about her family for a school project. This is what she wrote:

Brian – Dad. He and I have a really good relationship. It's great spending time together. We always joke around and I enjoy his company. I trust him totally and know that I could talk to him about anything. He's really smart so I know the advice he gives me is helpful even if I don't quite agree. I love and respect him a lot.

Anne – Mom. My mom and I have a good relationship too. I enjoy how I know she loves me. She makes some decisions for me that I wouldn't make myself, but when I look back, I see they were for the best. It's a total trust relationship. She has accomplished many great things in her life and that's what I admire.

Danielle – Sister. It's not possible for my sister and me to be any closer. We're like best friends and I always have a good time with her. Her experiences help her to know a lot about life. She encourages me to be the best I can be. I love her, look up to her and admire her strong will.

Dustin – Brother. My brother and I are friends. When we were little we always played Lego together. He's a lot quieter than I am. He's got a real sense of humor though. He makes everybody laugh at the most unexpected moments. I have a strong feeling he's going to be successful. The way he thinks is great. He keeps everything short, simple and to the point. He's a great guy and I want the best for him.

Considering what our family had been through, I cried when I read this for the first time. It's a good thing I didn't give up and quit, when it seemed like my life was over and all hope was lost.

I am now living the life I truly want to live. I have become a strong and emotionally healthy person. Hidden issues from my past have been exposed for what they are, cleaned up and dealt with.

Brian has regained my full trust. I trust him one hundred percent again, only the trust I have for him today is not blind or naïve. I understand that no one can know all of the future choices another individual will make. I believe our marriage will remain monogamous, *until death do us part*. At the same time, I am aware that an affair could happen. I base my trust today on Brian's proven behavior, and on the incredible degree of openness and honesty we share.

I'm excited about life and excited about my future. I am living a purpose-driven life, together with my first love, my best friend and the father of my children. We are free to be ourselves and free to choose. We enjoy real, honest, open communication with our best friends: each other. And we have hope for our future based on reality, not on a Cinderella fantasy.

What is reality? Reality is that I am not a perfect wife, and Brian is not a perfect husband, and ours is not a perfect marriage, but in the midst of all that imperfection, our love for one another is very real.

Brian: Would I want to go back to our marriage before the affair? Not a chance! Would I have liked to have gotten to this point some other way? Absolutely! Would I recommend an affair to others so they can reach a greater love and a better marriage? Absolutely not!

If you have experienced an affair, is rebuilding the marriage worth it? You bet it is! As long as you love each other and are willing to do the work.

Not only can Anne say, "My husband's affair became the best thing that ever happened to me." I can honestly say, what has transpired as a result of it has become one of the best things to happen to me as well!

We have moved our lives forward to a place which five years ago, we never knew existed. Not that we have reached marriage "nirvana" or don't have problems anymore. We do. But we are best friends. Without doubt, every bit of work and effort has been totally worth it.

Today, Anne and I share from our hearts openly and honestly with each other. We chose the right time to discuss sensitive issues, and are not fearful to share those thoughts that the other might have reacted negatively to in our pre-affair marriage.

We have learned to trust each other again, and have the deepest respect for what the other has to say. We recognize that we both love each other, so if any negative thoughts or feelings are shared, we understand it is for our benefit and not meant to hurt. All our conversation is for the purpose of building each other up and strengthening our marriage.

We are having fun together again, no longer allowing the pressures of life to spoil our marriage. That is to say, we don't focus solely on the difficult situations life challenges us with, rather keeping in mind what is important, namely our relationship. I am "dating" Anne once more, and since our kids are no longer kids, we have the freedom to date often.

I am more attracted to, more excited around, closer to, more sexually satisfied by, more deeply in love with Anne than ever before. Yet I have more freedom to be myself, and less pressure to be someone I'm not.

I/we have grown up.

One night a few years after the affair, I had a dream…

Brian and I were standing together holding hands on a cruise ship sailing through the Caribbean. We stood alone on the deck, standing against the railing and looking out over the turquoise blue waters. The warm wind was blowing and my soft chiffon dress was dancing gracefully in the breeze. In the distance the sun was setting and the sky's artwork displayed the most magnificent spectrum of nature's colors. Brian's hair was gray now and his face showed the lines of age, yet to me each line represented a moment of growth in his grace and character.

My hair was also an elegant gray and my face also showed lines, lines of passion, of giving and of joy. I looked into Brian's eyes and he looked into mine. We had shared a lifetime of happiness together and together we had weathered the storms of life. As we gazed into each other's eyes there was mutual admiration, respect and a very deep love. In that future moment of time, the affair itself had become insignificant, yet the lessons learned had become more precious than gold.

Waking up from my dream I was reminded that wherever my journey leads me, whatever obstacles I encounter, whatever battles I must fight, when it seems that all hope is lost … I should never give up, because it really is true: It ain't over 'til it's over.

C H A P T E R 2 5

Lessons
Learned

PREVENTING AFFAIRS

One of the biggest lessons we learned is that affairs happen to good people in good marriages. They are not merely the problem of an unlucky few, who just weren't really committed to each other or who were having serious marriage problems.

According to marital affairs expert Peggy Vaughan in her book, *The Monogamy Myth,* conservative estimates are that 60 percent of men and 40 percent of women will have an extramarital affair. If even half of the women having affairs (or 20 percent) are married to men not included in the 60 percent having affairs, then at least one partner will have an affair in approximately 80 percent of all marriages.

Brian and I have often asked ourselves, *Why did this have to happen to us? How could we have avoided it? Couldn't someone have gotten our attention in some other way?*

For me, the problem was that I was so sure that I had a great marriage, I'm not sure what could have gotten my attention. If someone had said to me, "You need to listen to your husband," I would have thought, *Yes, I'm doing that.* If someone had said, "You need to spend recreational time together," I would have thought, *We are.* If someone had said, "You need to have fun in your life," I would have thought, *For the most part we are. We have extra responsibilities right now and that's the way life is sometimes. You just have to make sacrifices.*

I was confident in Brian's commitment to me and mine to him. I don't think any "how-to" books could have awakened me to the dangers that were lurking in my relationship. But here are some things which could have helped.

BE INTROSPECTIVE

It doesn't matter how much you know if you are unable to be real with yourself and ask yourself questions such as: *Why do I feel this way? Why am I unhappy? Why do I feel attracted to this other person? Why don't I share the truth of how I feel with my mate?*

The first step to avoiding affairs is being able to understand and be honest with yourself. You cannot be honest with your mate until you have learned to be honest with yourself.

Most people who have had affairs never thought they would. They were people who meant their wedding vows one hundred percent and were totally committed to their marriages and to monogamy. *How can an affair happen then?*

In Brian's case, the affair happened in part because he wasn't being introspective "pre-affair." He did not even understand how unhappy he actually was. He was "sweeping it under the rug," "sucking it up" and "just dealing with it."

During the process of our healing one day Brian asked me, "Remember when I told you that the reason that you never had an affair was because I had been a good husband, and the reason why I had an affair was because you were a bad wife?"

I remembered, clearly.

"Well, I was wrong," he said. "It was easy for me to be a good husband because you understood yourself and were able to communicate your needs to me clearly. You never stood a chance of being a good wife, because I was not able to communicate my needs to you."

So even though I had read invaluable books such as Willard Harley's "His Needs, Her Needs," I was unable to apply the principles to our unique relationship, because Brian didn't recognize and understand his needs. Therefore he couldn't communicate his specific needs to me or how I could meet them. Although one can identify common emotional needs all husbands and wives have, meeting those needs is not accomplished in the same way for every person. It doesn't matter how many books you read, spouses can't meet each others needs unless they are both talking, to each other.

DEAL WITH ISSUES FROM THE PAST

If someone had asked me (or I had asked myself), "What baggage from your past or childhood are you bringing into this relationship that could be affecting you in a negative way?" I believe that could have helped me to wake up. If I had received some counseling focused around this poignant question. My problems were not marriage problems; they were personal problems, which were affecting my marriage negatively.

My biggest contribution to our relationship breakdown was one I was completely unaware of. It was the insecurities I had within myself. The "I'm unlovable" tape in my subconscious mind, made it difficult for me to receive love and honest communication (including constructive criticism). Simply put, I was too insecure. If you are carrying around baggage from your past, you are not really whole as a person and you don't have what it takes to really be a great spouse.

EDUCATE YOURSELF ABOUT AFFAIRS

Most people have relatively little accurate knowledge about affairs. Most people are very uncomfortable discussing the topic, so they don't. Contrary to the popular saying, what you don't know *does* hurt you. You must be informed. By reading responsible educational information about affairs (not the sensationalism often presented in the media), you can learn from the mistakes of others and avoid them in your own life.

DISCUSS AFFAIRS WITH YOUR SPOUSE

If you plan to stay married to the same person for a lifetime, it is unrealistic to think that neither one of you will ever be attracted to anyone else. Attractions will come. The question is what will you do with those attractions when they come?

Affairs need secrecy to happen. If we are unable to share temptations with our spouse because they punish us for doing so (by crying, getting depressed for days or getting angry), then the secrecy ingredient remains. Secrecy is to affairs, what sunlight and water is to plants. It helps them grow. Without it they die.

On the other hand if a man, for example, were able to come home and say to his wife, "I was attracted to a woman at work today," and instead of being angry the wife is able to say, "Why did you feel that way? Tell me about it. Do you think she might have been meeting one of your needs that I'm not right now?" The couple would be able to discuss their relationship, identify needs, change and meet each others needs, and by so doing, remove potential vulnerability to affairs.

OPEN, HONEST COMMUNICATION

Most couples are actually far from honest with one another. They are honest about subjects that aren't difficult, but dishonest about the things that really matter, the difficulties, frustrations and hurts in their relationship.

Here is an example: Let's assume a wife has gained over twenty-five percent of her body weight since marriage. She's not healthy, less energetic and quite honestly doesn't look that good. It's bothering her husband. It's happened gradually and she is not really aware how much it is affecting her. Her husband is careful to choose the right time, and is sensitive in his choice of words. He approaches her honestly.

"Honey, you are gaining weight and it really doesn't look so good. I'm concerned about your health, and it's bothering me." How many wives would be able to answer, "You know, you are right. Thank you for being honest with me. I'll start exercising and work on eating healthier."

Instead, how many of us would burst into tears, get depressed for several days, accuse our husbands of not loving us and tell them they were wrong for being so concerned about weight. Doing this would be punishing them for honesty, and sending a message not to be honest about potentially upsetting matters (like a future attraction to another woman).

Living with this kind of dishonesty in a relationship is living in a fairytale. One day you may be forced to wake up from the dream. Genuine, open, honest communication includes the ability to give and to receive constructive criticism.

LISTENING

It was true. I was not really listening to Brian. I never realized that when I became defensive when he shared things, rather than validating his feelings, I was in essence telling him that he was wrong.

I am still working on becoming a better listener. Listening does not mean I am just quiet, while Brian talks. It means I do not spend my time formulating my next response in my head while Brian (or anyone else) is speaking. I listen to what Brian is saying. I try to get into his skin. I listen for the understandable part without having to necessarily agree with him.

I ask myself, *What is he really saying? What is going on for him?* And when I feel that I do understand I say, "So what you're saying is …?" Many times it turns out I still haven't understood.

Most of all, I am careful not to interrupt and not to tell him that he is wrong, even if I disagree with what he is saying. Instead, I say things like, "I respect your opinion and I can understand why you feel that way. Right now I'm feeling ..."

As my husband, Brian needs to feel that I value and respect his opinions and advice.

Before the affair, I often came to him with a problem. He would present a solution, but I would not give it much weight unless another friend gave me the same advice. In this way, I was indirectly communicating to him that I didn't really hold his opinion to be of value, but rather the opinions of others to be of a greater value. This was disrespectful.

RECREATIONAL COMPANIONSHIP

A month before Brian's affair began, we had joined a local gym together. Brian had asked me to come and lift weights with him. The gym also offered a long distance running club. I preferred long distance running, so I joined this group instead of lifting weights with my husband.

I had no idea what a mistake I was making. I didn't realize this was not about fitness preferences. This was about my husband's need for recreational companionship.

According to Willard Harley, in his book "His Needs, Her Needs," recreational companionship is one of a man's top five needs within a marriage.

I also made a big mistake in the area of sports. Not only did I not join Brian, but I actually was guilty of criticizing him for watching sports. Now I sit and watch sports with Brian sometimes, because he enjoys my company while he watches. And guess what? I really do like hockey now! I've learned to understand the game and I'm genuinely interested.

FUN

Fun is not an option, rather a necessity. We had fallen into the trap that so many families do: work, work, work.

Midlife is a particularly vulnerable time for affairs because cou ples are dealing with aging parents on the one hand, unruly teenagers on the other, and their financial demands are the highest they've ever been. Their lives have become all about responsibility.

They are on a mundane treadmill, acting like martyrs. You cannot live this way no matter how strong you think you are. We have learned to revamp our budget and our time to include fun. And we make sure we don't do the same old things over and over, rather we make an effort to try new and different things together. This is what keeps life exciting. We have an affair … with each other.

FRIENDS AND MENTORS

The friendship that Darrell provided for Brian was invaluable. In fact, had they been close before the affair, it may not have happened. If couples desire to strengthen their relationship and prevent affairs, this is one important step they can take: develop and maintain close same-sex friendships.

Women tend to do this more naturally. Most men have to make extra effort to develop these friendships. Friendships don't happen by accident. They happen on purpose. We create them. We have to initiate them and continually put energy into cultivating them.

Brian had many friends and acquaintances. Anyone who knew him before would have thought he had lots of friends, and he did. The problem was he wasn't completely open and honest with his friends. He kept them at a certain distance. He did not discuss things that really mattered to him, like his hopes and dreams, as well as his disappointments and failures. His friends did not discuss things such as how well their marriages were or weren't going; neither did they create mutual accountability. Instead they usually discussed only non-personal topics, such as work, sports and vehicles.

SURVIVING AFFAIRS

Assuming you have read this book, (and didn't start with the last chapter), you will have learned through our story many keys in surviving an affair, both what to do and what not to do. You will also have gained insight into how to support someone through this experience: what works and what doesn't.

Here I've highlighted a few important points.

Affairs do not just go away. You can't just suck it up and get over it. You have to face it and deal with it.

EDUCATE YOURSELF — READ, READ, READ

Whether the relationship stays together or not, those who have recovered say that educating themselves was key to their success.

They read books and related articles, they seek out helpful websites, and they often join a support group or seek professional counseling. Usually recovery is achieved by combining several sources of support, rarely from one source alone.

A note regarding finding a counselor: often one that has been referred by a friend is a good option. Counselors are not all the same. If a certain counselor does not seem to be helping it is okay to switch and find another.

Resources and help for recovering from affairs (and other aspects of life, relationships and success) are available through our website www.passionatelife.ca.

SEVER ALL TIES WITH THE THIRD PARTY

If the couple intends to rebuild the relationship, it is first of all essential that *all* ties with the third party are severed. An unfaithful spouse cannot remain "just friends" with this person. Many times the person having the affair is quite reluctant to sever ties, and it may be necessary to deliver a strong ultimatum, such as the one I gave Brian.

Many times the betrayed spouse is afraid to deliver this strong message to their spouse, because they are afraid of being alone, and this is understandable. However, this same fear is unattractive to the spouse who has had an affair. It makes them feel trapped in the relationship.

It is human nature to enjoy the "chase" in marriage relationships, and freedom to breathe. We like a bit of a challenge. If one person is too easy, a push-over or doing all the giving, they devalue themselves. Instead, when we set healthy relationship boundaries and stand up for ourselves and what's right, we show others that we are valuable, and that makes us attractive to them. They respect us more, than when we give into unreasonable demands.

To learn more about how to effectively insist that your spouse break ties with the third party, I recommend the book "Love Must Be Tough" by Dr. James Dobson.

TALK, TALK, TALK AND OPENLY DISCUSS THE AFFAIR

The way Brian and I healed our marriage after the affair was through hours upon hours of dialogue. There was many a painful discussion, but through these discussions came understanding and healing. It is essential that the person who has had the affair be willing to discuss the details of the affair and answer all of their spouse's questions.

I have seen no better explanation as to why this is important than the analogy made by one man in a letter he wrote to his wife who had an affair. That letter has been reprinted in this book with permission, in the chapter entitled "Trouble with the Law."

AFFAIRS – NOT ABOUT SEX?

Prior to experiencing infidelity, I assumed affairs were about someone else being sexually more attractive than the spouse or in some other way better. This inaccurate assumption caused me to suffer much more than was necessary during my recovery, as I obsessed about my appearance and pressured myself to be the ultimate sex goddess.

I have learned that affairs often are about a friendship, not about sex at all, and that the real enticement of an affair is the reflection of oneself in the eyes of the adoring third party.

Keeping up one's physical appearance is important in relationships. According to Willard Harley in his book "His Needs, Her Needs," an attractive spouse is one of a man's top five needs in a marriage relationship. So there is value in discussing this topic as a couple, *honestly*.

In our marriage it was true that I had gained over thirty pounds since I married Brian eighteen years earlier, and this did matter to Brian. Yet this was not the cause of the affair. The real cause was that we were not able to openly discuss this issue (and other sensitive topics) without my becoming defensive.

It wasn't that my friend Lori was wrong in mentioning the value of working on keeping up my appearance to meet Brian's need for an attractive spouse. It was the incorrect timing of her well intentioned comment that was a problem.

When someone discovers their mate has been unfaithful, they will most likely become obsessive about appearance without any extra prodding, because their identity has been shattered. At this point, it is more important to understand that affairs do not mean you aren't pretty or sexy enough.

If one is overweight, there is value in returning to a healthy size, but that is best done in a responsible manner with a doctor's advice. During the painful affair recovery period, individuals should be careful to avoid eating disorders, and their friends should encourage them to maintain healthy eating patterns during the trauma.

If a marriage is based on a spouse's appearance, and a straying spouse returns home because their marriage partner suddenly becomes better looking, this is a very shallow relationship. If that's the one factor that brings the straying spouse home, the marriage probably isn't worth saving. There are many beautiful people in the world. No spouse can be the "prettiest" all the time. If being the "prettiest" could guarantee monogamy, then *why do the beautiful, rich and talented Hollywood movie stars also experience unfaithfulness?*

PATIENCE AND GIVING TO EACH OTHER

The person who has an affair must understand that this has been very painful for their spouse. Healing takes time. In our situation, it took two and a half years. This is actually a relatively short time period. We had more support than most, and Brian was exceptional in his strength and courage to do the work of healing. He had to be very patient with me for a long time, as I worked through the grief, the sadness and the anger. He had to answer my questions. And it had to happen at the pace with which I was ready to hear the truth. This he had to do, while he himself struggled with his own feelings of guilt, and while he was very much alone.

Generally there is a lot of support available for the person who has been betrayed, but the one who has been unfaithful is the bad guy, the loser, the one everyone hates. Brian is now providing support through our website for such individuals who are sorry for their actions, love their spouse and sincerely desire to rebuild their marriage.

In addition to Brian's patience, I also had to be patient and understanding towards him. I had to create an atmosphere that made Brian feel comfortable enough to answer my questions and to communicate with me about the affair and why it happened.

BOTH PARTIES MUST BE WILLING TO TAKE RESPONSIBILITY FOR THEIR PART

We all know that it was wrong for Brian to have an affair. And to be sure, I did not cause him to have the affair and am therefore not to blame. However, a major turning point in the healing of our relationship took place when I, for the first time, took responsibility for my part in the relationship breakdown.

It was six months from the time of initial disclosure of the affair before I was able to do this.

A FINAL NOTE

Marriages can heal after an affair and they can become much stronger. However, it is not always possible. Not every marriage is salvageable. One person alone cannot do the work of rebuilding. Both parties must do their part.

Having said that, whether still married or now single, anyone can create a great life after an affair.

Brian's affair was my personal wake up call. It was devastating, as anyone who has been there knows. Yet it forced me to grow up. I will never be the same again.

I have learned that I am a loveable person, and my security as an individual now comes from within.

As a young married woman, I based my identity and self-esteem on being a good wife and mother. My marriage was essential to my sense of identity, happiness and well-being. So when Brian told me of his affair and that he was leaving me, my whole world was shattered. During the recovery process, I have learned to know and value myself as an individual. I no longer need to be married, to be happy. I am able to be truly honest with others and, most importantly, truly honest with myself. I am no longer threatened by constructive criticism and I am no longer insecure.

Since the affair, and since I made it through the difficult recovery period, I have excelled in amazing ways in every area of my life. After the affair, I was unable to work at all for eight months. However, when I did return to my job, my employer commented that I had become a far better worker.

Within a couple of months my income doubled! I look after my health better now. I actually look and feel better than I did twenty years ago. I have more energy, more zeal and more enthusiasm for life. Since I have gotten over my insecurities, I experience far better relationships with my spouse, children and others. I also have more fun.

As sad as the affair was, I would not want to ever go back to what

I call my "pre-affair" existence. Many times, I have thought to myself, *If only I could have gotten here some other way. Why did I have to go through so much pain?* But I really don't know what else would have gotten my attention.

No matter what tragedies happen in our lives, we always have a choice, not a choice over what will happen to us, but a choice over how we will react to it. Will we become bitter or better? I chose to become better, and now my greatest tragedy has also become my greatest personal victory.

My husband's affair has become the best thing that ever happened to me!

E P I L O G U E

Since I chose to embrace Christianity at the age of twenty, my faith has been an important part of my life. I do not consider myself to be a religious person. Religion means you follow a long list of dos and don'ts. Rather I would say that God is my friend.

Originally, it was my intention to write a book about my recovery from the affair only, not a book about my faith. However, as I started to put it all down on paper, I saw that I could not tell my story accurately, while leaving my best friend, God, out.

During the painful recovery period, I was merely surviving one day at a time. It was later, when looking back, I saw all the miracles and provisions that had carried me through to healing, and an even better life on the other side of my tragedy.

From filling my living room with flowers the night before I was to find out, to providing a dedicated friend like Lori to encourage me daily, from my coworker calling me unexpectedly at just the right time, to another friend calling me to remind me of my favorite Bible verse, at the exact hour, I had decided the Bible wasn't true anymore. From Adrian Lee, barely more than a stranger at the time, reminding Brian of his values without having the slightest clue what he was doing or what was happening in Brian's life, to the unbelievable meeting I had with Helen, it is clear to me that something supernatural was at work in my life during that time.

To me it is apparent that there is more to this world than just what we can see, hear, touch, taste and smell. There is an unceasing war between good and evil going on.

When we human beings create something of value, there is always ingenuity, creativity, talent and design behind it. *Why then do we so easily believe that something as complex, beautiful and perfectly balanced as nature is an accident? Every animal, plant and natural resource, entire ecosystems the result of a coincidental big bang?*

If there is no God, where did my unquenchable desire to love and to be loved come from? And if I am merely an accident, and it doesn't matter whether I live or die, then where does my inner longing for purpose and meaning for my life come from?

When tragedy and suffering befall mankind, many people ask, *Why did God do this?* I say he didn't. He gave human beings freedom of choice, otherwise we would be robots. Most pain and suffering in the world are caused by people hurting other people and acting selfishly. It is God who rescues us when we call out to him, and he usually chooses to do that rescuing through other people, as he did with me.

RECOMMENDED RESOURCES
FOR RECOVERY FROM AFFAIRS

Support Groups

Beyond Affairs Network, www.dearpeggy.com. Support for those who have had affairs, are genuinely remorseful and seek support and advice for rebuilding their marriages, www.passionatelife.ca

Books

Love Must Be Tough, Dr. James Dobson
Not Just Friends, Shirley Glass
Beyond Affairs, Peggy Vaughan
The Monogamy Myth, Peggy Vaughan
Surviving an Affair, Willard Harley
His Needs, Her Needs, Willard Harley
Boundaries, Dr. Henry Cloud, Dr. John Townsend
Love is a Choice, Dr. Robert Hemfelt, Dr. Frank Minirth, Dr. Paul Meier
Feeling Good, David D. Burns M.D., cognitive therapy for depression
Healing for Damaged Emotions, David A. Seamands
Dealing With Your Husband's Secret Wars, Marsha Means, sexual addictions
Shattering Strongholds, Liberty Savard, Biblical perspective on prayer

Helpful Websites

www.passionatelife.ca
www.dearpeggy.com
www.marriagebuilders.com
www.smartmarriages.com

COMING SOON FROM
PASSIONATE LIFE SEMINARS
AND BRIAN AND ANNE BERCHT

Check our website www.passionatelife.ca for current free articles, specials, new books and seminars.

• A group study/discussion guide, as a companion for *"My Husband's Affair Became the Best Thing That Ever Happened to Me"* for couples wishing to prevent affairs in their own marriages. Coming soon

• *The Prince or the Pawn, Candid Truth About the Unfaithful,* Brian Bercht. Expected date available for sale June 30, 2005

• Marriage Enrichment Seminars

For information about these products or having Anne and/or Brian Bercht speak at your seminar, church or event, you can contact the authors at:

Passionate Life Seminars
P.O. Box 162
Abbotsford, British Columbia
V2S 4N8, Canada

Phone/Fax: 604.859.9393
Email: info@passsionatelife.ca

ISBN 141203320-9

9 781412 033206